The Thrifty Kitchen

Suzanne Gibbs & Kate Gibbs

LANTERN
an imprint of
PENGUIN BOOKS

We dedicate this book to the women in
our lives, past, present and future:

Kate's strong, wise and thrifty grandmothers, Marion Gibbs
and Margaret Fulton; Suzanne's late aunt, Jean Hatfield; and
Suzanne's late grandmother, Isabella Fulton, who inspired us through
stories, recipes and traditions passed down through four generations.

The women who inspire us every day with their amazing
love and generosity of spirit — from Suzanne's other darling
daughter, Louise Keats, to the best friend a woman
could ever have, Jannie Brown.

This book is for those women who show us that through
immense love, humour and strength, we can do anything
we put our minds and hearts to.

Contents

INTRODUCTION   ix

THRIFTY SHOPPING   xiii

CHAPTER 1   Breakfasts   1

Handy hints on storing and preparing eggs 2 • Make your own yoghurt 4
Oats four ways 6 • Melt-in-the-mouth French toast 8 • Pancakes and other sweet treats 11
Quick toast breakfasts 15 • The secret to perfectly poached eggs 16

CHAPTER 2   Work lunches and lunchbox foods   25

Leftovers for lunch 26 • What to keep on hand in your fridge and freezer 27
Three delicious hummus recipes 28 • Discover a shortcut to roasting capsicums 31
What to do with dried beans 35 • Sandwich inspiration 38 • Ava's packed lunches 48

CHAPTER 3   Weeknight meals   51

Quick and easy weeknight meals 52 • The versatile chickpea 54 • Tasty ways with canned fish 55–58
How to cook perfect pasta 71 • A classic throw-together stir-fry 72
How to dress up your lamb chops 75

CHAPTER 4   Meals from leftovers   83

What foods to keep and what to toss 84 • How to avoid food waste 85
A handy guide to storing leftovers 86 • Perfect mashed potato 88 • Fried rice three ways 92
Using up leftover cooked veggies 95 • Make a sweet curry from leftover meat 99

CHAPTER 5   Weekend meals to cook and keep   105

The best meals to save for later 106 • How to make your own stock 107
The ultimate lamb shank recipe 120 • The week's meals, planned ahead 123
Absolutely perfect gravy 125 • Fiona's weekend cook-ups 130

CHAPTER 6   What to do with all those . . .   133

Growing and using your own herbs 134 • Quick and easy apple sauce 136
Simple homemade mayonnaise 140 • Pesto – the great all-rounder 141 • How to cook eggplant 144
Preserve your own lemons 149 • Make your own chutneys and sauces 154

CHAPTER 7   Baking   165

Hints for baking success 166 • Baking for beginners 167
A super-easy homemade bread recipe – no need to knead! 168 • Choosing the right flour 170
All about meringues (including the classic pav) 174 • A simple cake to whip up for afternoon tea 182

CHAPTER 8   Entertaining on a budget   193

Quick fixes to feed a crowd 195 • Learn how to cook with mussels 198
Three flashy salads to impress your guests 200 • How to get your crackling crisp 205
Make pizza from scratch 212 • The softest, most chocolatey puddings you'll ever taste 221

ACKNOWLEDGEMENTS   222

INDEX   223

Introduction

How and what we eat lies at the heart of who we are. We divide our day into meals – breakfast, lunch and dinner – and much of our everyday life is spent thinking about food: when to eat, what to eat and who to eat it with. It's also an integral part of how we celebrate special occasions.

Cooking emphatically celebrates being alive – it's a way we can express our individuality as well as forging a sense of community amongst family, friends and even work colleagues. Chatting with your partner over a simmering pot of stew, negotiating with the kids about what's for dinner on Monday night, sharing your favourite brownie recipe with the office – all are ways of bringing people together. And by cooking our own food, we are immersing ourselves in a process: choosing what we'd like to eat, selecting the ingredients, deciphering a recipe and using our skills and instincts to produce a meal.

Creating meals from scratch, however, can occupy an enormous part of our lives – so much so that many of us often feel constrained by the time it takes and elect to take some shortcuts. The problem with this is that when we don't cook, we don't eat properly, nor do we learn about the foods we eat or look after ourselves through healthy, conscious eating. We become disengaged from food, thinking of it as purely physical sustenance rather than allowing it to nurture us. This detachment means we often don't have the skills to teach our children how to cook properly, and so the cycle continues. As cooking becomes less an everyday activity for some people, we tend to think of food in terms of what's available at the local takeaway, the sandwich place

near work or the petrol station. Even ready-made meals bought from expensive delicatessens, like ricotta ravioli with vine-ripened organic tomato sauce, are still essentially 'packet jobs', with no cooking required – at least not by us.

From a health perspective, it's clear that cooking your own food gives you ultimate control over what you put into your body, and you can make adjustments according to your own taste and nutritional needs. And, honestly, cooking will save you money. Think about it: compare the weekly cost of three homemade meals per day to buying takeaway or packaged food (make sure you include the two slices of toast you picked up with your morning coffee and the mid-afternoon emergency chocolate bar!). You'll find it's vastly cheaper to cook for yourself.

So, we all know how important eating well and cooking is, but before we jump on the 'let's discover our inner domestic goddess and forget about everything else we have to do' bandwagon, we're going to need to take a practical and sensible approach. This book is about finding ways to realistically integrate cooking into your day-to-day life, and not the other way round. We want to help you establish habits that are suitable for your particular circumstances – how you can best use your time to fit cooking into your life. We've given lots of useful advice along with the recipes, including some clever ways to be thrifty in the kitchen (often pearls of wisdom passed down from previous generations), so that your hard-earned money will go even further. And by happy coincidence, such a resourceful approach will reduce the amount of waste you generate and increase the variety of foods you eat, thereby helping you to tread more softly on the planet.

Suzanne

I was two years old when my mother, Margaret Fulton, and I went to live with my Aunt Jean and Uncle Bill in a town on the Hawkesbury River, just north of Sydney. They had a tiny cottage that we were all happy to squeeze into. My bath was an old cement laundry tub in which I would sit, surrounded by shelves heaving with jars of preserves that my mother and aunt had prepared using fruit from our orchard. To me, these jars of plums, apricots, peaches and tomatoes were sparkling jewels, and I was a princess.

Over the years we settled into a comfortable routine. By day we fished, foraged for oysters, tended the garden, milked the goats, fed the chickens and ducks and collected eggs. By night we sat around the table scaling fish, shelling peas and chatting about the day we'd had, before finally falling into bed and sleeping like logs. We didn't know it then, but we were pioneer greenies. We kept a compost heap, collected rainwater, mulched our fruit trees and enriched the soil with organic material (with a lot of help from our chickens and ducks). In the kitchen we were careful not to waste a thing. We caught only as much fish as we could eat, always making a soup from the heads and bones, and we rarely ate meat because it had to be bought from a shop.

I was happy and wanted for nothing, but it was a long time before I realised just how lucky I was. Lucky to be nurtured by resourceful people who knew how to grow food and make the most of unfamiliar produce (which in those days included garlic, eggplant, capsicum and zucchini, remember). Although the household income was small, the delicious meals we ate were inspirational. Money alone couldn't buy the knowledge and care that made so much of the natural ingredients, which had been passed down through generations of the Fulton clan.

Later, my mother and I went to live in a small terrace house in The Rocks in Sydney. This was well before she had written her first cookbook, and years before I decided to embark on a career in food. Every Saturday morning we would head off to the market and buy the freshest produce at the cheapest prices. We didn't have a lot but you would never have guessed it from the food at our table.

'Home we would come, like fishermen with our catch, excited about our bargains and faced with the difficult decision: what to cook first?'

And now my own family, which includes my husband Rob (whose boyhood ambition was to marry a Cordon Bleu cook!) and our two daughters Kate and Lulu, live by the same philosophy – that it's not necessary to spend a lot of money to eat well. We sometimes use expensive or rich ingredients, but with restraint. Beef fillet is not strictly out of bounds, but you don't need much. A little cream can make a great difference to a soup or sauce, but too much softens the flavour. We eat simply, the way I always have, and every meal is special. We cook together, set the table, share a bottle of wine and relax as we talk over the day's activities, not unlike generations of my family have always done.

Kate

I learned very early in life that eating was something to be treasured. From a young age, my sister and I would sit at the table and eat dinner with Mum and Dad. The four of us would always come together at mealtimes to share food and conversation – no television, no radio, no other distractions. Food was the uniting force, drawing us away from our individual activities to the table. And on Saturday mornings, I was the one still tucked up in bed after everyone else had got up, dressed and already finished a pot of tea. But the one thing that was sure to lure me into the kitchen was the soothing smell of Dad's homemade pikelets, and I was always up in time to flip the last few.

Everyone says their mother's cooking is the best they've ever had, and I would have to agree, especially since my mother was Cordon Bleu-trained and is passionate about cooking, and my grandmother, Margaret Fulton, is a veritable doyenne of Australian cuisine.

'People would always say to me, "You must eat very well at home", and they were right. There was always something simmering or baking in our house.'

It was all about choosing seasonal produce, using the right quantities and saving anything that could be used later on. A vast array of food would find its way into the kitchen: bags of mussels and pippies straight from the fish markets, dried pulses, strangely shaped vegetables. I was fascinated by all this, and became a permanent question-mark at my mother and grandmother's sides: What's that herb? Why do you sift the flour? What does bicarbonate of soda do? And now I'm glad I asked!

When I left home, I was keen to hold on to this intelligent and economical approach to food. At university, I always knew what to do with the remnants of food left in the bottom of the fridge at the end of the week – I'd make them into a hearty soup, stir-fry or risotto for my flatmates. Knowing how to store food, what to do with leftovers and which sauces were must-haves for the pantry did as much to help me get through university as studying. Later, as a cash-strapped journalist working in London, this approach to food was borne out of necessity as much as an appreciation for good, home-cooked meals.

Both my younger sister Lulu and I are keen cooks, and as adults we have embraced the practical habits instilled in us by our mother and grandmother. Lulu lives in the country, and this relative isolation means she has to think carefully about making the most of the ingredients she has to hand – she can't just pop to the shops. I live in Sydney with my fiancé Dan, and the expense of inner-city life means we need to watch what we spend on food. Instead of wasting money on expensive takeaways, we cook at home most nights. I'll make an Indian curry and freeze half for later, or Dan will make a pizza from scratch. As the now-iconic line from the film *The Castle* goes, 'Why would you eat out when this keeps coming up night after night?'

To me, being thrifty is about more than just saving money. It's about avoiding waste, looking after your health, appreciating each ingredient and having the desire and skills to cook for the people you love. And that sums up what this book is about.

Thrifty shopping

The first step to setting up a thrifty kitchen is to establish sensible, economical habits when shopping for food. Here we've put together a collection of foolproof tips and suggestions to help you save money without compromising on the quality and flavour of the food you and your family enjoy.

HOW AND WHERE TO SHOP?

If you can, the best thing to do is **shop locally and daily for your fresh produce**, buying only what you need, and no more, to avoid waste. Pick up a couple of bunches of basil going cheap and some lean chicken mince on the way home. Throw it together in a wok with some oil, garlic and fish sauce, cook some rice from your pantry to go with it and you've got a thrifty, delicious dinner in no time. And if you don't have specialist local shops nearby, popping into the supermarket on the way home may be just as handy.

Of course, not all of us have the luxury of a farmers' market, greengrocer, butcher or fishmonger within walking distance or on our way home, where we can pop in to get a couple of chicken thighs or a few zucchini for that night's dinner. If you have to drive a fair distance to get to the shops, it certainly doesn't make sense economically to go every day. Many of us find we have to buy our fresh produce on a weekly basis (some even less frequently), so you'll need a few tricks up your sleeve to make it last the week.

Have a think about the fresh produce that you and your family eat each week, and **include on your shopping list only what you know you'll get through**. Buy a whole bag of potatoes if the

family is spud-mad, but if you only have them once a week just take a handful; if you like chicken thigh fillets in curries as well as barbecued, buy enough for two meals and freeze half of them. While this might sound boring and predictable, most of us do eat the same kinds of dishes, week in, week out – it's the clever cook who spices things up with simple variations (and you'll find plenty of inspiration for how to do just that in this book). Keep in mind that a good squeeze of lemon juice and some fresh herbs can perk up almost any dish, so they should be permanent fixtures on your weekly list. Better still, grow your own parsley, mint and basil and you will have ready access to these versatile herbs (see page 134 for tips on growing your own herbs).

The best way of all to shop is to **choose food that is in season** – it's your guarantee that you're getting the best and paying less for it. There are great bargains to be had when you buy in season. At the beginning of summer, asparagus can be picked up for next to nothing, as can baby squash and capsicum, and for a few precious weeks you can get delicacies like raspberries at a reasonable price. Once you start to notice that something is getting a bit pricey, you can be sure it's not at its peak.

Making fresh produce last the week

- **Apples** are just about the only fruit that can be kept in the fridge without losing their flavour. With most other fruit, buy only what you will use in a few days.
- **Stone fruit** – when buying nectarines, mangoes, peaches or plums, choose perfectly ripe, just-ripe and firm ones. Eat the ripest ones first and leave the firm ones to ripen on the windowsill, and you'll be eating ripe fruit all week.
- **Lettuce** – buy a whole lettuce and store it, unwashed, in a snap-lock bag or airtight container in the crisper for up to a week. Keep it away from gas-producing fruit such as apples, pears or bananas, which will accelerate its deterioration. Wash and dry leaves thoroughly as you need them.
- **Meat portions** – keep in mind that 150–180 g of meat, chicken or fish per person per meal is sufficient, so stick to these quantities or use leftovers for another meal.

THE BIG SHOP

Weekly or fortnightly you should **stock up on those all-important pantry staples** that you rely on everyday. The number-one rule is to make a list of what you need, checking your fridge and pantry before you go. Most of us are like rabbits caught in the headlights when faced with the rows of brightly coloured boxes at the supermarket – we tend to wander the aisles in a daze, having no idea what we came in for, and end up filling our trolleys with things we'll never use. A list helps us stay focused and in control, and means we are less likely to be swayed by the marketing ploys that would see the ruin of our budgets and our waistlines.

Some of us are trying really hard to save money. If you find you're having to pull in the purse strings a bit, **don't be a snob about discounts**. The discount bins in supermarkets can be an excellent source of bargains, but most people pass them by, thinking they are full of lower-quality items. This is not always the case. Check the use-by date and only buy what you will use, but by all means snap up those bargains!

Look for weekly specials at the supermarket, but don't go stockpiling five boxes of cheese-and-onion-biscuits just because they're on sale (you'll soon be cursing when you discover the kids prefer the plain ones anyway!), and be wary of the two-for-one deals if the item is not something you usually eat a lot of. Use these specials to your advantage – don't be a sucker for an offer if the product is not appropriate for your household.

Remember that your kitchen is not a mini-supermarket, and you shouldn't buy things just because they look appealing, or in the vague hope they might come in handy. Even those spacious walk-in pantries can soon get cluttered with too many boxes of fancy cereal and flavoured olive oils that will never be used. When you're reaching for that jar of exotic marinade, ask yourself: will you be using it today, or tomorrow? Can you actually imagine the meal it is going to be used in? If not, don't buy it. Running a home is a bit like running a business. We want you to **start shopping smarter**; to try and avoid waste and recognise that a product is not necessarily better than the version you could make at home just because it has a fancy gold label on it.

Getting the best value at the supermarket

- **Cast your eyes up and down the shelves for cheaper options** – Many supermarkets put the most expensive items at eye-level.
- **Try the cheaper brand** – Paying more doesn't always mean you are getting a better product, and if you always buy the most expensive brands, you could end up spending as much as 30 per cent more on your overall bill than the shopper who buys the cheapest brand.
- **Check the ingredients** – For example, does the more expensive jar of jam actually contain more fruit? Labelling regulations now make it easier for us to know what the product we are buying contains – the ingredients must be listed in order of their proportions.
- **Take your calculator along** – Don't take it for granted that the larger the pack is, the better the value. Sometimes family packs are the best value, but sometimes they are not. Work it out yourself, and remember to take into account whether you're going to get through it all before the use-by date.

✻ If you really don't trust yourself not to make rash purchases, or you don't have easy access to a supermarket, try doing your grocery shopping online. You can shop in the peace and quiet of your home or office in a calm, controlled environment, with your list as guidance.

Think twice

Next time you're shopping, reconsider before filling up your trolley with the following items:

- **Packet cereal** – The cost of breakfast cereals can really add up, and they're not necessarily very good for you. A packet of rolled oats is your best bet, because with it you can make your own muesli or porridge (see pages 6–7 for oat-based breakfast ideas). The family will soon adjust, especially if you work at making it really special by adding some grated apple or other fresh fruit.
- **Jars or cans of marinades and curry pastes** – These can be great time-savers and have their place, but unless you know you will use them regularly (like your favourite Thai red curry paste, for instance), leave them on the supermarket shelf. And ready-made stir-in sauces, which are often laden with unwanted sugar, salt and preservatives, are best avoided.

- **Jam** – Check your fridge or pantry first: how many half-eaten jars of jam can you see? Make it a rule that you don't buy a new one until the last one has been finished, and the same goes for chutneys and mustards. It's easy to make your own quick raspberry jam: combine 500 g frozen raspberries with ¼ cup lemon juice in a large microwave-proof bowl, then microwave on the highest setting for 5 minutes. Stir in 1½ cups caster sugar and cook on high for another 20 minutes, lightly stirring every 5 minutes. Spoon into a sterilised jar (see page 152), seal, label and cool, ready to store.
- **Deli goods** – All those sliced meats, marinated artichokes and eggplants look good but can be really expensive. When it comes to sliced meat, buy only what you know you can use within a day or so – it won't last longer than that. The same goes for marinated vegetables, which can start to go mouldy after three days.

Saving on cleaning products

It's not difficult to spend a fortune on cleaning products for the home, and it's especially hard to save money when you're trying to buy organic or chemical-free products. Those specialty shops with aisle after aisle filled with gorgeous bottles of organic products to clean the oven, fridge, benchtops and sink are tempting, but the price will often bring you back to earth with a thud. And you probably already have one of the most effective cleaning products sitting in your pantry: baking soda. Here's a couple of ways it can come in handy.

- **To clean the inside of your oven**, scrub with wet steel wool then sprinkle generously with baking soda. Leave for a short time then rub clean with a damp cloth.
- **To keep your microwave clean**, practise some good ol' prevention – make sure you cover any food to be microwaved with plastic film or an upturned, microwave-safe plate. If you neglect to do this, and a simple wipe with a damp cloth won't budge the stuff that's sprayed all over the inside, mix ½ cup water with 3 teaspoons baking soda in a microwave-safe bowl. Place the bowl in the microwave on high for 2 minutes and 20 seconds, then remove. You should then be able to wipe the microwave clean easily.

STOCKING THE PANTRY

Aim to have your pantry stocked with essential ingredients that you can use to throw together a tasty meal at the last minute. You'll also find you'll save money by stocking up on staples. Here's a quick checklist of the items you'll need on hand in your pantry.

Packets of:
- Dried pasta (the best you can afford)
- Noodles, such as rice vermicelli and soba
- Rice, such as brown, basmati, arborio and jasmine
- Oats (for porridge, muesli and baking)
- Raisins, sultanas, currants or cranberries (for baking, porridge and healthy snacks)
- Flour, such as self-raising, plain, wholemeal and strong '00' bread flour
- Dried legumes, such as beans, chickpeas and lentils
- Couscous
- Cornmeal (polenta)
- Sea salt
- Sugar, such as caster, icing and brown (see page 167 for more information on different sugars and their uses)
- Dried yeast (to make your own bread and pizza bases)
- Cocoa powder
- Nuts, such as almonds, hazelnuts and cashews (all unsalted; for snacking or cooking with)
- Bicarbonate of soda
- Baking powder

Cans of:
- Fish, such as tuna, sardines, anchovies, mackerel and salmon (in oil or spring water)
- Curry pastes, such as Indian, Thai green or red (but not the stir-through sauces you just 'heat and eat')
- Chickpeas
- Lentils
- Cannellini beans
- Red kidney beans
- Tomatoes (whole and chopped)
- Coconut milk
- Golden syrup

Jars of:
- Olives (green and black, with stones in)
- Capers
- Dijon mustard

Vinegars, oils and sauces:
- **Balsamic vinegar** – This is great for salads. Experiment with white balsamic; we love its subtle flavour. Store at room temperature away from direct light, with the lid tightly closed.
- **Red- and white-wine vinegar** – Use on salads along with olive oil, or for giving a sauce a nice punch. Store at room temperature away from direct light, with the lid tightly closed.
- **Olive oil** – Use regular for cooking (don't waste the good, extra virgin stuff by cooking with it – the flavour will be lost), and save your finest extra virgin for dressing salads and for drizzling over dishes just before serving. Store at room temperature away from direct light, with the lid tightly closed.
- **Sesame oil** – Adds flavour to stir-fries, baked fish and steamed chicken. Best stored in the fridge to stop it going rancid.
- **Rice bran oil** – A healthy choice for cooking with, and great for adding to salads, marinades and dressings, especially for Asian dishes where you don't want the strong flavour of extra virgin olive oil. Store at room temperature away from direct light, with the lid tightly closed.
- **Passata** – This Italian-style crushed tomato sauce is invaluable in the kitchen (you can even make your own if you find you have a glut of tomatoes; see pages 160–1 for tomato sauce recipes). Use it as a quick base for spaghetti sauces, pizzas, soups, casseroles and pasta bakes. Once opened, store in the fridge and use within a few days.
- **Soy sauce** – If you like stir-fries and other Asian dishes, it's worthwhile getting a large bottle as you'll soon get through it. Look for salt-reduced soy or try kecap manis (see page 72), which is sweeter, thicker and less salty. Best stored in the fridge to retain flavour.
- **Tabasco** – This spicy sauce can really lift the flavour of simple fried eggs, chops, sausages or a Mexican meal. Best stored in the fridge to retain flavour.

Spices:
Don't clog your cupboards with a whole host of spices that you'll probably never use. Start with cinnamon, dried chillies, black peppercorns, paprika, curry powder, ground cumin, bay leaves and ginger, then see how you go.

* The thrifty cook always has the following on hand in the freezer: peas; broad beans; spinach; raspberries; frozen pastry, such as filo, shortcrust and puff; red chillies and kaffir lime leaves.

MEAT – GETTING YOUR MONEY'S WORTH

A friend of ours is constantly turning out intricate terrines, rillettes and pâtés. She buys liver, chicken mince and cheap cuts of pork and veal and adds herbs, bacon and fat to make smooth, salty, delicious creations. It will probably come as no surprise to learn that she has lived in Paris most of her life – the French invented *charcuterie,* and these types of dishes are much-loved in French households. The lesson here, of course, is that there is much more to meat than a barbecued steak. **The thrifty cook makes the most of every cut of meat**, and avoids waste by shying away from the singularity of mass production that would have us cooking only rump steak and chicken breasts. Take a moment to think about how much of the animal you eat. Since a beast has given up its life for your lunch, perhaps you owe it a little more consideration in terms of how much of it you're willing to eat.

For many of us, meat is among the most important and versatile foods. It supplies us with protein, iron and B vitamins. The fat gives us energy, has plenty of flavour and helps to keep the lean parts of the meat moist and succulent during cooking. Fortunately for the thrifty cook, **the cheaper cuts are just as nutritious as the expensive ones**. They can take longer to cook, but this is more than made up for by their delicious flavour. The upside is that everyone loves a long, slow-cooked casserole or roast – it's always worth the wait!

Now's the time to abolish any negative preconceptions you may have about cheaper cuts of meat. Don't assume that a lamb shoulder is going to be too fatty. You just need to trim it properly, and even though this will reduce the size of the joint slightly, you'll still be miles ahead in terms of value for money. Buy chicken necks, wings and giblets for making stock – or use the carcass of a roast chook. Gravy beef (also called shin beef) is an economical, richly flavoured cut with very little fat that can be cubed and cooked in a stew. Oxtail has a high proportion of bone, and needs long, slow cooking, but it rewards with a fantastic flavour. And why not consider offal? We believe it should be on the menu in every household. Tripe, kidneys and liver are nourishing, relatively cheap and delicious when cooked with flair. Many consider calves' liver a true delicacy when thinly sliced, lightly sautéed and served with a green salad.

So take a moment to open your mind to the endless possibilities at the meat counter. If you normally shop at a supermarket you might find it helpful to **visit your local butcher for a wider range of options**. For now, let's take a closer look at the best-value bits of each animal so you have an idea of what's available.

Lamb

It's unfortunate that we are encouraged to stick to just a few prime cuts of lamb, namely the leg, loin and the rack, when there are so many more economical and delicious cuts to be enjoyed. Many of these are becoming more widely available now, though you may have to cajole your butcher into supplying some of these lesser-known cuts.

Lamb shoulder – a shoulder of lamb, cut from the forequarter, is a wonderfully economical cut. Some shoulders have more fat than others, but the fat is easy to remove. This cut is very suitable for long, slow, moist cooking in curries, stews and casseroles. It can also be boned, stuffed and roasted, or cut into chops.

Shanks – you might find lamb shanks that are already 'french trimmed' but if not, ask your butcher to cut the knobbly end off. One shank per person should be enough, although hearty appetites will manage two. These are excellent cooked the night before you need them, so that you can remove the fat that has risen to the surface and set. They should be gently reheated to yield a lovely gelatinous gravy.

Best or scrag neck – economical compared with loin or chump chops, best neck chops, best neck cutlets and forequarter chops are good for grilling, frying or barbecuing. More difficult to get are scrag neck chops, which are tender, succulent and wonderful for soups and stews (think traditional Irish stew). Keep in mind that these have a high proportion of bone to flesh, so allow for extra to be sure there's enough meat.

Liver (or lamb's fry) – liver has outstanding nutritional properties and, when properly cooked, is as delicious as anything you will eat. It is best skinned and cut into thin slices (many butchers can do this for you). The slices should be dusted with seasoned flour and quickly pan-fried.

Lamb mince – this is usually made from lamb shoulder. It has a great flavour, but be aware of its high fat and water content. Generally speaking, the darker the mince, the less fat it contains – if you find a lot of moisture coming out of the mince when you fry it, it's a sure sign that water has been added. Try and buy premium lean mince when you can. Lamb mince is the traditional choice for Middle Eastern and Greek dishes, such as kofta kebabs and moussaka.

Beef

Blade – the blade is from the forequarter and can be butchered into several cuts. The oyster blade is good for grilling, barbecuing or braising; the barbecue blade is a good substitute for sirloin steak for barbecuing; and the bolar blade is delicious roasted.

Chuck – located under the blade, chuck is a great buy with excellent flavour. Use a whole piece for pot-roasting, or smaller pieces for curries, stews and casseroles.

Brisket – brisket, from the breast, is a fabulous cut that is mostly sold boned, as a corned (pickled) roll for boiling, or simply rolled for pot-roasting or boiling.

Oxtail – cubed oxtail meat cooked in soups and stews makes the most flavoursome and comforting winter dishes. Long, slow cooking is needed to bring out its rich flavour.

Shin or foreshank – this is cut into gravy beef and has a wonderfully deep flavour for stews and soups.

Beef mince – there are different grades of mince available, depending on the texture and fat content. The flavour of 'best' or 'premium' mince may be better, but it can be a little dry as it doesn't contain much fat. Choose coarsely ground mince for burgers or rissoles and finer premium mince for dishes cooked in liquid. Alternatively, buy a cheap cut of the relevant meat and mince it yourself using a sharp knife or a food processor.

Tongue – a whole ox tongue can be used in a variety of meals. Sold fresh, salted or smoked, tongue is one of the best cold meats for salads and sandwiches, but is also good served hot with a piquant caper or mustard sauce.

Tripe – the lining of the stomach of cattle (or sheep), tripe can be smooth or honeycombed and is nearly always sold partly cooked. Ask your butcher for it – most will have frozen tripe available. It will need to be blanched before use to freshen the flavour.

Chicken

Our favourite way to eat chicken is to roast a whole one so we can enjoy every last bit. But if you don't fancy a roast, here are some alternatives to the ubiquitous (and expensive) chicken breast.

Thighs – chicken thighs are cheaper than breasts and generally more flavoursome as they contain more fat (but you can trim most of this off, if you prefer). You can buy thigh fillets with the skin on or off, and they are incredibly versatile: good for stir-fries, curries or braises, they are also delicious roasted.

Wings and drumsticks – marinated in a sweet, sticky sauce, wings and drumsticks are a really economical way to serve a crowd at a party; they make great finger food. Drumsticks have a generous amount of flavoursome meat on them, and can be seasoned in endless ways then roasted for a delicious dinner.

Pork

Shoulder – this is an inexpensive cut of meat that can easily be transformed into a glorious meal. The shoulder is usually divided into the upper shoulder portion, called the collared butt or neck, and the lower portion called the picnic shoulder. This meaty pork cut is available bone-in or boneless. Pork shoulder roasts extremely well, especially if slow-roasted so that much of the fat is rendered out of the meat. It is also ideal for stews, braises and hearty curries, as well as being a good meat for the barbecue. Just trim off any unwanted fat if you're watching your weight.

Belly – the pork belly is the underside of the animal, from which streaky or American-style bacon is cut. This cut is very popular in Asian cuisine, where it is often marinated and slow-cooked in one piece to produce moist, fall-apart tender meat. Pork belly comes with or without skin.

Pork mince – probably the most inexpensive of minced meats, pork mince is made from either pork leg or shoulder. Use to make an economical bolognese sauce, pan-fried pork rissoles, hamburger patties or little Italian meatballs, as well as stir-fries and French terrines. Pork mince can also be combined with other minced meats, so experiment away!

Ribs – spare ribs are from the side or belly of the pig and are scrumptious pan-fried, barbecued, grilled or slow-roasted. Ribs team particularly well with a sticky sweet-and-sour sauce, making them a great barbecue dish. Look for meaty spare ribs with a reddish-pink colour.

This little piggie went to market . . .

Pork is the world's most popular meat. From spare ribs to trotters, almost the entire animal is eaten in some form or another. Trimmed pork is as lean as skinless chicken breast, and it's a good source of protein, thiamine, niacin, B6, B12, selenium, riboflavin, zinc and omega-3. However, fat has lots of flavour and pork with a little fat on it tastes markedly different to 'lean' pork, and is more likely to be moist and succulent.

Rabbit

It wasn't so long ago that rabbit was known as 'underground mutton'. Before the days of mass-produced chicken, rabbit, being very lean and usually wild, was considered good value. Australians would stew it and serve it with dumplings. Later, European immigrants introduced other rabbit dishes to our repertoire: rabbit cooked in mustard or with tomatoes and garlic.

Rabbit has now become gourmet fare, but still represents a good-value healthy meat with little waste. Speak to your butcher about the availability of rabbit – you might find you have to order it specially. Rabbit flesh tends to be dry, so take care not to over-cook it. The farmed rabbits available today don't need lengthy cooking time and will be done in less than 30 minutes.

To prepare a rabbit, separate it at the leg joints to give two thigh sections. Cut the loin into one or two sections through the backbone and cut the rib-cage section in two along the backbone. You should end up with five or six pieces.

Thanks for all the fish

These days, we all need to be aware which varieties of fish are sustainable and which are not. Some are in plentiful supply and can be pulled from the seas in great numbers without this having a huge effect on their overall population or their ecosystem. Others are severely overfished, which causes havoc in the underwater world. If we catch too much of one type of fish it may well disappear entirely, and other fish that rely on it for food will also suffer.

The general rule is that smaller fish such as sardines, mackerel and whiting are fine to eat. When buying fish for making fish and chips, avoid flake, which is another name for shark – it's one of the most threatened kinds of fish in Australia, in part because it takes so long to breed. Instead, go for flathead, barramundi, blue-eye trevalla, hoki, bream, mullet, yellow-eye mullet or snapper. Also on the okay list are yellowfin tuna and coral trout.

At the other end of the scale, on the 'absolutely overfished list', are Eastern gemfish (also called hake or silver kingfish), redfish (or red snapper), Southern bluefin tuna and Atlantic salmon. Also, remember not to touch orange roughy (which is also called deep-sea perch), sea perch and swordfish, as these are all caught on long lines, which damage other sea creatures. Avoid tiger prawns and go for Balmain or Moreton Bay bugs instead. Have oysters, but not the introduced Pacific variety. Don't buy baby octopus (which is imported), but rather look for squid or calamari. Happy shopping!

STORING FRESH MEAT, POULTRY AND FISH

Proper storage is essential to retain freshness and good condition. Fresh meat should be stored in the coldest part of the fridge on a rack over a plate or a tray, uncovered or loosely wrapped to allow for maximum air circulation (the meat may dry out a little, but this prevents bacterial growth). Lightly covering meat with greaseproof, baking or waxed paper is better than using plastic film. The very best option is a special container (with a corrugated base and air vents at the sides) that allows the contents to breathe but doesn't allow the meat to dry out. If you notice an off-smelling odour, you are best advised to discard the meat. Before storing chicken in the fridge for more than a day, be sure to take off its wrapping, wash it thoroughly and pat it dry with paper towel, then store as above. Fresh fish should be gutted and washed before storing as above.

When freezing meat, take off the wrapping and vapour-proof packaging to prevent freezer-burn (when white spots appear on the flesh). It may be tempting to simply use ordinary plastic bags, greaseproof paper or foil, but it's a false economy, particularly for long-term storage. Go for special freezer bags or wraps – they are strong and can be labelled, washed and re-used.

If freezing several pieces of meat, like a few chops or steaks, place each one in a separate bag or lay freezer wrap between them to make separation easier, and to prevent freezer burn. Remember to label and date the bag.

Thawing frozen meat and poultry

The best way to thaw frozen meat and poultry is to plan ahead and thaw it slowly in the fridge. Soaking it in hot water, or leaving it out on the bench for the day is a big no-no, not only for health reasons but also for maintaining the meat's quality. By thawing meat in the fridge slowly, you are keeping it at its best.

A couple of steaks to be eaten that night can be transferred from freezer to fridge in the morning, as long as they have been wrapped separately. If you plan to cook a frozen chicken the next night, take it out of the freezer and place in the refrigerator to thaw for 24 hours (if the chicken is large it may take longer – it would be safest to thaw in the fridge 2 days in advance, to make sure it is thoroughly defrosted before cooking). A whole turkey needs 2–3 days to thaw in the fridge.

The next best way to thaw is by using cold water. Place the raw meat or poultry in a heavy-duty snap-lock bag and submerge in cold tap water, changing the water occasionally. Use the microwave only when absolutely necessary, as some areas of the food can start to cook before the meat is fully thawed, which isn't pleasant. Frozen fish should be cooked directly from frozen.

Fresh meat, poultry and fish storage chart

Food	Fridge	Freezer
Beef	3–5 days	10–12 months
Beef mince	2–3 days	4–6 months
Lamb	3–5 days	10–12 months
Lamb mince	2–3 days	4–6 months
Liver	1–2 days	2–3 months
Pork	3–4 days	6–8 months
Pork mince	2–3 days	2–3 months
Poultry	2–3 days	5–6 months
Chicken mince	1–2 days	4–6 months
Rabbit	2–3 days	6–8 months
Fish – oily (such as salmon)	2–3 days	3–4 months
Fish – white	2–3 days	6–8 months
Shellfish	1–2 days	1 month
Uncooked meat patties	2 days	2–3 months

CHAPTER 1

Breakfasts

Breakfast is, without a doubt, the best meal of the day. It's the potential that makes it so great. You can run out the door with your bag slung over your shoulder, a hot coffee in one hand and a piece of buttered toast in the other. Or you can go all out with fresh fruit, eggs, crispy bacon, hash browns and towers of pancakes dripping with syrup: the options for the first meal of the day are limitless. Breakfast can cure the effects of a big night out, it can give you energy for the day ahead, it can bring everyone together to strategise, plan, reassure and relax. Without breakfast to spur us on, without the smell of coffee or bacon wafting through the hallways, many of us would find the start to the day much, much harder.

'Eat breakfast like an emperor, lunch like a king and supper like a church mouse', so the saying goes if you want to stay fit and healthy. Experts agree that people who start their day with a good breakfast are more efficient, more productive and noticeably better-tempered than those who don't.

It's long been the tradition of farmers' wives to send their husbands off to work with a solid breakfast. Large bowls of steaming porridge, followed by kippers, steak and eggs, mushrooms, piles of bacon rashers and still more piles of buttery toast. These large breakfasts were to prepare the men for a hard day's work in the fields, but you wouldn't want to eat that much every morning if you're going to sit at a desk all day. So how does Spanish-style toast, a quick omelette, or some homemade muesli sound? Pretty good, we think.

Prepare as much as you can the night before and you won't be getting hot under the collar while you're trying to iron your shirt, find your other shoe or flick through the onslaught of emails on your BlackBerry. Being organised is crucial. Even when you're in a mad rush, if you've got some low-fat yoghurt in the fridge, frozen berries in the freezer and roasted almonds in the pantry, with the mix of a spoon you'll have something delicious to tide you over until lunch.

Eggs are the great breakfast all-rounder: if you have a couple of eggs in the fridge, you have breakfast in minutes. A simple soft-boiled egg with buttered toast soldiers has to be the best remedy for hungry tummies in the morning. But eggs are also the basis of many other breakfast dishes – pikelets, French toast, frog in the hole . . . they're all delicious, quick and easy to whip up in the morning.

How safe are they?

If you're wondering how safe it is to consume raw eggs in drinks like Morning sunshine (see page 4), we can reassure you that fresh Australian eggs don't carry salmonella. The Australian Egg Corporation advises that fresh egg-based drinks must be consumed straight away (they're definitely *not* something to be saved for the next day), but otherwise consuming raw eggs in egg flips and homemade sauces like mayonnaise (see page 140) does not carry an increased risk of food poisoning. Be sure, though, to store homemade mayonnaise or other sauces containing raw egg in the fridge and use within a day of making.

Egg tips

- **Eggs love a cool climate** – keep your eggs in the fridge: they'll last longer and their flavour won't diminish. Write their use-by date on them in pencil if you're not storing them in the box.
- **Washed out** – don't wash eggs before storing them in the fridge as the water will seep into the egg – just give them a light wipe with a damp cloth if you have to. If you're boiling them, they're going to be cleaned in the process anyway.
- **Don't use them cold** – eggs should be brought to room temperature before cooking. If the egg is too cold when you plunge it into boiling water, the shell will crack, and cold eggs don't beat as well. Place the eggs in a bowl of room-temperature tap water for a couple of minutes before using to hasten this process.
- **The dip test** – to test how fresh an egg is, put it in a bowl of water. Stale eggs float, fresh ones sink. (As an egg ages, air gets beneath the shell.)
- **Spinning egg** – to test whether an egg is hard-boiled, spin it gently on a hard, flat surface. A wobbly spin indicates a raw egg.
- **Squeaky clean** – give your plates, eggcup and utensils a rinse straight after you've used them, as dried egg is sticky business and very hard to remove.

Chick, chick, chickens . . .

KATE > When I was young, our family lived on a large block in Sydney's inner west and we kept chickens in the backyard. My sister Lulu and I used to love chasing them round the garden, trying to put them safely back in their chookhouse at night. Our brood provided a constant supply of beautiful brown eggs. Lulu and I would go and say good morning to the chickens every day, and then rustle around in the hay to collect the eggs they'd left us.

We'd feed them fresh grain, pumpkin skin and seeds, capsicum seeds, fresh greens and potato peelings. Our neighbours would even drop off their scraps to give to the chooks, and we'd hand a few eggs over the back fence as thanks. Dad would give the chooks a regular supply of fresh sawdust to muck around in, and he also constructed an incredible chicken-wire fenced area so they had the run of a large corner of the garden. An enormous tree grew smack bang in the middle of their patch, and sometimes we'd find the chickens nesting in some of the lower branches. We also had an Indian Runner duck called Jemima, who laid gorgeous big pale eggs with a blue hue.

As well as enjoying these fantastic pets, we did love our eggs in the morning, and now we're both highly-skilled experts (eggsperts) at breakfasts involving eggs – coddled, scrambled, made into a frittata or just perfectly boiled with toast soldiers.

If you want to keep chickens or ducks in your garden, first check your local council regulations. There are numerous websites and books with more information on keeping your own poultry – just search online for relevant articles or check your local bookstore. Here are a few basic tips to get you started.

- **Make sure you have enough space** for them to scratch, peck and nest – there is nothing more depressing than sad-looking chickens or ducks that are cooped up all day.
- **They'll need protection** from the environment: shade from the sun and heat, shelter from the rain and somewhere quiet to lay so they're not constantly harassed by local cats, foxes and the like – you can buy small chicken huts for this purpose quite cheaply.
- **They'll also need a supply of fresh water** (either changed daily or provided by a drip system), as well as hay or sawdust (or both) to scratch about in. Feed them a varied diet – they'll love your

vegetable scraps plus a daily supply of pellets, which you can pick up from any good pet store and some larger garden suppliers.
- **They love to have plenty to do**, be it scratch in a patch of grass, peck around in some fresh newspaper or a light and bouncy ball to play with – you'll be surprised when they start pushing it around!
- **Give them company** – get at least two chooks so they're not lonely (remember, you'll get more, better-tasting eggs if they're happy!).
- **Provide your ducks** with a place to splash around in on really hot days – they love a little dip in one of those blow-up pools if you or a neighbour have one spare.
- **Ducks left free to run around** the garden will solve all your snail problems (but don't use any poisonous snail pellets or similar as they will harm the ducks as well).

Most importantly, look after your birds and treat them with the respect you would give any other pet, and you'll reap the rewards.

Morning sunshine

This is a nutritious meal-in-a-glass that should be in everyone's repertoire. A delicious egg-enriched drink is a great breakfast-on-the-run and an instant, light meal at any time of the day. Most of us are familiar with milk-based egg flips, but the orange juice takes this one to another dimension. You may recall Rocky Balboa drinking whole eggs before a workout; well, this is a much more elegant, tasty pick-me-up.

3–4 cubes ice
1 egg
1 tablespoon sugar or honey
1 cup ice-cold fresh orange juice
good pinch of grated nutmeg

1   Whiz the ice cubes, egg and sugar or honey together in an electric blender or a food processor until smooth. Add the orange juice and continue to blend until frothy.

2   Pour into a glass, top with grated nutmeg and serve.

Try these delicious variations:

- **Milky egg flip** – Use milk in place of the orange juice and add some vanilla extract if you like.
- **Fluffy egg flip** – Separate the egg and beat the yolk, honey and ice cubes together, then mix with 1 cup milk instead of orange juice. Beat the eggwhite until stiff, then fold into the milk mixture and serve immediately.
- **Pineapple sunrise** – Substitute the orange juice with pineapple juice. You could also add 1 tablespoon of coconut cream to this one for a 'pina colada'-inspired breakfast drink.

Speedy apple breakfast

Sure, you could just grab an apple and eat it on the run. Or you could turn it into a beautiful breakfast worth sitting down to.

LSA – a mix of ground linseed, sunflower seeds and almonds – is available from most supermarkets. You can make your own by combining linseeds, sunflower seeds and almonds in the ratio 3:2:1. Whiz them up in a blender and store them in the fridge.

1 apple
squeeze of lemon juice
1 tablespoon ground linseed, sunflower seeds and almonds (LSA) or chopped mixed nuts
1 tablespoon honey
2–3 tablespoons natural yoghurt
sliced fruits in season, to serve (optional)

1   Coarsely grate the unpeeled apple and stir through the lemon juice, LSA or chopped nuts, honey and yoghurt.

2   Dollop onto sliced fruit, if using, and serve.

Good culture: making your own yoghurt

If you love yoghurt and eat it regularly, why not make it yourself? Bought yoghurt is often full of preservatives, sugar and goodness knows what else. By making it yourself, you control exactly what goes in, and the quality is often much, much better. You'll need 1 large or several small sterilised containers (see page 152) with lids in which to set and store the yoghurt, a sugar or candy thermometer, and an 'incubator', such as a yoghurt maker, a Thermos flask or a container wrapped in a towel or blanket. Just heat 5 cups milk (adding ½ cup milk powder if you want an extra creamy yoghurt) in a large heavy-based saucepan over low heat until it reaches 80°C. Remove from the heat and cool until the milk temperature is 55°C. Meanwhile, place ¼ cup bought natural yoghurt (next time you can use your own) in a bowl or jug. Gradually stir in 1 cup of the warmed milk using a metal spoon, then quickly stir in the remaining milk. Pour into the incubator and leave in a warm spot for 4–6 hours, without disturbing, until set. Once set, transfer the yoghurt to a sterilised container and place in the fridge, where it will keep for up to 10 days.

Don't peel the apples before grating them for your Speedy apple breakfast, and you'll retain all the nutrients and fibre — just make sure you wash the apples well first.

Oats four ways

OLD-FASHIONED PORRIDGE is still one of the best and most economical breakfasts around. Some love their porridge the classic way, flavoured only with a little salt and served in a bowl with a bowl of cold milk alongside to dip spoonfuls of hot porridge into. Others like it with a little butter, salt and milk. But porridge with stewed fruit such as rhubarb, apples or prunes, sprinkled with a little wheatgerm and topped with milk or pouring cream, can also be sublime.

Muesli is another great oat-based breakfast. Bircher muesli was originally developed by Dr Bircher-Benner in his Zurich sanatorium – his attempt to make a healthy breakfast food. Traditionally, the oats are soaked in water or fruit juice overnight before being served the next day with grated apple, cream and toasted nuts. Muesli has taken on many transformations since its creation and toasted muesli has now become well known and loved. Whichever is your favourite, by making your own you're avoiding both the expensive and sugary 'gourmet' toasted mueslis and the cheaper products that may leave you wondering about the amount of flavour enhancers they contain.

Porridge with stewed rhubarb

SERVES 4

1⅓ cups rolled oats
500 g rhubarb, cut into 2 cm lengths
50 g caster sugar
½ teaspoon vanilla extract
pinch of salt
milk, buttermilk, cream or yoghurt, to serve

1   Place the oats in a medium-sized saucepan with 3 cups cold water, cover and leave overnight in the fridge.

2   Place the rhubarb, sugar and vanilla extract in a saucepan with ¼ cup water and place over medium heat. Slowly bring to a simmer, then reduce the heat to low and cook, uncovered, for about 5 minutes, until the rhubarb is tender but still holding its shape. Remove from the heat, and set aside to cool. If making in advance, transfer the cooked rhubarb to a bowl, cover and store in the fridge.

3   When you're ready to eat the porridge, add salt to the soaked oats and place over medium heat. Stir with a wooden spoon until the porridge starts to simmer. You may need to add a little more water. Reduce the heat to low and cook for about 10 minutes, stirring now and then, until the porridge is thick and creamy.

4   Serve hot topped with rhubarb and a dash of milk, buttermilk, cream, or yoghurt.

> **KATE >** I should have known, what with her being a Scot and all. The other day I made Grandma Fulton porridge for breakfast. Usually she is a gracious diner, handing out praise in abundance when we cook. But as she tasted my porridge she scrunched up her face. 'This tastes a little odd. Did you add salt?' I hadn't, thinking its absence was much better for our health. 'Katie,' she said, 'porridge only has two ingredients – salt and oats. Add them both.' We laughed, but I won't make that mistake again!

Microwave porridge

SERVES 1

⅓ cup rolled oats
pinch of salt

1   Place the oats, ¾ cup water and the salt in a microwave-safe bowl. Stir then cook in the microwave, uncovered, on a high setting for 2 minutes. Stir again and cook for a further minute.

2   Remove, stir and cover with a small plate or saucer for 1 minute. Stir again and serve.

Healthy and wise

Wheatgerm adds a great flavour to all cereals, porridge included. It's as healthy as can be – just a couple of spoonfuls each day will do wonders for your digestion. Just remember to store it in the fridge, as due to its high oil content, it will go rancid quite quickly in the cupboard.

Toasted muesli

MAKES 1.5 KG

⅓ cup vegetable oil
½–¾ cup honey
500 g rolled oats
1 cup sunflower seeds
1 cup slivered almonds
1 cup pumpkin seeds
1 cup wheatgerm
½ cup roughly chopped dried apricots
½ cup sultanas
milk, to serve
yoghurt and fresh fruit, to serve (optional)

1 Preheat oven to 180°C.

2 In a large bowl, mix the oil and honey together, then add the oats, sunflower seeds, almonds and pumpkin seeds. Stir with a large spoon so that everything is well coated with the honey mixture.

3 Spread this mixture evenly in a large baking dish. Bake for about 35 minutes or until golden brown, taking care to shake the dish every 10 minutes or so to make sure the muesli browns evenly. Remove from the oven and set aside to cool completely.

4 Toss through the wheatgerm, apricots and sultanas, then spoon into bowls and serve with milk, plus yoghurt and fresh fruit, if using.

✳ Store any leftover toasted muesli in an airtight container for up to 1 month. You can double these quantities to make a bigger batch.

Soft and crunchy muesli

SERVES 4

¼ cup rolled oats
juice of ½ a lemon or orange
1 tablespoon pouring cream
2 apples, washed and coarsely grated
2 tablespoons sunflower seeds
⅓ cup flaked or chopped almonds
⅓ cup raisins or sultanas
2 cups Toasted muesli (see left)
sliced kiwi fruit or strawberries, or whole blueberries
1–2 cups natural yoghurt or milk

1 Soak the oats in ¼ cup water for at least 30 minutes, or overnight in the fridge if possible. Add the lemon or orange juice, cream and grated apple, and mix well.

2 In a bowl, combine the sunflower seeds, almonds and raisins or sultanas. Divide the toasted muesli among four bowls and sprinkle each with some sunflower-seed mixture. Top with the oat mixture and some fresh fruit, then cover with the remaining sunflower-seed mixture. Serve with yoghurt or milk.

Bircher muesli with berries

SERVES 4

2 cups rolled oats
1 cup apple juice
1 cup coarsely grated apple
½ cup natural yoghurt
juice of ½ a lemon
1 tablespoon honey
1 cup mixed berries, such as strawberries and blueberries

1 Place the oats and apple juice in a medium-sized bowl, cover and soak for at least 1 hour, or overnight in the fridge if possible.

2 When ready to serve, add the grated apple, yoghurt, lemon juice and honey and mix until well combined. To serve, spoon into serving bowls and top with the mixed berries.

Melt-in-the-mouth French toast

SERVES 4

This is the best way to make French toast that's light, fluffy and delicious. If you're trying to eat less sugar, just sprinkle some over the toast rather than dredging it completely. Alternatively, skip the sugar altogether and drizzle with honey instead.

2 eggs
1 tablespoon sugar
1 teaspoon vanilla extract
¾ cup milk
4 thick slices day-old bread
sugar, for dredging
15 g unsalted butter
blueberries and maple syrup, to serve
thick cream and strawberry jam, to serve (optional)

✱ Use fruit loaf in place of regular bread for a spicy, fruity version.

1 In a shallow bowl, beat the eggs with a fork, then mix in the sugar, vanilla extract and milk. Add the bread slices and soak them briefly, turning a few times until all the egg mixture has been absorbed. Place some sugar in a separate bowl and set aside.

2 Melt the butter in a large frying pan over medium heat and fry the bread slices until golden on both sides. They should be puffed and still moist. Dredge the toast in the sugar and serve with blueberries and maple syrup. For a treat, add a dollop of thick cream and strawberry jam.

Try these delicious variations:

For a savoury option, omit the sugar and vanilla and add ½ teaspoon each of ground turmeric and ground cumin, a pinch of salt, 1 finely chopped green chilli, a handful of chopped coriander plus a finely diced onion to the egg mixture before you add the bread. Fry as above and instead of dredging with sugar, serve with a little natural yoghurt.

Make filled savoury French toast by using extra-thick slices of bread, then cutting a pocket through the centre. Fill with some ham and a slice of cheese, dip in the egg and milk mixture (omitting the sugar and vanilla) and fry as above.

Waste watcher

MADE TOO MANY?   *Once cooled, stack any leftover pancakes between small squares of plastic film, place in a snap-lock bag and freeze – they'll keep for at least a month. Thaw at room temperature for 30 minutes or so, or in the microwave on the lowest setting for just a few seconds.*

Ricotta pancakes

MAKES 10

Though these are not your French-style lace-like pancakes, the combination of ricotta and self-raising flour makes them light and incredibly tender, and they'll fill you up until lunchtime.

> 1 cup ricotta
> 2 tablespoons caster sugar
> 1 egg
> 1 cup milk
> 1 cup self-raising flour
> 20 g butter

1 Whisk the ricotta, sugar and egg together in a bowl. Lightly whisk in the milk and then the flour until just combined. Don't overdo it; the batter should still be a little lumpy.

2 Melt a little of the butter in a large, heavy-based frying pan over medium heat. Working in batches, pour ¼-cup measures of pancake mixture into the pan, leaving plenty of room between, then use the back of a spoon to spread them out to about 10 cm rounds. Cook for 1–2 minutes, until bubbles appear and the underside is golden. Flip and cook the other side.

3 Transfer the cooked pancakes to a plate and keep them warm under a clean tea towel while cooking the remaining mixture. Wipe the pan out with paper towel and add a little more butter between batches.

Try these delicious variations:

- **Top with sliced banana**, drizzle with golden syrup and sprinkle with brown sugar (pictured opposite).
- **Top with fresh berries** and yoghurt or lightly whipped cream
- **Top with jam** and whipped cream.
- **Sprinkle with caster sugar** and squeeze over some lemon juice
- **After spooning** the batter into the pan, lightly press blueberries or sliced strawberries into each pancake before you flip them.

Pikelets

MAKES 12

Hot pikelets, piled high and served with sweet jam and whipped cream, are the ultimate affordable luxury. These are the Aussie version of traditional Scottish pancakes, or girdle cakes. Just sit the family down at the breakfast table and keep the pikelets coming (you'll probably have to make a second batch to keep up with the 'more please' requests). Serve them warm or at room temperature with butter and honey, or jam and whipped cream.

> 1 cup self-raising flour
> ½ teaspoon salt
> 2 tablespoons sugar
> 1 egg, beaten
> 1 cup milk or buttermilk
> 30 g butter, melted, plus extra for cooking

1 Sift the flour with the salt into a bowl. Stir in the sugar and make a well in the centre.

2 Combine the beaten egg, milk or buttermilk and melted butter and mix well. Pour this into the dry ingredients and stir the mixture from the centre, gradually drawing in flour from the sides and mixing very lightly until just combined. Don't overdo it; the batter should still be a little lumpy. Test the consistency of the batter by dropping a tablespoon of mixture back into the bowl – if it doesn't drop easily it may need more milk.

3 Melt a little butter in a large, heavy-based frying pan over medium heat. Add tablespoonfuls of mixture to the pan, leaving room for each pikelet to spread a bit (you should be able to fit two or three in a large pan). Cook until bubbles have formed on the surface and the pikelet has risen. Flip and cook the other side.

4 Transfer the cooked pikelets to a plate and keep them warm under a clean tea towel while you cook the remaining mixture. Wipe the pan out with paper towel and add a little more butter between batches.

✱ Unlike other pancakes, the batter for pikelets should only be lightly mixed for best results – you don't need a smooth batter for these.

Apple and cinnamon breakfast muffins

MAKES 12

These are perfect for breakfast in bed with your newspaper and coffee on a Sunday morning. No need for butter – these light-as-air muffins use oil instead. And if you want to make them completely dairy-free, use soy milk in place of the cow's milk.

¾ cup firmly packed brown sugar
1 egg, lightly beaten
1 cup milk
½ cup vegetable oil
2 granny smith apples, cored
1½ cups self-raising flour
½ cup plain flour
1 teaspoon bicarbonate of soda
1½ teaspoons ground cinnamon
3 teaspoons caster sugar

1 Preheat oven to 180°C and butter a 12-hole (⅓-cup-capacity) muffin tin.

2 In a large bowl, whisk the brown sugar, beaten egg, milk and oil together. Finely chop one of the apples. Sift the flours, bicarbonate of soda and 1 teaspoon of the cinnamon and stir in with the chopped apple until just combined (take care not to overmix). Spoon the batter into the prepared muffin tin. Slice the remaining apple and arrange on top of the muffins. Bake for 20 minutes until risen and golden.

3 Combine the caster sugar and remaining cinnamon in a small bowl. Remove muffins from oven and leave to stand in the tin for 5 minutes, then transfer to a wire rack. Sprinkle with the cinnamon sugar while still hot. Serve warm or at room temperature.

Waste watcher

These will keep in the freezer for about a month. You can thaw them quickly by zapping them in the microwave on the lowest setting for just a few seconds.

Try these delicious variations:

- **Orange and pear** – Add the grated zest of ½ an orange to the sugar mixture before you whisk, and substitute the apple for the same amount of pear. Omit the cinnamon.
- **Raspberry and coconut** – Fold ¾ cup frozen raspberries and ¼ cup toasted desiccated coconut through the batter in place of the apple (omitting the cinnamon) then place a raspberry or two on top of each muffin before baking.
- **Lemon and poppy seed** – Add the grated zest of 1 lemon to the sugar mixture before you whisk, and add 1 tablespoon poppy seeds to the batter in place of the apple (omitting the cinnamon). Dissolve ¼ cup sugar in ¼ cup lemon juice and 2 tablespoons water and bring to a boil for 1 minute to make a syrup. Drizzle this syrup over the just-baked muffins, leaving them in the tin for about 3 minutes before turning them out onto a wire rack to cool.

When decorating these muffins with the sliced apple, create a pretty look by cutting the slices in half widthways and arranging in a fan shape as we've done here.

Bruschetta with ricotta, tomato and pesto

MAKES 4

This is the Italian version of garlic bread. Your basic bruschetta (pronounced br-oosk-etta) is so easy to do at home: just toast some ciabatta or other Italian bread and lightly rub with a cut clove of peeled garlic (it will actually grate onto the toasted bread), then drizzle with olive oil. You can then use this as a delicious base for anything you like.

4 thick slices ciabatta
1 clove garlic, halved
2 tablespoons extra virgin olive oil, plus a little
    extra for drizzling
1 handful baby rocket leaves
¾ cup ricotta
1 punnet cherry tomatoes, quartered
2 tablespoons baby or chopped capers
¼ cup homemade pesto (see page 141)
sea salt and freshly ground black pepper

1   Grill or toast the bread on both sides, then rub one side lightly with the garlic.

2   Arrange the toast on a platter and drizzle with half the oil. Divide the rocket leaves and the ricotta between each slice.

3   Toss the tomato in the remaining oil with the capers. Stir through the pesto and season with salt and pepper, then spoon onto the toast. Drizzle with more oil and serve immediately.

> **Try these delicious variations:**
> - **Diced tomato and chopped red onion** mixed with chopped basil.
> - **A small can of drained tuna**, diced tomato and a little chopped red onion mixed with chopped basil.
> - **A sliced hard-boiled egg** mixed with chopped parsley and seasoned with salt and pepper.

Spanish-style toast

SERVES 4

Toast features at breakfast in Spain just as it does here, however the toppings are quite different. Olive oil and honey or sugar is a favourite, as is this savoury combination of olive oil, tomato and anchovy fillets.

4 thick slices ciabatta or sourdough
1 ripe tomato
1–2 tablespoons extra virgin olive oil
4–8 anchovy fillets in oil, drained

1   Grill or toast the bread on both sides.

2   Cut the tomato in half and rub the toast with the tomato until completely soaked with juice, and you are left with only the tomato skins.

3   Sprinkle olive oil over the toast and arrange one or two anchovy fillets on top of each slice.

Asparagus soldiers

SERVES 4

Simple and elegant: a soft-boiled egg accompanied by freshly cooked spears of asparagus for dipping, just as kids love to do with toast. This is light, supremely quick and very nourishing.

1–2 bunches asparagus, well washed, woody ends discarded (apply pressure on the end of each spear and it will snap off where tender)
4 eggs
sea salt and freshly ground black pepper

1 Place the asparagus spears in a pan of salted boiling water and cook for 4–5 minutes or until tender. Transfer to a paper towel and cover to keep warm.

2 Meanwhile, place the eggs in a pan of water over medium heat. Bring to a simmer and cook for 3 minutes for soft-boiled eggs or 4 minutes for medium-boiled eggs. Place in eggcups on plates and serve the asparagus alongside. Season well and serve.

Frog in the hole

SERVES 2

This is a great one for kids, and it's not just about the name – it looks fun and tastes wonderful too. To add a more grown-up element, serve with the finest-quality ham, wilted spinach leaves (heated in the microwave for 20 seconds) and hollandaise sauce. But it's also lovely just like this.

2 slices wholemeal or seeded bread
2 eggs
butter, for frying
sea salt and freshly ground black pepper

1 Lightly toast the bread, then use an 8 cm-diameter round cutter or a similar-sized glass to cut a hole in the centre of each slice (save the cut-out centres to have with jam for afters).

2 Melt a little butter in a frying pan over medium heat. Fry the bread, turning once, until golden. Crack an egg directly into each hole and cook until the egg is done to your liking. Season and serve immediately.

Quick toast breakfasts

We may all adore our Vegemite, but sometimes toast calls for something different. Having trouble getting inspired? Try these:

- **Ricotta and avocado** – Our favourite breakfast on a busy weekday morning is a single piece of toasted sourdough or homemade bread topped with low-fat ricotta and a few slices of avocado. You don't need butter as the ricotta is so creamy and soft. Just season with salt and pepper to taste.
- **Bolognese** – Leftover bolognese or beef ragú makes the best topping for toast in the morning. Freeze a few small servings of cooled sauce in snap-lock bags, then as you need them just heat and pop on toast for breakfast – hearty and delicious.
- **Toasted sandwiches** – If you have one of those electric sandwich presses, you're sorted for toasted breakfast sandwiches. Experiment with herbs, sliced cherry tomatoes, leftover chicken or ham, or half a can of drained and flaked tuna and a little grated cheese. The combinations are endless.
- **Bacon and egg roll** – This is fabulous as a hangover cure or for a Friday morning treat. Fry a couple of rashers of bacon and an egg and pop them on a slice of toast. Add a couple of slices of avocado and some tomato salsa, then top with another piece of toast, wrap it all tightly in baking paper and take it to work in a paper bag – perfect to munch on with your morning coffee.

Poached eggs with rocket and prosciutto

SERVES 4

Although prosciutto might sound fancy and may cost more than some supermarket ham, its intense, salty flavour means a little goes a long way.

1 teaspoon white vinegar
4 eggs
1 good handful baby rocket leaves
1 teaspoon lemon juice
1 teaspoon olive oil
sea salt and freshly ground black pepper
4 thick slices bread, toasted
4 slices prosciutto

1 Bring a medium-sized pan of water to a boil over high heat and add the vinegar. Crack one egg into a cup and slip it into the just-boiling water.

2 Repeat with the remaining eggs and, as soon as the last egg is in, cover the pan and remove from the heat. If you like the yolk soft, remove after 3½ minutes, or 4 minutes if you prefer firmer yolks.

3 Place the rocket, lemon juice, oil, salt and pepper in a medium-sized bowl and toss well.

4 To serve, place a slice of hot toast on each plate and top with a poached egg, with the rocket leaves and prosciutto to the side. Finish with a grinding of pepper.

The secret to perfectly poached eggs

Quite simply, it's all down to the freshness of the eggs. If they are more than 5–6 days old, they will not hold their shape, so unless you are certain you are using absolutely fresh eggs, we suggest you add vinegar to the water as we've done here, to help hold the eggs together.

Open-faced omelette with tomato, green onions and pesto

SERVES 2

Just the quickest, easiest breakfast around, and a great way to use up things you might have lurking in the fridge. We've added pesto to this omelette, but if you don't have any to hand, use a little grated cheese, sliced ham or herbs from the garden.

2 eggs

2 eggwhites (left over from another dish or use frozen ones, thawed)

sea salt and freshly ground black pepper

1 teaspoon olive oil

2 roma tomatoes, sliced

2 green onions, thinly sliced

2 teaspoons homemade pesto (see page 141)

1   Preheat grill to high.

2   Place the eggs, eggwhites and 1 tablespoon water into a medium-sized bowl. Use a small balloon whisk or a fork to whisk the eggs lightly until just combined then season with plenty of pepper.

3   Heat half the oil in a small non-stick frying pan over medium heat and pour in half the egg mixture. As the egg begins to cook, arrange half the sliced tomato on the omelette and sprinkle half the green onions over the top. Cook for about 2 minutes or until almost set. Place the frying pan under the preheated grill to finish cooking the omelette, then slide it onto a plate and cover to keep warm.

4   Repeat with the remaining oil and mixture to make the second omelette. To serve, top the omelettes with a drizzle of pesto.

Healthy and wise

Eggs are rich in protein, vitamins and minerals, and low in kilojoules, each one containing just 5 g of fat. Most importantly, they are an inexpensive way to get your essential omega-3 fatty acids, which play a crucial role in brain function and development.

Ranchers' eggs

SERVES 4

These are eggs as made by generations of Mexican ranch hands using whatever ingredients were available – a few crumbled dried red chillies would be added for fire, but a dash of Tabasco works well too. Fresh eggs are essential for this, so the whites don't run away from the yolk.

2 tablespoons olive oil
1 clove garlic, finely chopped
1 large red onion, finely chopped
1 red capsicum, white insides and seeds removed, cut into thin strips or diced
1 punnet cherry tomatoes, halved *or* 1 × 425 g can chopped tomatoes
¼ cup chopped coriander, plus extra to garnish
dash of Tabasco sauce
sea salt and freshly ground black pepper
4 eggs
4 tortillas

1   Heat the oil in a heavy-based frying pan and cook the garlic, onion and capsicum over medium heat for about 5 minutes or until the capsicum is soft. Add the tomato and simmer for 5–6 minutes or until the sauce has slightly thickened. Add the coriander and season with Tabasco, salt and pepper.

2   Make four depressions in the tomato sauce, then break an egg into each hole. Cover the pan and cook over medium heat for 3–4 minutes, until the eggs are done to your liking.

3   Meanwhile, preheat a chargrill or another large frying pan on high and toast the tortillas, one at a time, until heated and browned. Keep warm.

4   Place a tortilla on each plate and, using an egg slice, transfer an egg with its surrounding sauce onto each one. Scatter with extra coriander and serve.

How to season your frying pan

When it comes to frying eggs, you'll need a pan you can trust. You could opt for a non-stick frying pan, but you must buy a good-quality one and treat it like royalty – use only wooden or plastic utensils, and don't let it get too hot. Even then, the coating will eventually wear away and the pan will need replacing. Your best bet is to invest in a good-quality, heavy cast-iron frying pan and season it well before its first use. Fill it three-quarters full with vegetable oil and add a teaspoon of salt. Bring to a gentle simmer over low heat; there should be only the slightest movement on the surface of the oil. Remove from the heat and leave overnight to cool. The next day, pour off and discard the oil and, using a dry cloth, rub in the salt left in the pan to give it a good clean. From now on, after every use, the pan should be cleaned only with a little salt and the oiled cloth (never washed with detergent). A pan that has been well cared for and regularly oiled will serve you well for life.

Potato, mint and feta rösti

MAKES 8

Potato pancakes, or rösti, are a great standby for breakfast, a quick supper dish or a snack. They are moreish, soft and melt-in-the-mouth, with a crisp brown crust. Who could resist? We've made a Greek-influenced version here, and we love them – the feta goes wonderfully with the potatoes. You could also make these plain and serve them alongside grilled sausages with a good dollop of tomato sauce or chutney.

3 large potatoes, peeled and coarsely grated
1 egg, lightly beaten
80 g feta, cut into small cubes
1 tablespoon chopped mint, plus extra leaves to garnish
1 baby salad onion or golden shallot, finely chopped
sea salt and freshly ground black pepper
15 g butter
2 tablespoons olive oil

1 Using both hands, squeeze out as much liquid as possible from the grated potato. Place it in a bowl and mix through the egg, feta, mint, onion or shallot and plenty of salt and pepper.

2 Heat the butter and oil in a large, heavy-based frying pan. Working in batches, drop ¼-cup measures of the potato mixture into the pan, patting down slightly with the back of a spoon to make rounds about 8 cm across. Fry for 3–4 minutes until the edges are golden brown and crisp, then turn the rösti and cook on the other side. Drain on paper towel and keep warm while you cook the remaining mixture.

3 To serve, add some extra mint leaves to the hot pan and fry until bright green and a little crisp, then scatter over the rösti.

Try these delicious variations:

- **Grate 1 large zucchini**, skin left on, along with 2 large potatoes, and omit the feta.
- **Grate 2 large potatoes** instead of 3 and add the fresh kernels from 1 cob of corn. Replace the feta with a little grated parmesan.

Use extra olive oil and omit the butter for a healthier, lower sat-fat option.

CHAPTER 2

Work lunches and lunchbox foods

You've had a good breakfast, but as the middle of the day draws near it's natural for those hunger pangs to make their presence felt. It's all too easy to nip out for a ham and mayo roll to eat at your desk, or to pop to the Thai restaurant opposite work that does a great chicken and basil stir-fry to go. But there are downsides to this approach. Firstly, it's likely to be bad for your health. The quantities of salt, sugar and oil in most takeaway meals are extremely high – that's probably why they taste so good. And if you're an office worker, you're probably not burning it off. Secondly, it can get pretty expensive. You deserve to treat yourself to a lunch out? Well, maybe, once in a while. Or maybe what you really deserve is a gorgeous homemade lunch that's healthy, delicious and much lighter on your wallet.

Let's work it out: if you buy a latte and toast for breakfast every morning, you're forking out around $8 a day. That's $40 a week and around $2000 a year. And that's just on coffee and toast. If you're also spending $10 a day on a quick lunch and a drink, the meals you're eating at work are costing you around $4500 a year. That's a holiday in Fiji for the family.

Our excuse, of course, is time – not enough of it. Once you've ironed the day's outfits, got the kids' uniforms on the right way round, found matching shoes for them and put a brush through your own hair, it's time to head off. But with good planning (and maybe getting up just 10 minutes earlier), you and your family can do away with the cost of buying lunch.

The trick is to make homemade packed lunches effortless – there is no way you're going to whip up a batch of mini-muffins, poach some chicken and make your own mayonnaise while you're still in your pyjamas. Have things on hand in the pantry, fridge or freezer that you know will streamline packed lunches through the week. Cook on the weekends or make extra at dinner time and use the freezer – you'll be so proud as you tuck into your bacon and corn muffins while everyone else in the office makes do with a soggy takeaway ham and cheese toastie.

Ensuring your kids actually eat the lunch you've packed for them is another matter, though. There will always be variables you can't control when sending them off into the world of trans-fatty temptations (you can't whisper advice in their ears as they line up for a hot, salty sausage roll at recess). When your kids are at school, you need to be much more creative in your efforts to sway their food choices. If you want them to eat well and not waste their precious pocket money on unhealthy foods, you'll have to focus on the often-thankless task of making an irresistible packed lunch.

Despite your best intentions, packed-lunch inspiration is not going to strike every day, so you'll need some quick fixes to shove into their lunchbox in 30 seconds flat, without having to resort to sugary and expensive muesli bars, soft drinks or packets of chips. And that's where we can help!

Waste watcher

LEFTOVERS FOR LUNCH   *Leftovers often make for great sandwiches the next day. A couple of slices of leftover roast beef on a roll with mustard and avocado, or some leftover tandoori chicken, a little yoghurt and cucumber in some pita bread are just two delicious lunches you can rustle up from last night's dinner.*

No more store-bought, individually wrapped treats . . .

Infinitely appealing in their simplicity and promised convenience, individually wrapped 'snack packs' are toxic both to the environment and your budget. We're all guilty of resorting to those neat packets of apparently nutritious muesli bars or little bags of baked-not-fried chips from time to time. But even if they're packaged in recyclable boxes and wrappers, or if they're organic, the single-serve treat is no way to teach your kids healthy, thrifty eating. Here are a couple of alternatives:

- **Keep your own supply of trail mix** by making your own granola or muesli (see page 7) and adding things like dried fruit, whole nuts or sunflower seeds. You can tailor this to your kids' tastes by omitting things they don't like and experimenting with different combinations. Just a handful or two of this trail mix is plenty for one day (remember, it's only a snack – too much of a good thing can be fattening and expensive). Some schools don't allow nuts, in case children with allergies get their little hands on them, so check the policy before you make the effort.
- **Make a tray of Fruity muesli bars** (see page 46) and wrap portions in small sandwich bags or plastic film and freeze. On hectic school mornings, throw one little frozen portion into a lunchbox – it will defrost in time for recess.

Freeze the sandwich loaf

No one wants a sandwich every day, even if you are creating little masterpieces between the bread. A loaf of bread seems like a cheap option for school lunches, but if not used within a few days it will often go stale, and you'll have to throw it out by Thursday. Buy a loaf of sliced bread (preferably wholemeal or something full of linseeds, pumpkin seeds and the like) and freeze it when you get home. Expel the air from the bag and wrap it up in a plastic supermarket bag. Frozen like this, it will keep for about three weeks. When scraping together a sandwich in time for the 7:35 a.m. bus, use the frozen bread. It will gradually defrost through the day and will keep your sandwiches fresh.

What to look for when you're shopping (and therefore avoid the bags of assorted mini chocolate bars):

- Tiny cans of tuna
- Small cans of mixed beans
- Grissini or bread sticks
- Punnets of cherry tomatoes
- Dried fruits
- Celery
- Carrots
- Avocados
- Small cucumbers
- Eggs for hard-boiling
- Sliced salami and other cold meats

What to keep on hand in your fridge or freezer:

- Tubs of homemade plain or Green-pea hummus (see page 28)
- Leftover cooked pasta
- Leftover cooked chicken, lamb, beef or meatballs
- Small tubs of fruit yoghurt – kept in the freezer they will be chilled and frosty for lunch. Pack little plastic spoons, or trust your kids to bring your best silver home again.
- Fried sliced eggplant (see page 145) and zucchini
- Roasted capsicum (see page 31)
- Sliced Turkish bread, baguette or bread rolls
- Flatbreads

Put a lid on it

Choose a container that is the right size for your lunch so the contents won't get thrown around too much. A leafy salad will be much tastier if it's not all damaged and bruised.

Tune in to tuna

An increasing number of us are having canned tuna for lunch (you can always tell when someone's made a tuna salad because they drain the fishy oil in the sink!). It's an excellent option, as it's perfectly contained and won't leak in your bag on the way to work.

Always buy dolphin-safe tuna, packed in olive oil if you can (or if you're watching your weight, tuna in springwater is a good option). A lot of brands offer 'gourmet' selections of tuna now, with all sorts of flavourings added. Just check the preservatives and additives on the label before you buy these – most of the time, you're probably better off adding your own black pepper and lemon juice.

Try this delicious salad: drain and flake a small can of tuna, chop up some parsley, a few cherry tomatoes and some leftover vegetables from the night before, or throw in a handful of cooked chickpeas or other pulses, then add a generous dollop of homemade pesto (see page 141) or natural yoghurt. A squeeze of lemon juice added at the last minute gives the salad a nice zing.

Easy, last-minute hummus

This is the most versatile dip around – it's healthy and so quick to make. Use it as a replacement for butter in sandwiches or as a dip for crackers or vegetable sticks.

¾ cup dried chickpeas, soaked overnight in enough water
    to cover *or* 1 × 400 g can chickpeas
juice of 2 lemons
1–2 large cloves garlic, crushed
pinch of salt
½ cup tahini paste
olive oil

1 If using dried chickpeas, drain and place in a saucepan with enough water to cover. Bring to a boil and cook over medium–high heat for 40–60 minutes, or until very soft. Drain well, saving at least ½ cup of the cooking liquid. If using canned chickpeas, drain (reserving ½ cup liquid) and rinse well.

2 Purée the chickpeas in a blender or food processor, adding a little of the lemon juice and enough of the reserved liquid to form a smooth paste.

3 Add some more lemon juice, the crushed garlic and salt and slowly mix in the tahini. Blend to a creamy paste, adding more lemon juice to taste.

4 Spoon the hummus into a plastic container and store in the fridge. Just a dollop or two should be enough to take to work or school to have with carrot sticks or crackers.

* If you're serving hummus to guests instead of packing it for lunch, you could reserve a few whole cooked chickpeas to use as a garnish. Spoon the hummus into a shallow bowl and make a small depression in the centre. Pour in a little olive oil, decorate with the reserved chickpeas and sprinkle with paprika or ground cayenne.

Green-pea hummus

Frozen peas are great to have on hand in the freezer – they're cheap and taste as good as fresh. This recipe is easy to whip up before work, and kids love the bright colour. Serve with some crackers, toasted Turkish-bread soldiers or sticks of celery.

360 g frozen peas
2 cloves garlic, crushed
1 teaspoon ground cumin
juice of 1 large lemon
2 tablespoons extra virgin olive oil
1 tablespoon tahini paste
sea salt and freshly ground black pepper
ground paprika, to garnish (optional)

1 Cook the peas according to the directions on the packet until just tender, then drain and refresh under cold running water. Drain again and pat dry with paper towel.

2 Place the garlic, cumin, three-quarters of the lemon juice, the olive oil and tahini in a food processor or blender and add the peas. Blend to a purée, add salt and pepper to taste and more lemon juice if needed.

3 Transfer the hummus to a bowl and sprinkle with paprika if serving as a dip, or pop into a plastic container and store in the fridge to eat later.

> **Try this delicious variation:**
>
> Make this hummus with our other favourite frozen vegetable – **broad beans**. Cook the broad beans according to the directions on the packet, then drain. When they're cool enough to handle, slip off the grey outer skins to reveal the bright green beans underneath, then add instead of the peas.

Healthy and wise

Cut down on the amount of oil you use in the hummus by using a little more lemon juice and a splash of water to get the right consistency. It won't be quite as rich but will still be delicious, and you'll feel better for it.

Bacon and corn muffins

MAKES 12

Hot muffins are delicious, but when cold these are perfect for a packed lunch. You can also serve them still warm, with or without butter, with soups or salads come dinnertime. For best results, do not overmix the batter — it should still look lumpy.

6 rashers bacon, rind removed, diced
1 cup plain flour
1 cup yellow cornmeal
1 tablespoon sugar
1 tablespoon baking powder
1 teaspoon salt
1 large egg
½ cup milk
60 g butter, melted
1 × 300 g can creamed corn

1 Preheat oven to 220°C and lightly grease a 12-hole (⅓-cup-capacity) muffin tin.

2 Cook the bacon in a frying pan over medium–high heat until crisp, then transfer to paper towel to drain.

3 Sift the dry ingredients into a bowl. In another bowl, combine the egg, milk, butter and corn, mixing well. Stir the wet ingredients into the dry ingredients very lightly, so that the batter is still lumpy, then fold in the cooked bacon.

4 Spoon the batter into the prepared tin. Bake for 15–20 minutes until the muffins are risen and golden. Cool for a few minutes before turning out onto a wire rack to cool completely.

> ### Rush, rush, don't miss the bus
>
> It really helps to have a store of homemade things like these muffins on hand that you can turn to on busy school and work mornings. Combine these with fresh fruit or vegetables and you have yourself a delicious lunch. Try these healthy and reliable combos, which will work for both you and the kids – just vary the proportions accordingly.
>
> - **Falafel pockets with eggplant** (see page 42) + 2 mandarins + Fruity muesli bars (see page 46).
> - **Bacon and corn muffins** (see above) + 5 cherry tomatoes + a small tub of Easy, last-minute hummus (see page 28) with crackers.
> - **toasted Turkish bread** + a can of tuna + celery sticks + a hard-boiled egg + a bunch of grapes.

*For a change, substitute the bacon in these muffins with ham, or add some halved cherry tomatoes or a handful of diced roasted capsicum (see opposite).

Roasted capsicum

Roasting or chargrilling capsicum gives it a soft texture and a delicious, smoky taste. You can keep this in the fridge to use all week in sandwiches or salads.

red capsicums
olive oil

1   To prepare capsicums for roasting, cut into quarters and flick out the seeds. Lay the quarters skin-side up on a baking tray and grill under a preheated grill for 5–10 minutes, or roast in a 220°C oven for 20 minutes until the skin is blackened and blistered.

2   Place the roasted capsicum in a paper or plastic bag, seal and leave for 10 minutes. Remove the capsicum and, using paper towel, gently scrape away the skin, rubbing off any blackened pieces. Avoid rinsing the flesh or the sweet juices will be lost.

3   To store, pack the roasted capsicum in a warm sterilised jar (see page 152). Fill to the top with olive oil, seal and store in the refrigerator for up to a week. Drain on paper towel before use.

Ways with roasted capsicum

Roasted strips of capsicum are great in an **antipasto spread**, and they can complete a simple **hummus sandwich**. At least one trendy cafe in Sydney serves roasted capsicum in a tuna, cheese, rocket and onion roll, and charges a small fortune for it. It's also wonderful on **homemade pizzas** (see page 214), or turned through a simple **pesto pasta** topped with some grated parmesan.

A shortcut — blister them instead

Haven't got time to roast and skin the capsicums? Here's another way of preparing them to use in sandwiches or salads. Halve 1 kg red capsicums, remove the seeds and white insides and cut the flesh into strips. Peel and slice 5 cloves garlic. Heat ½ cup olive oil in a large frying pan over high heat and fry the capsicum strips until they begin to scorch at the edges. Add the garlic and 2 tablespoons drained capers and fry for several minutes more, stirring to ensure the garlic doesn't burn. Add 2 tablespoons wine vinegar and season to taste, then cook for a further minute or so before removing from heat. Store in an airtight container in the fridge.

Chicken sausage rolls

MAKES 8

No strange offcuts of meat or unwanted fat in these little numbers. You know exactly what's in these homemade chicken sausage rolls, and they can be frozen to boot! They're great cold too – perfect for packed lunches. All the other kids at school will be *so* jealous.

700 g lean chicken mince
finely grated zest of ½ a lemon
2 tablespoons chopped flat-leaf parsley
1 teaspoon chopped thyme
sea salt and freshly ground black pepper
2 sheets frozen shortcrust pastry, thawed, halved
1 egg, lightly beaten
2 tablespoons sesame seeds

1 Preheat oven to 200°C. Line a baking tray with baking paper.

2 In a large bowl, mix the chicken mince with the lemon zest and herbs and season with salt and pepper.

3 Place a quarter of the mince mixture along the long edge of each pastry strip. Lightly brush the edges with water. Fold the pastry over the mince to form a roll, and press the edges together to seal.

4 Cut each roll in half and place on the baking tray. Brush with beaten egg and sprinkle with sesame seeds. Bake for 25 minutes until the pastry is golden.

> ## Try this delicious variation:
>
> Use the meat from four **good-quality beef sausages** in place of the chicken mince. Just remove the meat from the skins and mix with the herbs and salt and pepper (omitting the lemon zest), then proceed as above.

These sausage rolls can be frozen either before or after you cook them. If you've frozen them uncooked, there's no need to defrost them before cooking – just make sure you bake them for an extra 10 or 15 minutes. If you're using the oven to cook your evening meal it's a good idea to pop these in afterwards, so they're ready for the next day's lunch.

Tuna and bean salad with pita crisps

SERVES 2

Here, pita bread is brushed with a herby-paprika butter and then grilled until crisp and golden to accompany a delicious and healthy salad. Make the pita crisps the night before and store them in an airtight container.

2 small pita breads
1 tablespoon oil or melted butter
1 teaspoon chopped rosemary or oregano
½ teaspoon sweet or smoked paprika
1 × 210 g can tuna in oil, drained and flaked into bite-sized pieces
1 × 400 g can white beans or chickpeas, drained and rinsed
1 small cucumber, cut into chunks on the diagonal
1 large tomato, roughly chopped
½ red onion, sliced (optional)
lemon juice and olive oil, for drizzling
1 handful flat-leaf parsley or basil leaves, torn roughly

1   To make the pita crisps, preheat the grill to medium (or alternatively use a large, heavy-based frying pan). In a small bowl, combine the oil or butter with the rosemary or oregano and paprika. Split each pita open and brush the inside with the herb mixture. Cut each bread in half and place on a baking tray if grilling, then cook, turning once, until crisp on both sides. Alternatively, dry-fry over medium heat, turning once, until crisp on both sides. Set aside to cool, then store in an airtight container.

2   For the salad, toss together the tuna, beans or chickpeas, cucumber, tomato and onion, if using, in a bowl. Stir in lemon juice and olive oil to taste and add the herbs. Pack into small plastic tubs and store in the fridge.

Treating beans right

Dried beans, such as cannellini, borlotti, lima and haricot, are one of the thrifty cook's best friends. They are cheap and a fabulous source of protein, but they do require a little care in preparation and cooking to get them just right. The more gradual their rehydration, the better – a long, slow soak overnight in enough water to cover is best. Cook them over low heat and don't let the water boil or the beans will start to break up and lose their shape. And don't add any salt to simmering beans until they start to soften, as it can hamper the cooking process.

Ham and pasta salad

SERVES 4

This is perfect for when the kids (and you) are tired of plain old ham sandwiches. Plus, this crunchy salad can be a great way to use up leftover pasta and sneak some vegetables into their diets. Some children are not crazy about olives, in which case just leave them out.

350 g penne *or* 2 cups leftover cooked short pasta (not spaghetti or linguine)
1 head broccoli, cut into florets
2 thick slices ham, cut into strips
8 black olives, halved, stones removed
2 sticks celery, sliced
2 teaspoons Dijon mustard
½ cup homemade mayonnaise (see page 140)
sea salt and freshly ground black pepper
2 tablespoons snipped chives, chopped basil or chopped flat-leaf parsley

1 Cook the pasta in a large pan of boiling salted water until al dente, adding the broccoli florets towards the end of the cooking time to boil for a few minutes until tender. Drain together and refresh under cold running water.

2 Combine the ham, olives, celery, pasta and broccoli in a dish. Mix the mustard and mayonnaise in a small bowl and season to taste. Stir the mayonnaise through the salad and scatter with the chives, basil or parsley.

Try this delicious variation:

Just as easy and with plenty of flavour is a **tuna, lemon and caper pasta salad**. Drain and flake a 185 g can of tuna and combine with ¼ cup olive oil, 2 tablespoons baby capers, 1 or 2 crushed garlic cloves and ¼ cup lemon juice. Toss through 350 g cooked and drained penne, rigatoni or fusilli with ¼ cup chopped flat-leaf parsley and a good grinding of pepper. Serve at room temperature or chilled.

Change the look and texture of this salad by using different-shaped pasta such as fusilli or rigatoni. A squeeze of lemon juice at the end will add a nice zing.

Sandwich inspiration

THE NUMBER-ONE RULE when making sandwiches for a packed lunch is to avoid using fillings that will make the sandwich soggy. Vinegar-based or watery ingredients will ruin the bread and make everything pretty dismal. So be careful with things like tomatoes, horseradish, and pickles in brine – if you use them, place crisp lettuce or cheese between them and the bread.

A few more important tips: don't add too much salt to your sandwich as you'll find there's usually plenty of salt in the filling already (tuna, butter and cheese, for example). Use ingredients that are nutritious and filling, to help you last the day and avoid the 3 p.m. energy slump. Include plenty of greens in your sandwiches – it's a great way to get some salads and vegetables in your diet – and try some of the less-common greens such as watercress, snowpeas, fresh basil leaves and lettuces such as cos and baby varieties. If you find that bread made with wheat gives you a heavy tummy, experiment with rye, seeded loaves and other low-gluten breads. And lastly, pack an icepack next to your sandwich bag to help it survive the journey to work or school and pop the bag in the fridge when you get there if you can.

When it comes to sandwiches the options are endless, but opposite are four of our all-time favourite fillings that are sure to please everyone.

Healthy and wise

Try spreading avocado on your sandwiches instead of butter or margarine. It's much healthier and adds a lovely creamy taste. Ricotta is another good substitute for butter, as is hummus.

Perfect poached chicken

If you are cooking chicken especially for sandwiches, use breasts or thigh fillets and poach in a court bouillon (a fancy name for a quick stock, which can be as simple as water simmered with some peppercorns, onion slices and a bay leaf). Poach the chicken in this gently simmering liquid over a low heat for about 6–8 minutes; when cooked, the juices should run clear when the chicken is pierced with a knife.

Last-minute lifesavers

- **Mexican wrap** – Mix canned kidney beans with grated cheese, chopped jalapeño chillies, diced tomato, sour cream and chopped coriander. Spoon onto tortillas and wrap tightly.
- **Crunchy garden** – Halve a bread roll and spread with mayo, then top with shredded lettuce, sliced cucumber, sliced radishes, baby rocket, grated carrot and chopped parsley.
- **Hearty Italian** – Fill ciabatta slices with leftover roasted or blistered capsicum, eggplant and zucchini, some basil leaves and ricotta.
- **Curried egg wrap** – Cream 60 g butter with a good pinch of curry powder and a teaspoon each of Dijon mustard and lemon juice. Season, then fold through 4 chopped hard-boiled eggs. Spoon onto 2 chapatis, top with shredded lettuce and roll up.
- **Power booster** – Spread a wholegrain roll with mayonnaise and fill with lettuce, sliced Swiss cheese, alfalfa sprouts and sliced tomato.

Chicken and mayo

MAKES 2

150 g cooked chicken
2 tablespoons homemade mayonnaise (see page 140)
1 stick celery, finely sliced
sea salt and freshly ground black pepper
4 slices sandwich bread
softened butter, for spreading

1   Cut the chicken into small cubes, removing any skin and bone. Place in a bowl with the mayonnaise and celery and add salt and pepper to taste. Fold together lightly.

2   Butter the bread and divide the chicken mix between two slices. Top with the other slices of bread then cut each sandwich into halves or thirds and pop into a snap-lock bag.

 Add slivered almonds, chopped basil or tarragon, a slice of cheddar or a little watercress to the chicken and mayo mix to spice things up.

Tuna and artichoke

MAKES 2

1 × 425 g can tuna in oil, drained and flaked
6 artichoke quarters in oil, drained and sliced
juice and finely grated zest and of 1 lemon
freshly ground black pepper
half a baguette, cut into two and sliced lengthways
basil leaves, to garnish

1   Combine the tuna, artichoke, lemon zest and juice in a bowl and season well with pepper.

2   Fill the sliced baguettes with the tuna mixture and place a few basil leaves on top. Close then wrap in a folded sheet of baking paper to stop any drips. Tie with string or use a couple of rubber bands to secure.

Mozzarella and capsicum

MAKES 2

½ cup Roasted capsicum (see page 31), drained
   and thinly sliced
pinch of ground chilli (optional)
1 tablespoon chopped flat-leaf parsley
¾ cup fresh mozzarella, torn
extra virgin olive oil, for drizzling
4 slices grain bread

1   Combine the roasted capsicum, ground chilli, if using, parsley and mozzarella in a bowl. Drizzle with oil, then spread this mixture on two slices of the bread, top with the other slices and pop into a snap-lock bag.

Ricotta and grilled vegetable

MAKES 2

½ tablespoon olive oil
1 zucchini, thinly sliced lengthways
1 small eggplant, thinly sliced lengthways
½ cup ricotta
1 tablespoon snipped chives
freshly ground black pepper
half a loaf of Turkish bread, cut into two
   and sliced lengthways
basil leaves, to garnish

1   Heat the olive oil on a chargrill and cook the zucchini and eggplant slices for 3 minutes on each side, until charred and tender, then set aside to cool.

2   Combine the ricotta and chives in a bowl and season to taste, then spread half this mixture over one slice of Turkish bread. Top with half the vegetables and a few basil leaves and place another slice of bread on top. Repeat with the remaining ingredients and pop into a snap-lock bag.

Lamb and chickpea balls

MAKES ABOUT 30

Stretch, stretch, stretch – we're all about making more expensive ingredients go a long way. By adding chickpea purée to the lamb mince, these little pop-in-the-mouth meatballs are much more interesting than if they were just plain meat. You can substitute beef or chicken mince for the lamb, and perhaps omit the chilli if you're making them for children. These little morsels will last up to 3 days in an airtight container in the fridge, or you can pop the cooked leftovers into snap-lock bags and freeze for up to 3 months.

¼ cup olive oil

1 small brown onion, finely chopped

1 clove garlic, crushed

2 teaspoons ground cumin

1 teaspoon ground coriander

pinch of ground chilli

1 × 400 g can chickpeas, drained
and rinsed

400 g lean lamb mince

¼ cup chopped coriander

sea salt and freshly ground black pepper

small pita breads and salad leaves,
to serve

CORIANDER YOGHURT

1 cup Greek-style yoghurt

1 small cucumber, finely diced

1 tablespoon finely chopped coriander

sea salt and freshly ground black pepper

* These meatballs are delicious in a sandwich with a little cucumber, tomato and avocado, for a lunch to make your workmates green with envy. Of course, they are also perfect to serve hot for nibbles, with the coriander yoghurt on the side.

1   Heat 1 tablespoon of the oil in a frying pan over medium heat. Add the onion and garlic and cook for 2 minutes until soft. Add the ground spices and cook for another 2 minutes until fragrant. Remove this mixture from the pan and set aside.

2   Blend the chickpeas in a food processor until smooth, then transfer to a large bowl. Add the onion mixture, the lamb mince and the coriander and mix thoroughly with your hands, seasoning to taste with salt and pepper. Shape level tablespoons of mixture into small balls, until all the mixture has been used up.

3   Wipe out the frying pan with paper towel and heat the remaining oil over high heat. In batches, cook the meatballs for 6 minutes, tossing them frequently until browned all over and cooked through.

4   Prepare the coriander yoghurt by combining all the ingredients and seasoning to taste.

5   For a delicious work lunch, fill pita breads with some salad leaves and 2 or 3 meatballs. Pack the coriander yoghurt separately in a small container for adding at the last minute.

Falafel pockets with eggplant

MAKES 16 FALAFELS

Pita bread is available at supermarkets and makes a nice change from ordinary sandwich bread. Easy-to-make falafels can be prepared ahead of time and kept in the freezer, and they're great cold for lunch. Pop them frozen straight in the bread and they'll thaw in time for lunch.

1 eggplant, cut into 1 cm rounds
olive oil, for brushing
1 × 400 g can chickpeas, drained
  and rinsed
1 egg, lightly beaten
½ teaspoon each ground cumin, cayenne
  pepper and turmeric
1 tablespoon each chopped coriander and
  flat-leaf parsley

1 clove garlic, finely chopped
1 tablespoon tahini paste or olive oil
50 g fresh white breadcrumbs
sea salt and freshly ground black pepper
⅓ cup plain flour
rice bran, olive or vegetable oil, for frying
5 small pita breads
lettuce leaves or sliced tomato, to serve
hummus or natural yoghurt, to serve

1   Brush the eggplant slices with a little olive oil and fry or grill on both sides over medium heat until golden and tender. Set aside on paper towel to drain.

2   Purée the chickpeas in a food processor until smooth, then transfer to a large bowl. Add the egg, spices, herbs, garlic, tahini paste or olive oil, breadcrumbs, salt and pepper and a little water to bind, if needed. Combine the ingredients with your hands into a soft, firm mixture, then shape into small oval balls (you should get about 16) and roll in flour to coat.

3   Pour oil into a large frying pan to a depth of 5 mm and heat. When hot but not smoking, fry the falafels, in batches, for 3–4 minutes or until golden brown. Remove and drain on paper towel. If not using straight away, let them cool, then store them in the freezer in snap-lock bags – they will keep for up to 1 month.

4   To assemble the pockets, cut the pita bread in half and fill each pocket with a slice of fried eggplant, a lettuce leaf or 1–2 slices of tomato, a dollop of hummus or yoghurt and 3 falafels. For a quick lunch on the weekend, you might like to top toasted pita bread with hummus, eggplant, lettuce and falafels instead, as we've done here.

* Grilled or barbecued eggplant slices, perhaps sprinkled with a little cumin, olive oil and salt before cooking, are also great served with grilled chicken, lamb or beef and a green salad. Cook extra to include with these falafels for lunch.

If you've got a communal sandwich press at work, pop these falafel pockets in for a few minutes — they're lovely hot and crisp.

Try this delicious variation:

Add a warm, spicy, almost Christmassy scent to these by substit-uting **cranberries** for the sultanas and adding 1 teaspoon each of mixed spice and ginger with the cinnamon.

Cinnamon, sultana and buttermilk muffins

MAKES 12

This is domestic-goddess territory. What a difference it makes to a school day when there's a sweet muffin packed in the lunch box. The sultanas can be replaced with diced apple or pear, frozen blueberries or raspberries, or chopped dried apricots. You might even like to add a few chopped walnuts or pecans.

Buttermilk is made from cultured skim or low-fat milk. It's great to drink as it is but also adds a lovely tang and lightness to muffins and cakes.

1 cup plain flour
1 cup wholemeal flour
1 tablespoon baking powder
2 teaspoons ground cinnamon, plus extra for sprinkling
⅓ cup caster sugar, plus extra for sprinkling
¾ cup sultanas
1 egg
1½ cups buttermilk
¼ cup vegetable oil

1   Preheat oven to 200°C and lightly grease a 12-hole (⅓-cup-capacity) muffin tin.

2   Sift both flours together with the baking powder and cinnamon into a bowl, tipping in the bran left in the sieve from the wholemeal flour. Stir in the sugar and sultanas.

3   In another bowl, whisk the egg with the buttermilk and the oil, then gently fold this into the dry ingredients until just combined. The mixture should still be a little lumpy.

4   Spoon the batter into the prepared muffin tin. Mix some extra sugar and cinnamon together and sprinkle over the muffins. Bake for 15–20 minutes, until risen and golden. Cool for a few minutes before turning out onto a wire rack to cool completely.

Waste watcher

Muffins are perfect for freezing to eat later. If you like them buttered, cut them open and butter them, then pop them into a snap-lock bag, label with the date and name and take them out the morning you need them, packing them while still frozen. They will be thawed, fresh and scrumptious by lunchtime.

Don't have buttermilk?

Buttermilk is useful for baking because the acid in it reacts with the baking powder to make the batter rise. If you haven't got any buttermilk, substitute it with the same amount of milk to which you've added a tablespoon of lemon juice or a dollop of yoghurt.

Fruity muesli bars

MAKES 24

Forget those commercial muesli bars that are packed with preservatives and sugar – these beat them hands-down. You can vary the quantities of dried fruit or add chopped raisins according to your tastes.

The trick with this one is to press the mixture very firmly into the pan using a metal spoon or spatula so it all sticks together and ends up cutting nicely. Baking paper is also essential, so that the cooked mixture lifts out of the pan easily.

125 g unsalted butter
⅓ cup brown sugar
2 tablespoons honey
1½ cups rolled oats
½ cup self-raising flour
1 cup sultanas or dried cranberries
¼ cup sesame seeds
¼ cup sunflower seeds
½ cup chopped walnuts

* For packed lunches, just pop two or three muesli bars in a snap-lock bag, label with the date and freeze. Then just take them out the morning you need them – they'll defrost in time for recess.

1 Preheat oven to 180°C, and butter and line a 20 cm × 30 cm lamington tin (line the base and the two long sides, making sure the paper overhangs the side by 2 cm).

2 Melt the butter with the sugar and honey in a saucepan over medium heat. Stir, without letting it boil, until the sugar has dissolved. Stir in all the remaining ingredients.

3 Press the mixture firmly into the prepared tin and bake for about 30 minutes. Leave to cool completely in the tin before lifting out and cutting into 5 cm squares.

Try this delicious variation:

Sticky oat bars are also quick and easy to make and are another sweet treat for the school lunch-box or an afternoon nibble. Preheat the oven to 180°C and line a shallow 20 cm x 20 cm cake tin with baking paper. In a small saucepan, melt 125 g butter with ¾ cup brown sugar and ¼ cup golden syrup, then stir in 2¾ cups rolled oats and mix thoroughly. Turn into the prepared tin, smooth the top and bake for 25–30 minutes until golden brown. Leave to cool in the tin for a few minutes then cut into squares. Cool completely before removing from the tin.

Ava's packed lunches

'**THE REASON I LIKE** to do a nice school lunch for my daughter is that I feel like it's a little message from home. She has been out of the house all day and when she sits down at lunch there is a little something that her mummy has made for her,' says Meg Mason, of packing her five-year-old daughter Ava's school lunch. Her tip for making sure that Ava's lunch almost always gets eaten is to make sure that what she packs is appetising – she doesn't expect Ava to eat something she herself wouldn't like.

As she heads out the door in the morning, Ava slips on her oversized backpack filled with books, pencils and a lunchbox bursting with food specially made for her. Ava's school has a policy banning packaged food, which Meg is pleased about – the school doesn't want muesli-bar wrappers, cardboard juice boxes or chip packets creating unnecessary rubbish, and this has given Meg the impetus to find alternatives for Ava's lunchbox.

'Anything you buy that's pre-packed, like muesli bars or those cheese and biscuit dips, are really bad for them, and are more expensive than providing an equivalent from home,' says Meg. She plans ahead so she has lots of options to turn to on busy mornings. She always roasts an extra chicken if they're having it for dinner so she'll have plenty leftover for sandwiches. Every fortnight or so she makes a batch of mini muffins. 'We make them in little cupcake-sized trays and then wrap and freeze them,' she says. 'And small bags of popcorn are really good for an inexpensive treat – we make our own because the bought ones usually contain lots of salt and sugar.'

Any good lunchbox needs balance, so Meg always includes a sandwich or a small wrap plus something sweet like a thin slice of gingerbread cake (see recipe opposite). Also, she's mindful of the fact that they don't actually spend much time eating at school. 'They're busy chatting, or want to go and play.' A whole apple might not get eaten, but some chopped-up peaches probably will.

Meg has often tried things in Ava's school lunch that she may not yet have given her at home, like avocado or some tuna and bean salad. 'When they're at school, you can sneak things in and often they'll realise they quite like them!' she says.

Two-year-old Daphne stirs the cake mixture while Ava, 5, and mum Meg chat.

Meg's top tips

- Some of my more organised friends make a whole loaf's worth of sandwiches, which they then individually wrap and freeze. On school mornings, it's easy just to grab a frozen sandwich to throw in the lunchbox, and it will have thawed by lunchtime. Try and mix up the fillings: some chicken with parsley, some meatloaf and chutney, some ham with herbs and cheese.

- Remember that the food you've packed is going to have been sitting in a box for four hours by the time lunch comes around, so you have to be quite clever about the way you pack it. There are lots of good Thermos-type packs available, or you can get cold packs from the supermarket to keep food fresh.

- Try filling a drink bottle half-full with apple juice and freezing it, then fill it up with water in the morning and they'll have a nice cold drink for school. I spent a little bit more money on a good drink bottle because it keeps drinks nice and cold and doesn't leach flavour (plastic bottles can taint drinks).

Gingerbread cake

SERVES 8

This gingerbread cake is a lovely homemade treat for kids to combat that afternoon sugar slump.

- 185 g unsalted butter
- 1 cup brown sugar
- 1 tablespoon ground ginger
- 2 teaspoons ground cinnamon
- ½ teaspoon allspice
- 1 cup golden syrup
- 1 large egg, lightly beaten
- 1½ cups plain flour
- 1½ cups self-raising flour
- 1 cup milk mixed with 1 teaspoon bicarbonate of soda
- 1 cup sultanas or raisins (optional)

1 Preheat oven to 180°C and butter and line an 8-cup-capacity loaf tin with baking paper.

2 Cream the butter with the brown sugar and the spices until light and fluffy. Add the golden syrup and mix well. Add the beaten egg gradually, mixing between additions until thoroughly incorporated.

3 Sift the flours together and fold into the batter alternately with the milk mixture, then fold in the sultanas or raisins, if using.

4 Turn the batter into the prepared tin and bake for 1 hour and 20 minutes, until a skewer inserted in the centre comes out clean. Remove from the oven and leave to cool in the tin for 5 minutes before turning out onto a wire rack to cool completely.

* This cake is even better made a day or so before it's eaten, so it's perfect to make on the weekend, ready for the week's afternoon teas.

Don't be seduced by juice

Those colourful little boxes of juice might be convenient, but they are also packed with sugar. Researchers at Deakin University found that primary-school-age children who regularly consume juice and other fruit drinks are about twice as likely to be overweight or obese. Your average 250 ml serve of orange juice (with no added sugar) contains the equivalent of 6 teaspoons of sugar, only a fraction less than the 7 teaspoons found in cola. Apple juice also has 7 teaspoons, and the very popular Ribena drink has 9, compared to just 5 in cordial diluted with water (1 part cordial to 4 parts water). Grape juice – shock, horror – contains the equivalent of 13 teaspoons of sugar. Water has none. When traipsing up and down the supermarket aisles with the upcoming week's packed lunches in your mind's eye, only buy juice boxes for an occasional treat.

Lunchbox quick fixes

- A small bag of popcorn (about a handful, popped).
- An avocado and ham sandwich.
- A toasted cheese sandwich (they're delicious cold).
- A mix of sultanas, raisins, dried cranberries, dried apricots and dried figs packed in a little paper bag.
- Half an avocado, cut-side lightly rubbed with the lemon to prevent discoloration, packed with some crackers for scooping.
- A salad of canned tuna, drained, lightly blanched fresh green beans, lemon juice and a little chopped parsley.
- Fruit cut into cubes (except banana, which often goes mushy and brown), mixed together in a small container and kept fresh with a cold pack.

CHAPTER 3

Weeknight meals

If you work long hours, have children to bath or help with their homework, or you're simply looking for something quick and tasty to throw together in the evening, then this is the chapter for you.

Being a good cook is all about being able to make a great meal out of whatever is at hand. You don't need exotic, expensive ingredients: the key is to have a small selection of well-chosen pantry staples and to go for seasonal produce, which invariably will be cheaper, then let these dictate what you cook. You'll be surprised by the results.

The trick is simplicity. Unless you love whiling away your time cooking, keep the fuss to a minimum. But when you do cook, make sure you do it well. We all like to re-run our favourite dishes, but try to give them a little twist sometimes. Look at the fresh ingredients you buy and consider how you can use them in different ways throughout the week. A bag of eggplants, for example, is much more versatile, and a lot cheaper, than a packet of frozen meat pies. You can cook the eggplants in a tomato sauce for a pasta dish, add them to a curry, or grill slices to have with chops or steak.

Then, having put the effort into cooking a meal, you may as well sit down and eat together. Take the time to set the table and create a nice atmosphere. Mealtimes are best spent together, discussing your day, telling stories and making each other laugh.

EASY WEEKNIGHT MEALS

We know all too well what it's like trying to be innovative with the evening meal, day in, day out. So, here are some very simple ideas for fabulous dinners that you can turn to any night of the week, and you'll virtually have dinner on the table within 30 minutes. We've included some recipes for the kids, but they're so good you'll love them too.

Crispy chicken parcels (serves 4)

Slice 2 chicken breast fillets lengthways to make 4 thin, flat fillets. Spread 1 tablespoon ricotta and a sprinkling of parmesan on each fillet and wrap in a slice of prosciutto. Heat some oil in a large frying pan and fry the chicken parcels for 3 minutes each side, until cooked through. Remove the parcels, then add a knob of butter to the pan and cook until a nutty brown colour, without burning. Add a squeeze of lemon juice to the pan, stir, then drizzle over the parcels. Serve with steamed vegetables.

Carbonara poached eggs (serves 4)

Cook 300 g linguine in a large pan of boiling salted water until al dente. Drain, reserving ⅓ cup of the cooking liquid. Return the linguine to the pan, stir through the reserved cooking liquid and ¼ cup extra virgin olive oil, and season. Meanwhile, poach 4 eggs in water for 3 minutes. Divide the pasta between four plates, top with a poached egg, some shaved parmesan and an extra drizzle of olive oil. Serve with steamed asparagus or a green salad.

Light tuna salad with a spud (serves 4)

Toss together 1 × 425 g can tuna in oil, drained, 1 grated carrot, 1 chopped celery stalk, a generous dollop of Greek yoghurt and some flat-leaf parsley. Wrap 4 potatoes in paper towel and pop in the microwave for 3 minutes on high (or longer if the potatoes are large). Serve a potato per person with salad on the side.

Greek-inspired lentil salad (serves 2)

Combine 1 × 400 g can rinsed and drained organic lentils with 1 cup halved cherry tomatoes, ½ cup crumbled feta, ½ a small red onion, chopped, and a small bunch of mint, chopped. Drizzle with olive oil and lemon juice, and serve as is or with lamb chops.

Thai-can-do chicken curry (serves 4)

Fry 1 tablespoon red curry paste with a third of a 400 ml can coconut milk in a wok for 3 minutes. Add the remaining coconut milk, 1 chicken stock cube, a quarter of a pineapple cored and cut into bite-sized wedges, 2 tablespoons soy sauce, 1 tablespoon fish sauce, 2 shredded kaffir lime leaves and the shredded meat from a barbecued chicken or Chinese roast duck. Heat through then stir in a large handful of cherry tomatoes and serve with steamed rice.

Miso chicken soup (serves 4–6)

Shred the meat from a barbecued or leftover roast chicken, discarding the skin, and set aside. Combine 2 cups water with 5 cups chicken stock in a pan and bring to a boil over medium heat. Stir in 1 carrot, cut into thin strips, and 2 cups sliced shiitake mushrooms, and simmer for 5 minutes. Add the chicken and ¼ cup miso paste then simmer, stirring gently, for 3 minutes. Serve garnished with finely sliced green onions.

Pork chops with fennel and pear salad (serves 4)

Thinly slice 1 large fennel bulb and 1 pear, toss together and arrange on plates. Drizzle with olive oil and lemon juice, season, and top with shaved parmesan. Meanwhile, rub 4 pork chops with the grated zest of 1 lemon and 1 teaspoon fennel seeds. Pan-fry the chops in olive oil for 3 minutes each side until cooked, then remove the pan from the heat and splash over the juice of a lemon. Serve on the fennel and pear salad.

Easy, one-pan chicken (serves 4)

Heat some olive oil in a pan and brown 8 chicken thigh fillets. Add 1 sprig rosemary, chopped, stir through and set aside. In the same pan, heat a little more olive oil over and add 1 finely sliced red onion, cooking for 5 minutes. Toss in 3 sliced garlic cloves, 2 chopped anchovy fillets, 1 × 400 g can chopped tomatoes, 1 tablespoon capers and 1 cup wine. Return the chicken to the pan, cover and cook for 20 minutes, then serve with a green salad.

Moroccan chicken couscous (serves 4)

Boil 2 diced zucchini and 250 g diced pumpkin in 3 cups chicken stock for 5 minutes. Add 1 tablespoon olive oil, 2 tablespoons sliced preserved lemon and 2 cups instant couscous. Turn off the heat and leave covered for 5 minutes. Season 4 chicken thigh fillets and grill for 4 minutes each side until cooked and golden, then slice. Serve the couscous topped with sliced chicken and garnished with snipped mint leaves and a dusting of paprika.

Summery cold gazpacho (serves 2)

Whiz 2 slices of bread in the food processor to make breadcrumbs. Add 1 × 400 g can chopped tomatoes, a sliced cucumber, a sliced red capsicum, 2 cloves garlic and a small chopped red onion and process to a chunky purée. Chill, then serve ladled into bowls, dressed with a splash of red-wine vinegar, a dash of olive oil, some salt, pepper and Tabasco, with crusty bread alongside.

Steamed fish and green bean salad (serves 4)

Steam 500 g green beans until tender then toss with 1 cup crumbled feta and ¼ cup toasted pine nuts. Drizzle with olive oil, a squeeze of lemon juice, and season with plenty of pepper. Season 4 fish fillets with salt and pepper, drizzle with a little olive oil and grill for a few minutes each side until cooked, then serve with the salad.

Penne with zucchini, lemon and mint (serves 4)

Cook 500 g penne in a large pan of boiling salted water until al dente, then drain. Meanwhile, heat ¼ cup oil in a frying pan, add 2 crushed garlic cloves and 3 grated zucchini and cook for 2 minutes, stirring until soft. Add ¾ cup ricotta and cook until heated through. Combine the zucchini mixture with the pasta and toss in 1 cup torn mint leaves, ½ cup roasted slivered almonds and the juice of ½ a lemon, stir and serve immediately.

The quickest Thai beef salad in the world (serves 4)

Pan-fry or barbecue 2 seasoned sirloin or blade steaks until medium–rare, then cover and set aside. On a large platter, arrange lettuce leaves, 1 long cucumber, thinly sliced lengthways into ribbons, 1 bunch torn mint leaves, 2 sliced green onions, 1 cup halved cherry tomatoes and 1–2 sliced chillies. Meanwhile, combine the juice of 1 large lime or ½ a lemon and 2 tablespoons fish sauce with 1 teaspoon sugar. Slice the steak into thin strips, scatter over the salad and drizzle with the dressing. Sprinkle with chopped roasted peanuts to serve.

They love babycinos, here come baby-burgers (serves 4)

Grate 1 zucchini and squeeze out any excess juice. Combine this with 1 grated carrot, 400 g chicken mince, ½ cup breadcrumbs, 1 × 125 g can drained corn kernels and 1 egg in a bowl. Mix lightly and shape into patties. Heat 1 tablespoon olive oil in a frying pan, then cook the burgers for 5 minutes on each side, until cooked through. Serve on toasted Turkish bread with sliced tomatoes, cucumbers and lettuce, and chutney or tomato sauce.

Sausage and broccoli pasta (serves 4)

Squeeze the meat from the skin of 4 sausages into small chunks and fry in a little olive oil until cooked. Meanwhile, cook 375 g fusilli in a large pan of boiling salted water until al dente, adding a small head of broccoli or cauliflower cut into florets to the water 5 minutes before the end of the cooking time. Drain the pasta and veggies and toss through the sausage meat. Grate a little cheese over the top and serve.

Sticky chicken (serves 4)

Combine ¼ cup oyster sauce, 2 tablespoons teriyaki sauce and 1 tablespoon honey, and brush a little of this mixture over 4 small chicken breast fillets. Place the fillets on a baking tray and roast in a 200°C oven for 6–8 minutes until cooked through. Meanwhile, fry 1 tablespoon grated ginger and 1 sliced garlic clove in a little rice bran oil for a minute or so, then add some bok choy, sugar snap peas or broccoli florets and cook for 3–4 minutes. Stir in the rest of the sauce and serve with the chicken.

Easy vegetable soup (serves 2)

Fry 1 chopped onion in 1 tablespoon olive oil. Add 2 cups chicken stock and 2 large potatoes, chopped, and simmer for 10 minutes. Add 1 small head broccoli, cut into florets, and cook for another 5 minutes until the veggies are tender. Cool slightly then blend until smooth. Stir in a little water or milk to thin if needed.

Comfort mince on toast (serves 4)

Cook 1 finely chopped onion in 1 tablespoon rice bran oil in a large frying pan for 3 minutes until soft. Add 500 g beef mince, stirring to break up any lumps, and cook for 5 minutes. Stir in 1 tablespoon plain flour and cook for 2 minutes. Add 1 cup beef, chicken or vegetable stock, 2 teaspoons Worcestershire sauce and 1 cup frozen peas, stir, then cover and simmer for 10 minutes. Serve on hot buttered toast, scattered with some freshly chopped flat-leaf parsley.

Italian chickpea and pasta soup

SERVES 4

It's dishes like this Italian soup that prove time and again that food can be economical yet still nutritious and delicious. Chickpeas and pasta provide the base here, and the rosemary, garlic and parsley bring a rich, fresh flavour. It's even more economical if you grow your own herbs (see page 134).

1 × 400 g can chickpeas, drained and rinsed
3–4 cups chicken or vegetable stock or water
2 tablespoons chopped rosemary
250 g pasta (either small shapes or spaghetti broken into short lengths)
2 tablespoons olive oil
2 rashers bacon or slices pancetta, diced (optional)
2 cloves garlic, finely chopped
⅓ cup freshly chopped flat-leaf parsley
sea salt and freshly ground black pepper
freshly grated parmesan, to serve

1   Tip about half the chickpeas into a blender or food processor and purée, adding a little water if needed. When smooth, transfer to a large saucepan with the remaining whole chickpeas, 3 cups of stock and the rosemary.

2   Bring to a boil and add the pasta. Cook for about 8–10 minutes until the pasta is tender. Add another cup of stock if needed to give a soup consistency.

3   Meanwhile, heat the oil in a frying pan over medium heat and fry the bacon, if using, the garlic and the parsley until softened. Add three-quarters of this mixture to the soup for the last 5 minutes of cooking.

4   Season the soup with salt and pepper, ladle into bowls and garnish with a little of the remaining garlic and parsley mixture. Serve with a bowl of grated parmesan on the side.

The versatile chickpea

Chickpeas, also known as garbanzos, are another legume we couldn't do without. Not only are they the star ingredient in hummus (see page 28), but they're fantastic added to salads, stews and soups to add flavour and bulk up the meal. As with dried beans, a long soaking time and gentle cooking results in a tender chickpea that will hold its shape. Soak overnight, if possible, covered in plenty of water, then drain and transfer to a saucepan, adding enough fresh water to cover. Bring to a boil over medium heat, then reduce the heat to low and simmer, covered, for 1½–2 hours or until tender. Add salt to taste, if needed, after draining the chickpeas (adding salt during the cooking time will slow the process down).

Salmon, leek and potato chowder

SERVES 4

Go back in time and drop in on Grandma as she serves up the dinner: take a deep breath and notice the smell of the home-cooked meal, the starched linen, the relaxed mood that comes with the family eating together – now you're ready for the absolute homeliness of this chowder. It's a wholesome soup that will inspire you to invest in a 1950s floral apron and a Bakelite radio.

30 g butter

2 leeks, well washed and finely sliced

4 potatoes, diced

2 tablespoons plain flour

4 cups fish or vegetable stock

1 × 415 g can red salmon, drained, skin and bones removed

1 cup hot milk

sea salt and freshly ground black pepper

2 tablespoons chopped dill

1   Melt the butter in a large, heavy-based saucepan over medium heat. Add the leek and cook, stirring, for 5 minutes until soft and pale golden. Add the potato and flour and stir until the potato is well coated.

2   Add the stock and cook, stirring continuously, for 10 minutes, until it boils and thickens slightly. Reduce the heat, add the salmon and hot milk and stir until heated through, without letting it boil. Season to taste with salt and pepper, stir through the chopped dill and serve.

✱ Instead of using tinned salmon, you could use up leftover cooked fresh salmon from the night before, or whip a fresh salmon fillet into the micro-wave, cover and heat on low for a few minutes, before flaking and adding to the chowder to cook through.

Try these delicious variations:

- **Corn chowder** – Substitute the salmon with 2 cups corn kernels and use flat-leaf parsley instead of dill to sprinkle on top. Try this with a dash of Tabasco.
- **Asparagus and salmon chowder** – Simply add a drained can of asparagus pieces or freshly cooked asparagus, cut into short lengths, along with the salmon.
- **Mussel chowder** – Use 2 diced carrots instead of the potato, and 2 stalks chopped celery in place of the leek. Cook these in the butter along with 2 rashers diced bacon. Substitute the salmon with 2 cups roughly chopped shelled steamed mussels, and scatter with flat-leaf parsley or chives instead of dill.

Waste watcher

THE GREAT CHEESE FREEZE *The difference between cheese at its prime, as opposed to being something old socks smell of, is about a month. While much French cheese improves with age – the smellier, the better – the ever-popular cheddar is definitely best eaten fresh. Before it's time to scrape the mould off a block of cheddar with a knife, take the time to grate it coarsely, pop it into a snap-lock bag and freeze it. It will last in the freezer for at least two months, and can be used to cook with straight from the freezer.*

Crunchy tuna and egg mornay

SERVES 4

You're going to love this. Forget the stuff they serve at boarding school and turn your mind to something your mum might have given the family on a rainy afternoon, but with a modern twist. Traditionally, tuna mornay doesn't include pasta – nor, come to think of it, does it include peas – but both help make it a more substantial meal. This version has all the elements of a classic tuna mornay: a creamy cheese sauce, hard-boiled eggs, chunks of tuna and crunchy crumbs on top. Sitting down to this is like putting on your favourite pair of comfy slippers.

250 g macaroni or other small pasta

2 thick slices day-old white bread, crusts removed, coarsely torn

60 g butter

¼ cup plain flour

3 cups milk

120 g coarsely grated cheddar

1 × 425 g can tuna in brine, drained and flaked

150 g frozen peas

3 hard-boiled eggs, sliced

1 Preheat oven to 180°C. Cook the pasta in a large pan of boiling salted water until al dente, then drain and transfer to a large bowl. Meanwhile, place the bread in a food processor and pulse a couple of times until coarsely chopped.

2 Melt the butter in a saucepan over low–medium heat. Add the flour and cook, stirring, for 1 minute or until foaming. Remove from the heat and gradually stir in the milk, then place over medium heat and cook for 5 minutes, stirring constantly, until the mixture thickens. Reduce heat to low and cook for 2 minutes. Add two-thirds of the cheddar and stir in until melted.

3 Add the cheese sauce, tuna and peas to the cooked pasta and stir until just combined. Spoon half this mixture into a 2-litre-capacity ovenproof dish. Lay the eggs evenly over the top, then add the remaining mixture.

4 Combine the breadcrumbs and remaining cheddar in a bowl and sprinkle over the mornay. Bake for 15 minutes or until golden, then serve at the table.

Try these delicious variations:

- If you grow your own herbs, chop up some **flat-leaf parsley** and add it to the pasta mixture.
- Another good addition to this is thin slices of **fresh tomato**, placed in a single layer on top of the pasta (just under the breadcrumb and cheese mixture) before baking – the tomatoes add moisture and a lovely fresh flavour.

Smooth saucing

As the French know, the sauce used in a dish is everything. If you're going to bother making a sauce at all, it pays to do it properly. This mornay would be nothing without its smooth, creamy cheese sauce, which binds all the elements together. But a lumpy, thick sauce is definitely going to spoil things, so let's start by getting that right. The secret to a smooth sauce is temperature. The roux (the mixture of fat – in this case, butter – and flour) needs to be at a different temperature from the liquid added to it: hot added to hot equals lumps. Take a look at the recipe here. The butter is melted, then flour is stirred in over the heat for a minute or so, and while it is still hot, the cold milk is stirred in. Keep on stirring and by the time the sauce has thickened, it will also be smooth. Stir in a figure-of-eight shape and, if you do see lumps starting to form, use a whisk to smooth the sauce out.

Slightly spicy salmon fish cakes

SERVES 4

Fussy eaters

Catering to fusspots is never easy, but you can experiment with these fish cakes by leaving out what they don't like (except for the potatoes), and adding things they do. For kids or those with simpler tastes, leave out the coriander and curry paste, and try chopped parsley if you have it growing. For vegetarians, leave out the salmon and replace it with spinach or any leftover veggies from the fridge, cut into 1 cm chunks. Frozen peas, stirred into the mixture before shaping the patties, are a nice addition too.

Homemade fish cakes taste so much better than the ready-made ones from the supermarket frozen-food section. These are sophisticated and delicious, and taste so fresh that you'd swear the fish had been pulled from the sea that morning. Plus, they're cheap to make and you know exactly what's in them. The bonus is that you're saving loads of time by using ingredients you probably have in the pantry anyway: curry paste, a can of salmon, breadcrumbs and some potatoes. Look for a jar of good Indian-style chutney to serve with the salmon cakes – or use your own homemade version (see page 154). Accompany with a green salad to make a complete meal.

4 potatoes, halved
1 × 210 g can pink or red salmon, drained
1 red, white or brown onion, finely chopped
1 tablespoon curry paste
1 tablespoon chopped coriander

¼ cup plain flour
1 egg, lightly beaten
¾ cup dried breadcrumbs
olive oil, for cooking
lemon wedges and Indian-style chutney, to serve

1 Place the potatoes in a large saucepan of salted water, bring to a boil and then simmer, covered, until easily pierced with a fork (about 20 minutes). Drain, return to the pan and toss over low heat for a few minutes until the potatoes are thoroughly dry. Mash well until smooth.

2 Flake the salmon into a bowl. Add the mashed potato, onion, curry paste and coriander and season to taste. Mix well to combine. Shape into eight round patties, then dip each one into the flour, brush with beaten egg and coat with breadcrumbs. Chill for 30 minutes.

3 In a large, heavy-based frying pan, heat a generous drizzle of oil over medium heat and fry the patties in batches until golden brown and heated through, adding more oil as necessary. Serve with lemon wedges and an Indian-style chutney.

Pink vs. red salmon

Pink salmon is not just the one that a certain major fish cannery throws away. It is quite a bit cheaper than red and has a milder taste. Here the milder flavour works because it's made up for with additions like curry paste and coriander. Red salmon, while more expensive, is the best option for salads. If you're not already familiar with canned fish, don't be put off by the skin and bones. They've been processed to be soft and will blend into other ingredients; the bones, in particular, are an excellent source of calcium. Salmon, either pink or red, is great to have on hand, not least because it's so good for you, providing omega-3 fatty acids that help prevent heart disease.

Instant potatoes?

If your time doesn't run to cooking the potatoes for these fish cakes yourself, use instant mashed potato instead, made according to the instructions on the packet (you'll need 2 cups of mash). Don't fret about using instant mash if you're short of time. Potatoes are hardly expensive, but cooking them can be costly in terms of time when you're yet to bath the kids, make the bed and iron your shirts for tomorrow! The thing about instant mash is that if you're going to use it, it's important to buy the best quality you can afford. Instant mash is nutritionally similar to real-life potatoes, but lower in vitamin C, so it's not quite as healthy as the real thing. The texture is definitely different, and so we wouldn't necessarily recommend it to accompany a fillet of beef, but in recipes like this it works well as a sort of 'fast food'. Some will turn their noses up at the idea of using processed food, but actually the practice of drying and grinding starchy root vegetables is thought to date back before the advent of agriculture as a great way to transport food and store it for long periods.

Very retro curried eggs

SERVES 4

Curried eggs have been a Sunday-night special for generations of Australians, and are an excellent option when you want to keep cooking to a minimum. You'll probably already have the ingredients on hand to make this creamy sauce to serve with hard-boiled eggs. Make it as spicy or as mild as you like, and jazz it up with crisp-fried onions and coriander. No need to wait until Sunday!

Make your own crisp-fried onions in the microwave (see below left) or buy crisp-fried shallots from Asian food stores.

* Prepare your crisp-fried onions in the microwave – a great trick that surprises everyone. Slice 2 white or brown onions thinly and place on a microwave-safe plate. Drizzle with a little rice bran or peanut oil. Microwave on the highest setting for about 5 minutes until the onion starts to brown, stirring several times to encourage even browning – keep a careful eye on the onion to make sure it doesn't burn.

1 tablespoon olive oil
1 small white or brown onion, finely chopped
1–2 teaspoons curry powder
2 tablespoons plain flour
1½ cups milk
1 granny smith apple, peeled and grated
2 tablespoons fruit chutney
1 tablespoon chopped coriander, plus extra sprigs to garnish
sea salt and freshly ground black pepper
6–8 hard-boiled eggs, peeled and halved
steamed rice and crisp-fried shallots or onions, to serve

1   Heat the oil in a heavy-based saucepan over medium heat. Add the onion and cook, stirring, for 3 minutes until soft. Add the curry powder and flour and cook for 1 minute, stirring. Add the milk and slowly bring to a boil, whisking until the sauce begins to thicken. Stir in the apple and chutney and simmer for 3 minutes. Add the chopped coriander and season to taste.

2   To serve, arrange the boiled eggs on a plate of steamed rice, spoon over the curry sauce and top with extra coriander and some crisp-fried shallots or onions.

The lowdown on boiling eggs

If your eggs have been in the fridge and you haven't had time to take them out in advance, place them in a pan of water and bring to a boil. Start timing when the water is boiling and **cook for 3 minutes to soft-boil or 5 minutes to hard-boil**. If your eggs are at room temperature, bring a pan of water to a rolling boil and use a spoon to lower in each egg. Reduce the heat a little and start timing once the water has reached a simmer. **Soft-boiled eggs** with the whites just set and the yolks still creamy **are ready in 4 minutes**, or **5 minutes for perfectly set whites** and yolks that are still a tiny bit soft inside. **For hard-boiled eggs, cook for 7 minutes**, drain and, to avoid a green tinge around the yolk, cool immediately by placing in a bowl of iced water (they will cool quicker if you crack the shells lightly). Unfortunately, the fresher the egg, the more difficult it is to shell: the shells of just-laid eggs stick as if they've been super-glued. Crack the shells all over and roll the egg between your hands to loosen before shelling.

Fish florentine

SERVES 4

This is a great way of frying fish fillets as they do in Florence. The egg seals in the moisture and flavours of the fish as it cooks. Give each piece of fish plenty of room in the pan (cook them in batches if you need to).

For an exotic flavour, try drizzling a little kecap manis (a sweet sticky soy sauce, see page 72) or a little soy sauce over the cooked fish.

4 fish fillets, such as barramundi, blue eye or flathead (about 180 g each)

plain flour seasoned with salt and pepper, for dusting

2 eggs, beaten

2–3 tablespoons rice bran or olive oil

sea salt, optional

lemon wedges, to serve

1　Cut the fillets diagonally into two or three longish sections and coat with the seasoned flour, then dip the floured fish pieces in the beaten egg to coat evenly.

2　Meanwhile, heat the oil in a large frying pan over medium–high heat and fry the fish pieces for 2–3 minutes each side until golden and cooked. Drain on paper towel, sprinkle with a little salt, if using, and serve immediately with lemon wedges.

Try this delicious variation:

You can use **chicken instead of fish** for an equally tasty result. You'll need 6 chicken thigh fillets, trimmed of fat and cut in half lengthways. Combine 2 tablespoons lemon juice with 1 tablespoon chopped flat-leaf parsley and some salt and pepper in a shallow bowl. Toss the chicken pieces through this mixture, then coat in seasoned flour and dip in beaten egg. Fry in a little rice bran or olive oil for 5–6 minutes, turning several times, until the chicken is golden and crusty outside, and the juices run clear when the flesh is pierced with a skewer. Drain on paper towel and serve with wedges of lemon.

How to combat kitchen whiffs #1

Preparing and cooking fish can leave your kitchen a bit pongy if you don't follow a few basic rules:

- **Clean the fish on sheets of newspaper**, then wrap up the waste in the paper and tie it all up in a plastic bag before throwing it in the outside rubbish bin.
- After baking fish in the oven, **toss a few curls of orange or lemon peel in the switched-off oven** and leave them there for 20 minutes or so to eliminate any fishy odours.
- A few tablespoons of **white vinegar added to the washing-up water** removes fishy smells from pans and plates.

Sardine and chilli spaghettini

SERVES 4

Sardines must rank among the best of all canned foods, and some brands are even considered a delicacy in Europe. While many people are fans of sardines canned in tomato purée or some other sauce, when cooking it's best to steer clear of those with fancy flavours, as it limits what you can do with them. Choose sardines in spring water, oil or, if you want to be really daring, oil with a slice of lemon.

400 g spaghettini, spaghetti or angel-hair pasta
¼ cup olive oil
3 cloves garlic, crushed
1–1½ teaspoons chilli flakes
1 punnet cherry tomatoes, quartered
1–2 × 110 g can sardines in oil or spring water, drained and lightly mashed
handful of basil leaves
sea salt and freshly ground black pepper

1   Cook the pasta in a large pan of boiling salted water until al dente, then drain, reserving ¼ cup of the cooking liquid.

2   Wipe the pan out with a tea towel, add the oil and heat over medium heat. Fry the garlic, chilli and tomatoes for 2 minutes, until the tomatoes are soft but still holding their shape. Add the sardines and cooked pasta and toss until heated through. Stir through the reserved cooking liquid and the basil leaves, season to taste and serve.

What else can you do with canned sardines?

- Try mashing a can of drained sardines with a little lemon juice and mixing with 2 cups well-seasoned mashed potato, then form into patties, coat with egg and breadcrumbs and fry to make delicious **fish cakes**.
- Thinly spread drained sardines with Dijon mustard, **dip them in egg and breadcrumbs, and fry**. Serve on fingers of hot buttered toast.
- Pop a sardine inside a big **baked potato**, top with grated cheese and brown under a hot grill.
- Make a **sardine butter** to serve on toast by mashing up the drained contents of a can of sardines with two hard-boiled eggs, 60 g butter and a good squeeze of lemon juice.
- Layering sliced potato and onion with drained sardines turns a **potato gratin** into a complete meal. Top with some buttered breadcrumbs before baking to make a crusty topping.

If you want to 'green' this dish up a little, toss through some chopped flat-leaf parsley or some baby rocket leaves.

Thai green chicken curry

SERVES 4

Some of the most versatile ingredients to be found on pantry shelves are Asian-influenced, like coconut cream and Thai green and red curry pastes. These curry pastes are a boon if you enjoy exotic flavours but are not sure how to recreate them. Green curry paste can be very hot, so tread carefully.

Don't shake the can of coconut milk before you open it – that way you can use the coconut cream that will have risen to the surface to fry the paste.

1 × 270 g can coconut milk
1 tablespoon green curry paste
1 teaspoon grated ginger (optional)
600 g chicken thigh fillets, trimmed of fat and cut into bite-sized pieces
150 g frozen peas
a little chicken stock or water (optional)
1 tablespoon fish sauce
10–12 basil or Thai basil leaves
steamed rice, to serve

1 Scoop the creamy top layer from the coconut milk into a wok or medium-sized saucepan. Add the curry paste and stir-fry over low heat for a minute or so until fragrant. Stir in the ginger, if using. Add the chicken pieces and increase the heat to medium–high, then stir-fry for 2 minutes.

2 Add the rest of the coconut milk, the peas and some chicken stock or water if you like your curry a bit more saucy. Simmer over low heat for 8–10 minutes until the chicken is cooked. Add the fish sauce and basil leaves, mixing in gently, then serve with steamed rice.

A lighter option

If you want to make this taste like your local Thai takeaway's version, you're going to have to up the fat content considerably – adding some oil and using coconut cream instead of milk. But we're opting for a much healthier version here, one you can enjoy once a week without fearing the onslaught of extra cushioning around your hips. We've used coconut milk, which is much lower in fat than coconut cream (and for an even lighter result, try light coconut milk, or use half coconut milk and half water or stock). Many store-bought curry pastes are saturated in oil, and not always particularly good-quality oil at that. Some have no added oil, and are just a happy mix of spices, making the result much more flavoursome and healthy. Check the ingredients and go for the latter version for a healthier curry.

---

* Grow basil leaves in your garden or in pots outside so you have constant access to this versatile herb (see page 134 for advice on how to grow herbs). Or try fresh kaffir lime leaves – store them in the freezer in a small snap-lock bag, slice one leaf finely and add to the curry paste for extra flavour.

Green vs. red

Thai curry paste is not a dry spice blend like those used in Northern Indian curries, but a paste made from a blend of mostly fresh ingredients. The green curry paste is hotter than its red counterpart, and is made with fresh chillies instead of dried. When you're buying curry paste, choose one that doesn't have too much oil added (you can tell the amount there is by how high it's ranked on the list of ingredients). Curry paste will keep for months in the fridge if opened, and almost forever in your pantry un-opened. Experiment with the amount of paste you add, depending on how hot you like it.

Spaghetti puttanesca

SERVES 6

Pasta alla puttanesca comes from Naples, and literally means 'pasta the way a whore would make it', probably because it was a fast, cheap meal that prostitutes could prepare in the time between customers (although some say the reference relates to the sauce's hot, spicy flavour!). With a well-stocked pantry, you'll have all the ingredients needed for this already on hand, so it makes for a great last-minute meal in the evening. You can omit the anchovies if you wish, but they do give a rich flavour and are certainly not overbearing.

3 tomatoes, peeled (see below) and roughly chopped *or* 1 × 400 g can
    peeled chopped tomatoes
¼ cup olive oil
3 cloves garlic, finely chopped
3 teaspoons capers, chopped
16 black olives, stones removed
1 small red chilli, finely chopped
1 tablespoon finely chopped oregano
sea salt (optional) and freshly ground black pepper
500 g spaghetti
4–6 anchovy fillets in oil, drained and chopped
freshly grated parmesan, to serve

1   In a large, heavy-based pan, heat the oil over medium heat, add the garlic and cook until lightly coloured. Add the chopped tomato and any juice, stir well, then add the capers, olives, chilli, oregano, salt (if using – remember anchovies and capers are very salty) and pepper to taste. Cook for about 20 minutes, stirring occasionally.

2   Meanwhile, cook the spaghetti in a large pan of boiling salted water until al dente (when the spaghetti is almost cooked, add the anchovies to the water just to blanch them). Drain and place in a large serving bowl. Pour over the sauce and serve with plenty of grated parmesan.

Peeling tomatoes

An easy way to remove skins from tomatoes is by plunging them into boiling water, slowly counting to 10, then removing them and cooling immediately in iced water. Use a small paring knife to cut a small slit at the stalk-end of each tomato to enable you to slip off the skins.

Squid with capsicum and lemon

SERVES 4

If you love seafood, squid is a great choice in terms of sustainability, and its flavour is perfect for a dish like this.

Always try to buy whole squid, the smallest size you can find. Prepare it yourself as it's sure to have more flavour and be more tender than the tubes you can buy ready-prepared.

750 g whole squid *or* 500 g cleaned squid

¼ cup olive oil

1 red capsicum, white insides and seeds removed, cut into thin strips

2 cloves garlic, crushed

1 teaspoon chilli flakes

juice and finely grated zest of 1 lemon

2 tablespoons chopped flat-leaf parsley

sea salt and freshly ground black pepper

1   If you've bought whole squid, prepare it by pulling carefully just below the head and removing the insides and the hard spine. For large squid, remove the skin by slipping your finger underneath and pulling off. Cut the tentacles off below the head, cut into small lengths and reserve, discarding the eyes and hard beak. Rinse and then cut the body (or tube) into rings.

2   Heat the oil in a large frying pan over medium heat. Add the capsicum and fry for a minute or so, then add the garlic, chilli flakes and lemon zest. Cook for about 5 minutes until the capsicum is soft.

3   Increase the heat to high, add the squid pieces and cook for a minute or two until the squid is opaque, tender and just cooked. Remove the pan from the heat and stir in the lemon juice. Transfer to a serving dish, sprinkle with parsley and salt and pepper, and serve.

* Try this as an elegant entrée for 6–8 people, or you could make it as part of a mezze or tapas spread. Squid, though cheap, looks really impressive when paired with other ingredients. Borrow from the Italians and Spanish and add breadcrumbs, tomatoes, anchovies or capers – they are all a great match. Crusty bread is an essential accompaniment for mopping up the delicious sauce.

Vietnamese chicken with vermicelli

SERVES 4

★ Experiment with bamboo shoots and baby corn, which you can buy in cans from most supermarkets and Asian food stores. They're great to have on hand when you're throwing together stir-fries like this one. Just slice them lengthways and pop into the wok with the chicken.

This dish is a regular feature in our kitchens, and it's sure to be just as popular in yours as it's quick, low in fat and has a light yet punchy flavour. It's just a matter of remembering to pick up some chicken on the way home, or taking some out of the freezer and popping it in the fridge in the morning. For this dish, thigh fillets are better than breast because they're more flavour-some, moist and – joy of joys – cheaper.

We keep vermicelli noodles on hand at all times to have this fabulous dish at our fingertips. You can of course serve this without the tomato and cucumber salad, but it does add a lovely freshness to the meal.

200 g rice vermicelli noodles

1 tablespoon oil

500 g chicken thigh fillets, trimmed of fat and cut into bite-sized pieces

2 white or brown onions, halved and sliced lengthways

1 teaspoon freshly grated ginger

2 tablespoons fish sauce

1 tablespoon soy sauce (preferably the reduced-salt variety)

freshly ground black pepper

coriander sprigs, to serve

TOMATO AND CUCUMBER SALAD

2 tomatoes, sliced

1 small cucumber, peeled and sliced

1 red or green onion, halved and sliced lengthways

sugar, malt vinegar, sea salt and freshly ground black pepper, to taste

1 Put the noodles into a large bowl and cover with cold water. Leave to stand for 10 minutes, until softened and limp, then drain.

2 To make the salad, toss the sliced tomato, cucumber and onion together in a bowl. Dress with a sprinkling of sugar, a dash of vinegar and season with salt and pepper to taste.

3 Place a wok over high heat, add the oil and swirl to coat the inside of the wok. Add the chicken, onion and ginger and stir-fry for 3–4 minutes. Add the fish sauce, soy sauce, a good grinding of pepper and ¼ cup water. Bring to a boil and simmer for 3 minutes. Gently stir in the noodles, return to the boil and cook for a further 3 minutes or until the chicken is cooked and the noodles are tender (add another splash of water if the mixture dries out).

4 Transfer to a serving dish, garnish with coriander and serve immediately with the salad.

Waste watcher

Stir-fries are a great way to use up veggie odds and ends. You can throw in some broccoli florets, snowpeas or even capsicum strips – just fry them first until tender, then add them to the wok when the chicken is nearly cooked.

Spaghetti carbonara

SERVES 4

This is proper carbonara: just pasta, pancetta, eggs and parmesan. No fattening cream, butter, or expensive mascarpone. The eggs are added when the pan is off the heat – they will cook in the residual heat of the pasta to make a rich, golden, satiny sauce. You're using fresh eggs, so there's no need to be squeamish about soft-cooked eggs. The freshly ground black pepper is essential, as the dish is named because the pepper looks like a deposit of coal soot (*carbonara*).

400 g spaghetti
⅓ cup olive oil
150 g pancetta, diced
3 eggs, beaten
¾ cup freshly grated parmesan or pecorino
freshly ground black pepper

1 Cook the spaghetti in a large pan of boiling salted water until al dente, then drain and return to the pan. Meanwhile, heat the oil in a frying pan and fry the pancetta for 3–4 minutes over medium heat until golden and crisp.

2 Add the pasta to the pan and toss over low–medium heat until thoroughly coated. Remove from the heat and add the beaten egg, stirring constantly so that it quickly cooks into a smooth creamy sauce. Stir through half the cheese and a good grinding of black pepper.

3 Pile into serving bowls and serve with the remaining cheese and some more pepper.

Raising the bar – a fancy way of serving carbonara

Take an extra 4 eggs (1 per person) and crack them, separating the whites (but reserving for another use – remember you can freeze them) and returning the yolks to the best-looking half of the shells. Set them aside in the carton to hold them steady while you proceed with the dish, then just before serving, place an eggshell with the yolk in the centre of each bowl of spaghetti. Each person tips the egg yolk from its half-shell onto the pasta, setting the shell aside, and stirs it through while the pasta is still piping hot. You could be dining silver-service!

How to store your parmesan

If you've splashed out and bought yourself a nice big wedge of parmesan, it's important not to waste a skerrick of it by letting it dry out in the back of the fridge. Parmesan has a very low moisture content so it's particularly prone to drying out. Keep your parmesan tightly wrapped in wax paper then in foil, and store it in the warmest part of your fridge (generally the door). Try to remember to take it out of the fridge 15 minutes or so before you need to use it so that any moisture lost can be reabsorbed from the air.

Try these delicious variations:

- Add **150 g sliced mushrooms**, pan-fried in a little butter, to the spaghetti when you stir through the pancetta.
- Add **1–2 cups frozen peas** to the pasta water a few minutes before it is cooked and drain them together, adding to the sauce at the end.

Pasta and beans with pork ragú

SERVES 4

Quick, easy, filling and cheap, this hearty pasta ticks all the right boxes. Kids love it, and it's a great way to get healthy beans into their diet.

250 g pasta shells or penne
¼ cup olive oil
1 red, white or brown onion, finely chopped
1 carrot, diced
1 bunch flat-leaf parsley, stems finely chopped, leaves chopped and reserved
2 cloves garlic, finely chopped
1 teaspoon dried oregano
500 g lean pork mince
1 × 400 g can chopped tomatoes
⅓ cup black olives, stones removed
1 × 400 g can cannellini beans, drained and rinsed
sea salt and freshly ground black pepper
freshly grated parmesan, to serve

1   Cook the pasta in a large pan of boiling salted water until al dente, then drain.

2   Meanwhile, heat the oil in a large frying pan over medium heat and fry the onion, carrot, parsley stems, garlic and oregano for about 10 minutes, until the onion is soft. Increase the heat to high, add the pork mince and fry for about 5 minutes, stirring to break up any lumps. Add the tomatoes, olives and beans, stir and simmer for 5–10 minutes until the sauce is thick and fragrant, then season to taste with salt and pepper.

3   Add the drained pasta and the parsley leaves to the pan and toss for another minute over medium–high heat, then serve immediately with plenty of grated parmesan.

Waste watcher

HIT A SNAG?   *If you haven't had time to go to the butcher and you have some Italian sausages in the freezer, you can replace the pork mince used here with the same amount of sausage meat. Just cut the thawed sausages open, squeeze out the meat and cook as described.*

How to cook perfect pasta

Follow these guidelines and you'll have perfect pasta every time:

- Generally speaking, **allow 80–100 g of pasta per person**, depending on what else you're serving it with and whether it's for a main course or an entrée.
- **Use a large pan** with plenty of room for the pasta to cook evenly without sticking together.
- For **every 250 g of pasta, use 3.5 litres of water** with 1 teaspoon salt added (do not add oil – although it prevents the pasta sticking together, it also stops the sauce clinging to the pasta).
- Have the **water boiling vigorously before adding the pasta**, and drop the pasta in a handful at a time so the water stays on the boil. Stir a few times, then leave to boil vigorously.
- **Cooked pasta should be tender but firm** – al dente, as the Italians call it, which means 'firm to the bite'.
- When cooked, **remove the pan immediately from the heat and drain**, but do not rinse as the starch on the cooked pasta encourages the sauce to cling.

Red beef and pumpkin stir-fry

SERVES 4

You'll be sitting at the table enjoying this steaming stir-fry faster than you could have run up the road and ordered a takeaway – it's quick, simple and very satisfying. Keep fish sauce, kecap manis and Thai red curry paste on hand as you'll be turning to this recipe again and again.

1 tablespoon rice bran or vegetable oil
600 g pumpkin, peeled and cut into bite-sized pieces
1–2 tablespoons red curry paste
500 g blade steak, thinly sliced
1 bunch green onions, cut into 2 cm lengths
¼ cup kecap manis (see left)
1–2 tablespoons fish sauce
½ bunch coriander, leaves and stems chopped
¼ cup crushed peanuts
steamed rice, to serve

1   Heat the oil in a wok or large frying pan over high heat. Stir-fry the pumpkin for 5 minutes or until it is tender, then remove and set aside.

2   Add half the curry paste to the wok and cook for 1–2 minutes until fragrant. Add half the beef and brown for 5 minutes, then remove and set aside. Repeat with the remaining curry paste and beef.

3   Return all the beef to the wok along with the chopped green onions, kecap manis, fish sauce and ½ cup water and toss to combine. Simmer for 3–5 minutes, until the sauce has reduced slightly and the beef is cooked through.

4   Toss through the stir-fried pumpkin and simmer for a further 2 minutes. Stir through the coriander and top with peanuts, then serve with steamed rice.

Healthy and wise

Chicken thigh fillets are a great choice for this stir-fry. They're moist and flavoursome, but they do have a bit of fat on them (which is probably why they taste so good!). Take the time to cut away as much of the visible fat as you can – you'll be doing your heart a big favour.

What's kecap manis?

This is a thick, sweet soy sauce used in Indonesian and Malaysian cooking. It is sweeter and less salty than regular soy sauce (due to the addition of palm sugar), and gives a wonderful rich flavour to noodle and dark meat dishes. Use it sparingly though: a little goes a long way.

Try these delicious variations:

- Use an **Indian curry paste** instead of a Thai red curry paste.
- Use **cashews** instead of peanuts.
- Use **sweet potato** instead of pumpkin.
- Use **chicken or pork, or even firm tofu** cut into chunks, instead of beef.
- **Leave out** the coriander.

Use the leaves and stems from the coriander — they have plenty of flavour and can be chopped along with the leaves. Just make sure they are washed really well to remove any sand or grit. The roots are used primarily for making curry pastes.

Lamb chops with anchovy sauce and bean purée

SERVES 4

Here's an easy way to dress up lamb chops. The ingredients list may be a little longer than for other weekday meals, but it's all simple stuff you may well have on hand anyway. It's the combination of all these flavours that take the lamb chops to a new dimension. Don't like anchovies? Just leave them out and use some grated lemon zest or chopped capers instead.

4 thick lamb chump chops
plain flour seasoned with salt and pepper, for dusting
1 tablespoon olive oil
1 × 50 g can anchovy fillets in oil, drained and chopped
2 tablespoons chopped flat-leaf parsley
2 tablespoons extra virgin olive oil
juice of ½ a lemon

BEAN PURÉE

2 tablespoons olive oil
1 small white or brown onion, roughly chopped
1 clove garlic, crushed
2 × 400 g cans cannellini beans, drained and rinsed
⅔ cup chicken stock or water
sea salt and freshly ground black pepper
1 tablespoon extra virgin olive oil
good squeeze of lemon juice

1 To make the bean purée, heat the olive oil in a saucepan over medium heat and cook the onion for 5 minutes until soft but not coloured. Add the garlic, beans and stock or water, season with salt and pepper and cook for about 5 minutes. Remove from the heat, leave to cool slightly, then use a stab blender or food processor to make a purée, adding the extra virgin olive oil and lemon juice while you mix. Keep the purée warm while you cook the chops.

2 Dust the chops thoroughly in the flour, shaking off any excess. In a large, heavy-based frying pan, heat the oil over medium heat and cook the chops for 6–8 minutes, turning them once.

3 Meanwhile, combine the anchovies and parsley in a bowl and stir in the extra virgin olive oil and lemon juice. Serve the chops on the bean purée with some anchovy sauce spooned over.

Healthy and wise

This bean purée is a healthy, low-GI alternative to mashed potato. Another good low-GI option is cauliflower purée – just steam some cauliflower, add a little butter or oil and purée in a blender.

Roast chicken with tomato and fennel

SERVES 4

Just throw everything in a roasting tin and pop it in the oven, and by the time you've helped the kids with their homework and done a load of washing, it's time to eat.

2 tablespoons olive oil
4 chicken marylands (leg and thigh portions)
2 red, white or brown onions, peeled and
   cut into segments
½ teaspoon saffron threads (optional)
1 large bulb fennel, trimmed and thickly sliced
4 cloves garlic
1 strip orange zest
1 punnet cherry tomatoes *or* 1 × 400 g can chopped tomatoes
1 teaspoon sweet paprika
sea salt and freshly ground black pepper

* Potatoes, cut into small chunks and added to the roasting tin before it goes in the oven, go really well with this chicken, as do steamed zucchini or peas. Fettuccine is also a good accompaniment – the saffron-tomatoey sauce goes beautifully with pasta. Or just serve with lots of crusty bread for mopping up the sauce.

1 Preheat oven to 200°C. Heat the oil over medium heat in a roasting tin and brown the chicken pieces for 2–3 minutes each side. Remove the chicken and set aside, then add the onions, cooking for a few minutes until lightly coloured.

2 Meanwhile, soak the saffron threads, if using, in ¼ cup hot water for a few minutes to soften and release the flavour.

3 Return the browned chicken pieces to the roasting tin and arrange the fennel slices, garlic cloves, orange zest and tomatoes around the chicken pieces. Sprinkle over the saffron and its soaking water, if using, then season with paprika and salt and pepper.

4 Bake for 20–30 minutes until the chicken is cooked through (you may need to add a little more water during cooking if the dish starts to dry out). Serve immediately.

Fish and risoni stew

SERVES 4

Risoni is pasta shaped like small grains of rice that you'll find in the pasta section of the super-market. You can make this a really cheap meal by using drained flaked canned tuna instead of fresh fish, folded through at the end.

1 tablespoon olive oil

1 white or brown onion, finely chopped

3 cloves garlic, crushed

1–2 teaspoons finely chopped red chilli (optional)

1 × 400 g can chopped tomatoes

½ cup white wine *or* juice of 1 lemon with enough water added to make ½ cup

½ cup risoni

500 g firm white fish such as flathead, blue eye or snapper, cut into chunks

crusty bread, to serve (optional)

GREMOLATA

½ cup finely chopped flat-leaf parsley

1 clove garlic, chopped

2 teaspoons finely grated lemon zest

1 Make the gremolata by mixing all the ingredients together, then set aside.

2 In a heavy-based saucepan with a lid, heat the oil over medium heat and fry the onion until soft. Add the garlic and chilli, if using, and cook for 1 minute, without letting them burn. Add the tomato and white wine and bring to a boil, then reduce the heat to low, cover and simmer for about 10 minutes.

3 Add the risoni to the pan with 1 cup water and simmer for 5 minutes. Add the fish to the pan, cover and simmer gently for 5–8 minutes until tender. Add a little more wine or water to the pan if the sauce has become too thick.

4 Serve scattered with the gremolata.

Healthy and wise

Fish is low in saturated fat and a great source of omega-3 fatty acids. However, some types of fish may contain high levels of mercury and other environmental contaminants. Levels of these contaminants are generally higher in older, larger fish, such as shark or orange roughy, so steer clear of these varieties.

Gremolata is a classic Italian garnish traditionally served with osso bucco, and we love the fresh tang it imparts to meaty casseroles, fish stews and grilled or barbecued fish. Use the freshest garlic you can find for the best flavour.

Japanese chicken donburi

SERVES 4

This is a favourite comfort-food meal in Japan – everything is soft, easy to eat and nourishing. The chicken is simmered in Japanese sauces and served with rice and a warm egg-enriched dashi broth. If you happen to have chicken breasts, by all means use them instead of the thigh fillets – just take care not to overcook them.

1⅓ cups jasmine rice

2–3 green onions

400 g chicken thigh fillets, fat removed, flesh cut into 2 cm cubes

1 tablespoon rice wine or dry sherry

2 tablespoons soy sauce

1 cup dashi broth

2 tablespoons white vinegar

1 tablespoon sugar

4 fresh shiitake mushrooms, thinly sliced

6 eggs, lightly beaten

1 Rinse the rice in a sieve under cold running water until the water runs clear. Bring 2⅔ cups water to a boil in a heavy-based saucepan with a lid. Sprinkle in the rice, stir once, then cover. Reduce the heat to low and cook for about 12 minutes until the rice is cooked (try not to lift the lid more than once to check the rice). Add more water if necessary if the liquid has absorbed before the rice is quite cooked. Set aside and keep warm.

2 Thinly slice the green onions on the diagonal and place in iced water for about 5 minutes to curl the ends.

3 Place the chicken in a bowl with the rice wine or sherry and half the soy sauce, and set aside. Put the dashi broth, the remaining soy, the vinegar and the sugar into a saucepan and stir over medium heat for 4–5 minutes until the sugar dissolves.

4 Add the chicken, marinade and mushrooms to the broth mixture and simmer over medium heat for 4–5 minutes until the chicken is cooked. Pour the beaten egg into the broth, cover and remove from the heat. Leave to stand for 3–4 minutes until the egg is just set.

5 Divide the cooked rice between serving bowls and spoon over the chicken and egg mixture. Drain the green onion and scatter over before serving.

* Instant dashi broth powder, which is made from dried fish (bonito), is a staple in Japan. It forms the base for miso soup and other broths and cooking liquids. You'll find it in the Asian section of many supermarkets, or at Asian food stores. You only need ¼ teaspoon mixed with 1 cup boiling water to make the amount needed here.

CHAPTER 4

Meals from leftovers

Clever cooks don't throw away leftovers. As the minister said to his wife when she set down her casserole with a flourish and waited for grace, 'It seems to me that I have blessed a good deal of this material before.'

Leftover pasta and vegetables can be transformed into a hearty bake or soup, roast lamb can shine again in a shepherd's pie and roast chicken can feature in a stir-fry. You don't have to eat the same thing for days on end; leftover food can be reinvented as a completely new meal for another night. The trick is to be aware of how much you throw away as you're clearing up after a meal — too many scrapings in the bin and you should think about the way you shop, serve and eat. Good cooks treasure leftovers, knowing these sundry items will help make another meal.

And although thrifty cooks rarely have unexpected leftovers, there are times when appetites just aren't as hearty and there's more rice, pasta, vegetables or meat than is needed for one meal.

There are practical and intelligent ways to deal with leftovers to prevent half a cooked chicken going off in the fridge or cooked vegetables being tossed in the bin. Many of us waste a huge amount of money and food by throwing out what we can't eat in one go, but there is another way.

First, consider how you actually present a meal to your guests, your family, yourself. Try serving the meal on one or two large platters placed in the centre of the table instead of on individual plates. This way, everyone can help themselves and take exactly what they need. It's encouraging for picky eaters, especially children, who can decide for themselves how much they feel like eating. They may come back for seconds, but the take-as-you-need system avoids the half-eaten steak being thrown away, and generally reduces the amount of leftover food that can't be re-used.

The tricky part for the home economist is to keep an eye out for those we might call 'pelicans', whose 'eyes can hold more than their belly can'. Try to keep enough for another meal back in the kitchen, so that everything is not eaten up at the table for the sake of it. That way, if someone could do with a bit more, you can offer it; you hold the purse strings, so to speak. Think about running the kitchen as if you were running a business. Everyone feeling they're satisfied is one thing, but being a bit too greedy, overeating, or thinking things must be polished off is quite another (remember – it takes our stomach almost 20 minutes to tell the brain we've had enough to eat). You want to have enough leftovers to be worthwhile putting towards another meal. Tiny bits of this and that just become a nuisance.

Secondly as soon as the meal is over, pack those precious leftovers away carefully – before the dishes are done! The sooner you store them, the better they will be. When they are cool, get them into airtight containers or snap-lock bags and into the refrigerator or freezer, depending on when you plan to use them.

It's important to limit the number of leftover ingredients you use in a new dish in order to retain some semblance of novelty. Make sure you introduce freshness and colour by adding ingredients like chopped flat-leaf parsley, finely grated lemon zest or chopped tomatoes. And remember to create a nice contrast in texture. Most leftover ingredients are soft, so a little crunch of something crisp like capsicum, celery, nuts or bacon is usually welcome. Remember too that leftovers don't necessarily need to be cooked again. Meat, chicken, fish and vegetables, in particular, only need to be reheated or they start to lose their flavour.

WHAT TO KEEP:

- Boiled or mashed potatoes
- Rice and pasta
- Chicken, lamb, beef or fish (especially tuna and salmon)
- Ham and turkey
- Vegetables
- Gravy

WHAT TO TOSS:

- Once dressed, a green salad has to be eaten. Try making a smaller salad, and if that goes down quickly you can pop back to the kitchen with the bowl and add fresh leaves to toss through the existing dressing.
- If you've used something once in a leftover dish, avoid reheating it again – it could start to become a health hazard.
- Discovered something at the back of the fridge you forgot about and may have kept for too long? Never taste food that looks strange or smells unpleasant to see if you can still use it – discard it, just to be on the safe side.
- Is it mouldy? What you see is only the tip of the iceberg as mould tends to spread under the surface. You might be able to save some hard cheese, salami, and fruits and vegetables by cutting the mould out and removing a large area around it, but most mouldy food should be discarded.

REINVENT LEFTOVERS TO CREATE:

- Filled savoury pancakes and omelettes
- Cottage and shepherd's pies
- Soups
- Mornays
- Curries
- A range of pasta dishes and pasta bakes
- Soufflés
- Chicken or meat pies
- Savoury pastries
- Hash browns
- Moussaka
- Fabulous sandwiches and rolls for lunch
- Rice and bean salads
- Fried rice
- Fish cakes, rissoles and croquettes
- Pâtés and potted meats

Don't let good food go to waste: the general rules

- **Make a shopping list**, and check the pantry and fridge before you shop. Avoid impulse buys and, generally speaking, if you're not going to cook fresh ingredients that night or the next night, don't buy them.
- **Avoid buying large packs of meat** unless you're confident you can use them in the next 2 days, or freeze them immediately on the day of purchase to use on another occasion.
- **Be realistic** about how much food you need, and become familiar with healthy portion sizes. Meat, fish and poultry servings should be no more than 180 g per person to stay within healthy guidelines. Allow for one potato or ½ cup rice and 1–2 cups salad or vegetables per person.
- **Rather than waste ingredients**, make double the amount of dishes such as lasagne or curry, and freeze them for other occasions, remembering to label with how many they will serve. You'll be helping to cut your energy bills, not to mention saving yourself time!
- **Invest in good-quality storage containers** and snap-lock bags, and pack leftover stews or casseroles, cooked rice, mashed potato or cooked pasta in the freezer. Don't forget to label and date these items, and check your freezer regularly so that you eat those items closest to their use-by date first.

Leftover meat 'done up'

The proper term for dishes made with leftover cooked meat is a *rechauffe*, but by any name, we all know them as leftovers 'done up'. There's an art to this, though – a good leftover dish should be more than just cooked offcuts thrown together in a random fashion. Shepherd's or cottage pies, moussakas, croquettes, rissoles: all call for care and skill and, as we've said before, rely on the clever combination of leftovers with good fresh ingredients. The first skill to learn is how to reheat meat properly. It should be finely diced, and any fat, skin or sinew should be removed. If you are combining the leftover meat with any leftover gravy or sauce, make sure the sauce is warmed before the cold leftover meat is added, preferably in the top of a double boiler or in a saucepan over the lowest possible heat. This is to prevent the meat becoming tough and shrinking, and also to help the flavour of the sauce penetrate the meat.

*There's lots you can do with leftover lamb like this slow-roasted shoulder (see page 209), but a good way to use it again is to reheat it in one large piece under the grill so the outside goes nice and crispy.

KEEPING LEFTOVERS SAFE

- Make sure your hands are very clean when handling leftovers and always use clean tongs, forks, knives or spoons to prevent any contamination.
- Store leftovers in separate sealed containers to avoid cross-contamination.
- Chill leftovers as soon as possible. If they are to be frozen, freeze them as soon as possible.
- When preparing leftovers, use plastic or non-porous cutting boards that can be put in the dishwasher or scrubbed thoroughly.
- Make sure leftovers haven't been placed on a plate or cutting board where raw meats have been previously cut, without washing it thoroughly in hot soapy water first.
- As a general rule, use up your refrigerated leftovers within 3–4 days (see the chart below for storage time-limits for specific foods).
- Avoid, if possible, defrosting frozen leftovers on the sink or bench. It's usually best to use the fridge to thaw.

STORING LEFTOVERS

The following are estimates of safe refrigerator and freezer storage time-limits.

Type of food	Stored in fridge	Stored in freezer
Vegetable soups and stews	3–4 days	1–2 months
Vegetable soups and stews (meat added)	1–2 days	1–2 months
Mashed potato	3–4 days	1–2 months
Cooked potatoes and carrots	3–4 days	Best not frozen
Cooked green vegetables	2–3 days	1 month
Cooked rice	2–3 days	1–2 months
Cooked pasta	2–3 days	1–2 months
Sliced ham	2–3 days	Best not frozen
Cooked meat and casseroles	3–4 days	2–3 months
Cooked poultry	3–4 days	2–3 months
Cooked fish	2–3 days	1 month
Cooked meat patties	2–3 days	1–2 months
Hard-boiled eggs	2–3 days	Best not frozen
Raw eggwhites	1 week	2–3 months
Raw egg yolks	2 days (covered with water)	1–2 months
Gravy and meat stocks	1–2 days	2–3 months

Getting to know your fridge

A refrigerator is not just a storage area; it is an essential kitchen tool. Though its temperature should be at or below 3°C, in reality all refrigerators have warm and cool spots, dry and humid spots. Rather than being an inconvenience, this can actually make the refrigerator even more useful. Why? Because foods differ in their storage requirements. Here's a quick guide.

Cool zones

The meat compartment (if your fridge has one) and the back of the middle and bottom shelves. This is the best place to store:

- raw poultry, large cuts of meat, fish and shellfish (the latter placed on top of snap-lock bags of ice inside a deep container)
- prepared foods, cooked meats (in snap-lock bags) and leftovers
- fruits such as oranges, grapes, apples
- raw steaks, chops, minced meats, diced meats
- eggs, still in the carton
- butter, in a butter dish

The bottom shelf of the door is the best place to store:

- milk, yoghurt and sour cream

Moderate to cool zones

The chiller is the best place to store:

- leafy greens, asparagus, celery, broccoli, cauliflower
- cheese, wrapped first in baking or waxed paper then foil

Moderate zones

The front of the top and middle shelves are the best places to store:

- delicate fruits such as melons and tomatoes
- vegetables such as green beans

The butter compartment is the best place for:

- fresh herbs, washed and wrapped in paper towel, then placed in an airtight plastic container

Warm zones

The front of the bottom shelf, and the middle shelves of the door. This is the best place for:

- mangoes and other sub-tropical fruits (in snap-lock bags punched with air holes for breathing)
- mushrooms and corn (kept in their original packaging)
- condiments
- drinks

How to combat kitchen whiffs #2

Furry cheese, shrivelled carrots, leftovers with a greenish hue . . . the number-one secret for keeping your fridge smelling nice is to avoid leaving food in there past its prime. Ideally, the food in your fridge should have a pretty fast turnaround time – if it doesn't, chances are you're buying too much, or you're not using up your leftovers. Here are a few tips on keeping food odours at bay in your fridge:

- Some people swear by keeping a natural sponge in the salad crisper to keep fruit and veggies fresh for longer.
- Store cheese in an airtight box with a sugar cube added to keep it fresh.
- Always store eggs pointy-end down – it makes them last longer.
- Store eggs in the main part of the fridge where it's colder, rather than in the door.
- Wipe the insides of the fridge down with 1 tablespoon bicarbonate of soda dissolved in 1 litre warm water every 2 weeks or so to keep smells at bay.
- A handful of charcoal or kitty litter, placed in a small bowl in the fridge and left for a day or two, will also eliminate most odours.
- If you've just cleaned the fridge out and you want to freshen it up a bit, try leaving an orange spiked with cloves, or a cotton-wool ball soaked in vanilla extract in a small dish or egg cup, in there for as long as the nice aroma lasts.

Is it freezer burn?

Patches of white on frozen foods are a sure sign they've passed their use-by date. Wrapping food correctly for storage in the freezer can maximise storage times.

Skordalia

MAKES 2 CUPS

This is one of the best ways of using up leftover mashed potato. A Greek dish, it's traditionally served with hot or cold fish or shellfish, fried or boiled vegetables, or grilled chicken, or you could serve it as a dip with some toasted sourdough alongside.

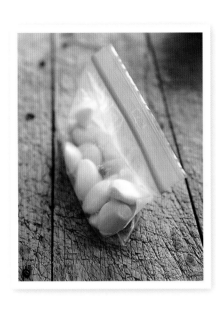

2 slices stale-ish white bread, crusts removed
4–6 cloves garlic
½ teaspoon salt
1 cup mashed potato (see below)
⅓ cup olive oil
1 tablespoon lemon juice
1 tablespoon white vinegar
sea salt and freshly ground black pepper
sliced toasted sourdough, to serve

1   In a shallow bowl, soak the bread with enough water to cover for 5 minutes, then squeeze dry and set aside.

2   Crush the garlic with the salt and place in a food processor with the mashed potato and bread. Pulse for a few seconds until smooth.

3   Add the olive oil, lemon juice and vinegar and process until smooth and creamy (but avoid over-processing or the oil will start to separate). Add salt and pepper to taste, then transfer to a bowl. Cover and chill in the fridge until ready to use – it will keep for up to 2 days. Serve with slices of toasted sourdough.

The perfect creamy mashed potatoes

Cutting potatoes too small or overcooking makes them water-soaked and they'll lose flavour. A perfectly cooked spud for mashing should break under the pressure of a fork but not be too mushy. To serve 4–6 people, peel 6 medium-sized potatoes and place in a saucepan with cold, lightly salted water to cover. Cook with the lid on for 20–30 minutes, until the potatoes are easily pierced with a fork. Drain well, then return the pan to the heat and toss for a minute or two until the potatoes are dry. Mash with a potato masher or put through a potato ricer. Beat the mashed potato with a wooden spoon until very smooth, then add a knob of butter and gradually beat in ½–1 cup hot milk (adding cold milk to potato makes it sticky), until light and fluffy. Season to taste.

To keep mashed potato warm without spoiling, cook and mash the potatoes as described above, then press down well into the saucepan with the potato masher or a spoon, packing tightly and smoothing the top. Add a knob of butter and spoon about ⅓ cup hot milk over, cover with a tight-fitting lid and leave in a warm place. Before serving, beat well, adding more hot milk if necessary. The potatoes will keep warm for up to 20 minutes.

Chickpea, pea and bean salad with aïoli

SERVES 4

This delicious, healthy salad has plenty of flavour and is filled with vegetables and diced cooked meat – a good way of using up leftovers. Leave out the diced meat for a tasty vegetarian option.

250 g green beans, trimmed and cut into
  thick matchsticks
2 carrots, cut into thick matchsticks
2 zucchini, cut into thick matchsticks
250 g snowpeas or sugar snap peas
1 cup shelled broad beans
1 × 400 g can chickpeas,
  drained and rinsed
1 × 400 g can cannellini beans,
  drained and rinsed
1 cup diced cooked ham, fish, chicken,
  turkey or pork
2 hard-boiled eggs, finely chopped

2 tablespoons chopped flat-leaf parsley
crusty bread, to serve (optional)

AÏOLI
4 cloves garlic, crushed with
  1 teaspoon salt
1 egg yolk
1 cup olive oil
1 tablespoon lemon juice
sea salt and freshly ground black pepper

1 To make the aïoli, place the crushed garlic in a bowl and whisk in the egg yolk. Gradually add ¼ cup of the olive oil, drop by drop, then the lemon juice, whisking all the time until the mixture thickens nicely. Whisk in the rest of the olive oil, a little at a time, until you have a wonderfully thick and golden mayonnaise. Season to taste.

2 Steam the vegetables or cook them in batches in boiling water until just tender, then drain. Combine them with the drained chickpeas and cannellini beans, and transfer to a serving dish.

3 Fold through the aïoli and the diced meat, then sprinkle with the chopped egg and parsley. Serve warm or cold with plenty of crusty bread, if you like.

* If you want a short cut, make the aïoli in a food processor by firstly mixing the garlic with the egg yolk then, with the motor running, gradually adding the oil and then the lemon juice. Or for the simplest option, add some crushed garlic to 1 cup ready-made egg mayonnaise.

Fried rice three ways

ALL THROUGHOUT ASIA, steaming sizzling woks constantly turn out variations of this staple. In Indonesia, Thailand, Malaysia and China they might add chicken or pork, a little curry paste, and any fresh vegetables they have to hand. Here, we have the best of all worlds because we can experiment with other countries' versions of this fabulous dish. Fried rice is easy for the cook because it caters for the less adventurous, yet keeps the foodies satisfied. It's a great way to use up leftover rice and any vegetables overstaying their welcome in the bottom drawer of the fridge. This is one of the easiest, quickest meals to cook at home. Experiment with the following three versions, then try your own combinations.

Fried rice

SERVES 4

This is your basic fried-rice recipe, and a great way to use up meat and vegetables left over from a previous meal.

> 2 tablespoons rice bran, peanut or vegetable oil
> 3 eggs, lightly beaten
> 3 green onions, chopped
> 1 carrot, diced
> 125–250 g sliced or diced cooked meat or seafood,
>   such as leftover pork, chicken, prawns or bacon
>   (or you can use firm tofu)
> 5 cups cold cooked long-grain rice
> 1 cup frozen peas
> 1 tablespoon soy sauce, or to taste

1   Heat the oil in a wok or large frying pan, add the beaten egg and fry over low heat, turning the omelette once, until golden. Transfer to a plate and leave to cool. Add the green onion, carrot and meat and stir-fry for 30 seconds.

2   Add the cooked rice and peas and stir-fry for another 2 minutes. Cut the cooled omelette into strips and return to the pan, cooking for 1 minute. Add the soy sauce and stir until combined. Pile on to a serving dish and serve piping hot.

✻ What other vegetables can you use? Take a look in the fridge. See any capsicum you can cut into strips, or Chinese cabbage you could shred? Sliced mushrooms, chopped leek, bean sprouts and sliced celery are all good as well.

Egg fried rice

SERVES 4

The perfect meal for the hungry, time-poor, budget-conscious person (and, not surprisingly, a hit with students!). This simple version of an Asian classic is so easy you can even whip it up before work to take for your lunch.

> 2 tablespoons rice bran, peanut or vegetable oil
> 4 eggs, lightly beaten
> 5 cups cold cooked long-grain rice
> 1 tablespoon soy sauce, or to taste

1   Heat the oil in a wok or large frying pan, add the beaten egg and stir-fry until lightly scrambled.

2   Tip in the cooked rice and mix with the beaten egg until combined and heated through, then add the soy sauce and toss through again. Serve straight away or pack up for lunch.

Leftover rice

There are so many things that can be done with cooked rice that it pays to have a supply on hand. Whenever you're cooking rice, cook double, with the knowledge that you've got another great meal in the making. It is best stored in a shallow plastic container and will keep for several days, as long as it's covered and put in the fridge as soon as it's cooled. Then just reheat it in the microwave or by placing it in a bowl over a pan of simmering water until piping hot.

Cooked rice freezes very well too, so if you're caught out with too much there's no need to waste it. Just pack it into an airtight container or snap-lock bag and freeze for up to 2 months.

Healthy and wise

Sure, you could resort to your local Chinese takeaway for your fried-rice fix, but then you really don't know what's in it. Although the ubiquitous flavour enhancer monosodium glutamate (MSG), widely used in Asian food, has not been shown to be a significant health hazard, anecdotal evidence suggests that many people experience palpitations, numbness in the back of the neck and hot flushes about 20 minutes after consuming food containing it. In Australia, processed foods must be labelled as containing MSG, but at restaurants and when ordering takeaways, it's best to request that no MSG be used, if you're sensitive to it.

Thai-style fried rice

SERVES 4

This is a spicy version of fried rice. With a hint of curry paste, garlic, and crunchy green beans for texture, this will have even fast-food snobs coming back for seconds. Although there are quite a few ingredients, you should have most of them in your pantry anyway, so all you'll need is some leftover rice and a little fresh chicken or pork or a handful of prawns.

¼ cup rice bran, peanut or vegetable oil

200 g green beans, cut into short lengths

2 large onions, chopped

2 cloves garlic, chopped

1 tablespoon red curry paste

250 g chicken thigh fillet or lean pork, finely sliced
  or 250 g small green prawns, shelled

3 eggs, lightly beaten

5 cups cold cooked long-grain rice

2 tablespoons fish sauce

handful coriander sprigs, to garnish

1 Heat the oil in a large wok or frying pan over high heat, then add the beans, onion and garlic, stir-frying until the garlic starts to colour. Add the curry paste and stir well.

2 Toss in the meat or prawns and stir-fry for 2–3 minutes until almost cooked. Make a well in the centre of the mixture, then pour in the beaten egg and stir until lightly scrambled. Add the rice and stir-fry, tossing so that everything is mixed together and heated through.

3 Add the fish sauce and stir-fry for a further minute until well combined. Pile onto a serving platter and garnish with coriander.

✱ Fish sauce and curry paste are Asian basics that you should always have on hand. You can pick up a large bottle of fish sauce for next to nothing, and it lasts for ages in the fridge. This recipe is a great way to use up any leftover Thai curry paste – it will stay fragrant and fresh in the fridge for several weeks.

A foolproof way of steaming rice

Measure your rice and use one and a half to twice the amount of water to cook it. So for 1 cup of rice you'll need 1½–2 cups water (long-grain rice needs a little more water than medium- or short-grain rice). Rinse the rice in a sieve under cold running water, until the water run-off is clear. Bring the water to a boil in a heavy-based saucepan with a lid (the heavier, the better for preventing the rice catching on the base of the pan). Slowly sprinkle in the rice, stir once, then cover. Reduce the heat to very low and cook for about 12 minutes without lifting the lid, until the last few minutes of cooking to check it's not drying out or burning. Add a little more water if necessary, or if there is too much, cook a little longer with the lid off to evaporate the extra. Rice should be tender but still firm to the bite. Remove from the heat but keep the lid on until you're ready to use it. Use a fork to fluff up the rice before serving.

Get the rice right for frying

The trick to perfect fried rice is to pre-cook the rice a good few hours beforehand at the very least, or the day before if you can. This ensures that the grains don't stick together while you're frying them. Spread cooked long-grain rice out on a tray to cool, cover with a clean tea towel and keep in the fridge until you need it. If you aren't ready to use the rice within a day, transfer it to an airtight container and store in the fridge or freezer (see page 92).

If you're hankering for some fried rice but don't have any leftover cooked rice, you'll need to make sure the rice you cook fresh has as little starch in it as possible to prevent it sticking. Place your cooked rice into a large bowl and cover with cold water. Put your hands in the bowl and mix the rice until the water turns cloudy and milky. Tip the rice into a large sieve to drain, then rinse well under cold running water. Tip the rice onto a large tray, spreading it out, and pat off excess moisture with some paper towel or a clean tea towel.

Quick minestrone

SERVES 4

If you've got some leftover cooked vegetables, feel free to use them in this soup, remembering they'll just need gentle reheating. One of the tricks to using leftovers is to add a fresh element, either in the form of herbs, lemon juice or vegetables, to give the dish a lift, so make sure you add some fresh ones as well.

3 cups chicken or vegetable stock
1 × 400 g can chopped tomatoes
300 g mixed vegetables, such as beans, peas, asparagus, broad beans, cauliflower, broccoli or broccolini, cut into short lengths
140 g cooked small pasta shapes or spaghetti, broken into 5 cm lengths
1 × 400 g can cannellini or butter beans, drained and rinsed
2–3 tablespoons pesto (see page 141)
⅓ cup freshly grated parmesan

1 Bring the stock and tomatoes to a boil in a saucepan over high heat, then add the vegetables. Reduce the heat to medium and simmer for about 8 minutes, until soft and just tender.

2 Stir in the pasta, drained beans and half the pesto. Reheat gently and ladle into bowls, topping each serving with a dollop of the remaining pesto. Serve piping hot with grated parmesan.

Grated vegetable hash brown

SERVES 4

This is great to whip up when you have an assortment of veggies rolling around in the bottom of the fridge at the end of the week (although not strictly 'leftovers', these odds and ends are often overlooked and can end up being discarded). The frying itself takes some time, but when you're tucking into this golden, sweet and nutty hash brown, you'll think it's worth the effort. Use whatever vegetables you have on hand – finely shredded cabbage or grated sweet potato can be used in place of the zucchini.

2 zucchini, coarsely grated
2 potatoes, peeled and coarsely grated
1 parsnip, scrubbed and coarsely grated
1 tablespoon olive oil
1 large red, white or brown onion, finely chopped
2 cloves garlic, finely chopped
sea salt and freshly ground black pepper
2 tablespoons chopped mixed herbs such as sage, flat-leaf parsley and thyme

1 Squeeze out any excess moisture from the grated veggies.

2 In a heavy-based frying pan, heat the oil over medium heat. Add the onion and cook for about 5 minutes, stirring, until softened. Add the grated veggies, garlic and herbs and continue to cook for 5 minutes, stirring occasionally.

3 Season with salt and pepper to taste and reduce the heat to low. Cook for 10 minutes, loosening the base now and then with a spatula to prevent it sticking.

4 Meanwhile, preheat your grill. Remove the pan from the heat and place under the hot grill just long enough to brown the top. Slide the hash brown onto a serving plate, and serve immediately, cut into wedges.

Lemon and mushroom chicken pie

SERVES 4

No chicken leftovers? This pie is so good it's worth picking up a barbecued chicken especially on the way home. Remember to keep a packet of puff pastry on hand in the freezer to make light work of meals like this.

15 g butter *or* 1 tablespoon oil
1 white or brown onion, finely chopped
125 g button mushrooms, sliced
3 green onions, sliced
400 g cooked chicken, skin removed, flesh sliced
finely grated zest of 1 lemon
¼ cup light sour cream
sea salt and freshly ground black pepper
2 tablespoons chopped flat-leaf parsley or a mixture of
   flat-leaf parsley and chives
1 sheet puff pastry
milk, for brushing
creamy mashed potato and steamed green vegetables
   or a green salad, to serve

1 Preheat oven to 200°C. Melt the butter or heat the oil in a frying pan over medium–high heat, and cook the onion for 3 minutes until softened. Add the mushrooms and green onions and cook another 2 minutes, until softened and lightly coloured. Stir through the chicken and lemon zest.

2 Place the chicken and mushroom mixture in a 6-cup-capacity baking or gratin dish. Dollop the sour cream over and season generously with salt and pepper.

3 Top with the pastry sheet and pinch around the edges to seal, cutting away any excess pastry, and make a small slit in the centre to let the steam escape. Brush with a little milk and then bake for 25 minutes, until the pastry has risen and is crisp and golden. Serve with creamy mashed potato and steamed green vegetables or follow with a green salad.

Rice-stuffed capsicum

SERVES 4–6

We discovered, when throwing scraps to our chickens recently, that they love capsicum seeds – they're like caviar to them. So if you have chooks, spoil them with the seeds, while you enjoy the baked capsicum halves, filled with yummy leftover meat, herbs, rice and cheese.

4 green or red capsicums, cut in half crossways,
   white insides and seeds removed
30 g butter *or* 2 tablespoons oil
1 red onion, finely chopped
250 g cooked chicken, pork, beef or lamb, diced
1 tomato, diced
1 cup cooked rice
¼ cup chopped flat-leaf parsley or coriander
sea salt and freshly ground black pepper
½–⅔ cup grated cheese

1 Preheat oven to 200°C and lightly butter a large baking dish. Drop the capsicum halves into a large pan of boiling salted water and cook for 3 minutes until softened. Drain and set aside.

2 Melt the butter or heat the oil in a small frying pan and cook the onion over medium heat for 5 minutes, until soft and light golden. Transfer to a bowl and add the diced meat, tomato, cooked rice, parsley or coriander and plenty of salt and pepper.

3 Arrange the capsicum halves in the baking dish and fill with the rice and meat mixture. Sprinkle with grated cheese and bake for 15–20 minutes, until nicely browned and heated through.

Sweetish colonial curry

SERVES 6–8

This is a very well-loved, typically Australian dish. Use any leftover meat – pork, lamb, chicken, etc. – and serve this curry on its own or with rice and a green salad.

30 g butter
¼ cup slivered almonds
1 cup sliced celery
1 large white or brown onion, finely chopped
½ stick cinnamon
2 teaspoons curry powder
2 tablespoons plain flour
1½ cups chicken stock
2 cups cooked chicken, pork or lamb strips, or a combination
2 tablespoons sultanas
½ cup cream
steamed rice and a green salad, to serve

1 Melt half the butter in a heavy-based saucepan over medium heat. Add the almonds and cook, stirring, until they are lightly coloured, then remove with a slotted spoon and set aside. Add the remaining butter and fry the celery, onion and cinnamon stick for about 5 minutes, until the onion is soft.

2 Sprinkle the curry powder over and cook for 2 minutes, stirring. Add the flour and cook for 1 minute. Gradually add the stock and bring to a boil, stirring constantly. Reduce the heat, add the meat, sultanas and cream, and heat through. Sprinkle with the almonds and serve with steamed rice, then follow with a green salad.

All about almonds

If you've bought your almonds with the brown skins still on them, it means they have not been blanched. Whole, skinned almonds are called **blanched almonds**. You can easily blanch them yourself – just drop them into a pan of rapidly boiling water then immediately remove from heat. Stir, cover and leave for 3–4 minutes. Test by scooping one out: carefully see if the skin will slip off easily; if not, leave for another minute. Drain the almonds and rinse them in cold water, then drain them again thoroughly and transfer to a plate. Press the skins with your fingers to slip them off, then dry the skinned almonds thoroughly.

Slivered almonds are blanched almonds split in half then cut lengthways into thin pieces, and **flaked almonds** are blanched almonds shaved into fine flakes.

Fettuccine with chicken and tomato cream

SERVES 4

This creamy, fresh tomato sauce is delicious folded through pasta with fine strips of chicken or ham. It's a great way to use up leftover roast chicken.

500 g ripe tomatoes, roughly chopped *or* 400 g can chopped tomatoes
2 sprigs oregano
500 g cooked chicken or ham, cut into strips
sea salt and freshly ground black pepper
1 cup cream *or* ½ cup evaporated milk
30 g butter
10 basil leaves
300 g fettuccine or linguine

1   In a wide, shallow pan, cook the tomato with the oregano for 10 minutes, then push through a coarse sieve (to make a smoother sauce, you could purée the tomato in a food processor before pushing it through a sieve, as we've done here).

2   Return the tomato to the pan, add the chicken or ham strips and a little salt, and warm through over low heat.

3   Pour the cream or evaporated milk into another pan and heat gently. Stir in the butter and cook gently for a few minutes to reduce. Stir the cream into the tomato mixture and add the basil leaves. Season to taste with salt and pepper.

4   Meanwhile, cook the pasta in a large pan of boiling salted water until al dente, then drain and add to the sauce, tossing through gently. Serve immediately.

Healthy and wise

Don't miss out on these beautiful flavours just because you're scared you mightn't be able to do up the zipper on your favourite dress! You can replace the cream with light cream, full-cream milk or light evaporated milk, and just use half the amount of butter — you'll still get the same silky texture and flavour.

Lamb, eggplant and potato pie

SERVES 4–6

This is a variation on shepherd's pie, using leftover cooked lamb – and if you have 3–4 cups leftover mashed potato, you can even skip cooking the potatoes. If it's leftover cooked beef you have, not lamb, use that instead – it works just as well.

½ cup olive oil
1 eggplant, cut into thick rounds
1 large red, white or brown onion, chopped
2 cloves garlic, finely chopped
1 teaspoon ground cinnamon
1–2 tablespoons each chopped mint and flat-leaf parsley
3 large tomatoes, roughly chopped
sea salt and freshly ground black pepper
750 g cooked lean lamb, finely chopped
4 potatoes, peeled and cut into chunks
30 g butter
½ cup hot milk

1 Preheat oven to 180°C and oil or butter a 2-litre-capacity baking dish.

2 Heat ⅓ cup of the oil in a large, heavy-based frying pan over medium–high heat and, working in batches, fry the eggplant for 3–4 minutes on each side until just coloured, then set aside to drain on paper towel.

3 Wipe out the pan with paper towel and heat the remaining oil. Cook the onion, stirring, until softened. Add the garlic and cook, stirring, for 1 minute. Add the cinnamon, mint and parsley and cook, stirring, for 1 minute. Add the tomato and salt and pepper to taste and cook, stirring, for 10 minutes, or until the sauce has thickened. Fold through the cooked lamb and remove the pan from the heat.

4 Meanwhile, cook the potatoes in boiling salted water until tender. Drain well, then dry over low heat before mashing with the butter and hot milk until light and fluffy. Season with a little salt and pepper.

5 Line the baking dish with half the eggplant, then top with the lamb mixture and the remaining eggplant. Spread the mashed potato over the eggplant and make indents on the surface with a spoon. Bake for 30–40 minutes, until the pie is bubbling and lightly coloured on top.

Prefer the original?

If you hanker for traditional shepherd's pie, leave out the eggplant, and cook the onion as in step 3. Instead of tomatoes and herbs, add some gravy left over from the roast plus a little water or stock to moisten if necessary. Fold through the cooked lamb and spoon this mixture into the dish between two layers of sliced tomato. Top with the creamy mashed potato and bake as described.

CHAPTER 5

Weekend meals to cook and keep

The weekend is a chance for you to gather your thoughts about food. What do you really want to eat come Monday? And if you don't have time to pop out to the supermarket on Thursday night, will you be buying a disappointingly soggy sandwich on Friday? And then find you're too shattered to cook come the evening, so you fork out nearly a quarter of your day's wages for some take-away food for the family? Don't feel bad – it happens to us all now and then. But instead we want to encourage you to use the spare time you have on weekends to prepare a couple of simple and delicious homemade meals to have on hand during the week.

There's only one thing standing in the way of this Nigella-like vision of domestic bliss, and that is that some people see cooking as a chore (hard to believe, we know!) and feel they deserve a break from all this drudgery on the weekends. Now, we're not asking you to change who you are, we're just trying to encourage you to see things a little differently. Cooking on the weekend is an entirely different beast from the frenzied weeknight routine. It can be incredibly fulfilling – even relaxing – especially when you give yourself enough time to do things at a gentle pace, and remind yourself that you are putting credit in the 'food bank' to use up during the week. And if you have kids who are old enough to help in the kitchen, get them involved too so it feels like a real family effort.

So, what to cook? All it takes is a bit of planning: sit down with the family, ask everyone to nominate their two favourite dinners and make a list based on this (of course, suggestions like duck à l'orange can be taken with a pinch of salt – what you want is a list of simple dishes that will keep well in the fridge or freezer). Use this chapter as a starting point, scour other recipe books and magazines for inspiration, then come up with a master list of meals you know the whole family will enjoy. Then you can make one or two of these dishes every weekend to pop in the freezer, and you'll have meals ready to go for at least two nights each week (and isn't it this same convenience that attracts us to takeaway food in the first place?). You'll save yourself time, money and a good deal of angst and frustration during the week.

All the recipes in this chapter are designed to be cooked on the weekend, then stored in the fridge or freezer for future meals. Because some of them involve slow-cooking, you'll be able to get one going and then start on another, virtually halving your time in the kitchen.

The best meals to save for later

- **Pasta bakes** – refrigerate or freeze uncooked, ready to pop into the oven for a meal during the week.
- **Meatloaf** – cook it ahead, then slice and freeze in batches in snap-lock bags to have in sandwiches or with salad for lunch.
- **Soups** – both creamy puréed soups and chunky soups freeze well, and will warm and nourish you at the end of a busy day.
- **Stews, casseroles and curries** – these dishes often taste even better a few days after being cooked. They're easy to throw together on the weekend, and their high liquid content means they thaw and reheat beautifully.

STOCK – AN IMPORTANT BREW

Stock, the liquid produced from slowly simmering meats and vegetables in water, provides the foundation for soups, sauces, stews and braises the world over. It gives dishes body and flavour, and can mean the difference between an ordinary meal and something really exceptional. Beef stock is brown or a light golden colour; poultry and veal stock is white-ish, and fish stock is clear.

A thrifty kitchen would be incomplete without some stock ready and waiting in the fridge or freezer, and it's so simple to make yourself. There are many ways to cook and flavour stock, and some methods have been passed down through generations. We've found that there are two golden rules to follow in order to make flavourful, versatile stock: simmer it slowly over low heat; and don't over-season it, as this limits the ways you can use it.

Making a batch of stock is the perfect pastime for those wintry weekend afternoons. To make your own, you'll need a large stockpot or heavy-based saucepan with a close-fitting lid (you don't want the precious liquid to evaporate too quickly and fill the kitchen with steam). Stocks keep for a week in the refrigerator, or they can be frozen for 2–3 months.

Chicken stock

MAKES ABOUT 6 CUPS

500 g chicken bones (thighs, necks, wings or backs)
  or 1 chicken carcass
1 small onion
1 small carrot
1 teaspoon salt
1 bouquet garni (a bay leaf, a few sprigs of parsley and thyme
  and a few black peppercorns, tied with kitchen string)

1 Place all the ingredients in a large stockpot or heavy-based saucepan with enough water to cover. Bring to a boil over low heat, skimming the surface now and then to remove any fat or scum.

2 Partially cover and simmer for 1–2 hours, then strain through a fine sieve, discarding the solids, and leave to cool. Refrigerate or freeze until needed. Remove any surface fat before using.

Beef stock

MAKES ABOUT 8 CUPS

1.5 kg beef bones (shank, marrow, rib bones or a combination – ask your butcher to saw these into pieces for you),
  any large chunks of meat removed and chopped
500 g chopped gravy beef or chuck steak
1 carrot, thickly sliced
1 onion, thickly sliced
2 teaspoons salt
1 bouquet garni (a bay leaf, a few sprigs of parsley and thyme
  and a few black peppercorns, tied with kitchen string)

1 Preheat oven to 200°C. Place the bones, chopped meat and vegetables in a large roasting tin and brown in the oven for about 20 minutes.

2 Transfer everything to a large stockpot or heavy-based saucepan and add the salt, bouquet garni and enough water to cover all the ingredients. Bring to a boil over low heat, skimming the surface now and then to remove any fat or scum.

3 Partially cover and simmer for 3–4 hours, then strain through a fine sieve, discarding the solids, and leave to cool. Refrigerate or freeze until needed. Remove any surface fat before using.

Fish stock

MAKES ABOUT 5 CUPS

1–2 kg fish trimmings – bones, heads (without gills) and
  skin or shells of any white-fleshed fish or shellfish
1 cup white wine or the juice of a lemon plus enough
  water to make 1 cup
1 bouquet garni (a bay leaf, a few sprigs of parsley and thyme
  and a few black peppercorns, tied with kitchen string)

1 Place all the ingredients in a large stockpot or heavy-based saucepan with enough water to cover. Bring to a boil over low heat, skimming the surface now and then to remove any scum.

2 Partially cover and simmer for 20 minutes, then strain through a fine sieve, discarding the solids, and leave to cool. Refrigerate or freeze until needed. Remove any surface fat before using.

* Save any crab, lobster or prawn heads by packing them in snap-lock bags and freezing them. They will keep for up to 1 month and be on hand to toss in the stockpot when you want to make some fish stock.

Vegetable stock

MAKES ABOUT 4 CUPS

1 onion, chopped
1 leek, white part only, chopped
3 stalks celery, chopped
1 parsnip or turnip, chopped
1 x 3 cm piece ginger, finely chopped
1 cup chopped mushrooms
12 black peppercorns
1 teaspoon sea salt
1 bouquet garni (a bay leaf, a few sprigs of parsley and thyme
  and a few black peppercorns, tied with kitchen string)

1 Place all the ingredients in a large stockpot or heavy-based saucepan with enough water to cover. Bring to a boil over low heat, partially cover and simmer for 1 hour.

2 Pour the stock through a colander set over a bowl, pressing the vegetables against the sides of the colander to extract the juices, then discard the solids. Strain the liquid through a fine sieve, then leave to cool. Refrigerate or freeze until needed.

French vegetable soup with pistou

SERVES 6–8

The great thing about this soup is that you can make it when you have odds and ends to use up, and you've got something healthy to eat during the week. *Pistou*, the French version of pesto, is a paste of tomato, basil, garlic and cheese, which gives the soup a punch of flavour at the end.

30 g butter
400 g dried borlotti beans or 500 g freshly shelled borlotti beans
1 large white or brown onion, finely chopped
500 g green beans, trimmed and cut into 3 cm lengths
3 zucchini, thinly sliced
6 potatoes, cut into 2 cm dice
1–2 teaspoons salt
½ cup small pasta shapes, such as macaroni or egg vermicelli broken into 2 cm lengths

PISTOU

1 cup basil leaves
4 cloves garlic
1 large ripe tomato, peeled (see page 65) and chopped
1 tablespoon tomato paste
½ cup freshly grated parmesan or Swiss cheese
¼ cup olive oil

* You can use frozen vegetables, such as broad beans and peas, in place of the zucchini and green beans. It's not your traditional French vegetable soup, but if it works for you, go for it!

1 If using dried beans, soak them overnight in a large bowl of water. Drain and tip into a large saucepan with enough fresh water to cover. Bring to a boil, cover and simmer over low heat for 15 minutes, then drain.

2 Melt the butter in a large deep pan, then add the vegetables and beans and cook over medium heat for about 5 minutes until the vegetables have softened. Pour in 3½ litres water and bring to a boil over high heat. Add the salt, reduce heat to low, then cover and simmer for 1 hour. Add the pasta and cook for a further 15 minutes.

3 Meanwhile, make the *pistou* by blending the basil leaves with the garlic in a food processor or blender. Add the chopped tomato, tomato paste and cheese and purée to a paste, adding the oil gradually as you mix.

4 Serve the soup piping hot and add a dollop of *pistou* and a grinding of pepper to each bowl.

Waste watcher

If you want to freeze this soup you can, but keep in mind it won't have a long storage life in the freezer – vegetables lose a lot of their texture if frozen too long, so try to use it within 2 months.

Turkish bean salad

SERVES 6

This bean dish is packed with flavour and is something you could serve with grilled meat for an evening meal, leaving plenty of leftovers for lunch the next day. Pack it up along with some sliced feta and pita bread and you have a delicious lunch that will be the envy of everyone.

500 g dried red kidney beans
juice of 1 lemon
½ cup olive oil
2 red, white or brown onions, chopped
3 cloves garlic, chopped
1 potato, diced
2 mild green chillies, seeds removed, finely diced
2 carrots, diced
6 tomatoes, diced
sea salt
1 cup chopped flat-leaf parsley
lemon wedges, to garnish (optional)

1   Soak the dried beans overnight in a large bowl of water. Drain and tip into a large saucepan with enough fresh water to cover by 2 cm. Bring to a boil and cook for 40 minutes, or until tender but not mushy. Drain the beans, reserving 1½ cups cooking water. Add the lemon juice to the cooking water and set aside.

2   Heat the oil in a large, heavy-based saucepan over low heat. Fry the onion for about 5 minutes until soft. Add the garlic, potato, chilli and carrot and cook for another 5 minutes. Add the tomato, beans and reserved cooking water, and season with salt to taste. Continue to cook for another 20 minutes.

3   Stir in the parsley, reserving a little to garnish. Serve the salad at room temperature, sprinkled with the reserved parsley and accompanied by lemon wedges to squeeze over if you like.

What else can you do with dried kidney beans?

Try making this **tasty pasta dish** to serve 4. Soak 1 cup dried red kidney beans in water to cover overnight. Drain and cook in a saucepan with fresh water to cover for 30 minutes, until partially cooked. Meanwhile, cook 375 g short pasta in a large pan of boiling salted water until al dente, then drain. Bring a small pan of salted water to the boil and add 125 g baby green beans, halved lengthways, and blanch for 3 minutes or until tender, then set aside. Heat ⅓ cup olive oil in a large, heavy-based frying pan and fry 2 finely chopped cloves garlic until aromatic. Add the grated zest and juice of 1 lemon, the drained kidney beans, ¼ cup chopped flat-leaf parsley, the pasta and green beans and mix everything together, then heat through. Season to taste and serve.

Tomato and zucchini bake

SERVES 8

This is one of those old-fashioned country recipes that always surprises, because it's so yummy and smells just wonderful when baking. It can be eaten warm or cool any time of the day and can be dressed up or down, whatever the occasion (at Christmas, it makes a festive brunch to go with sliced ham or even smoked salmon). You can be creative by topping it with extra zucchini slices or alternating zucchini and tomato slices. For vegetarians, simply leave out the bacon – it's still just as good.

4 zucchini, coarsely grated
3 rashers bacon, finely chopped
1 large onion, finely chopped
1 cup self-raising flour
5 eggs, lightly beaten
1 cup grated cheese
¼ cup rice bran oil
sea salt and freshly ground black pepper
1–2 tomatoes, sliced

1   Preheat oven to 200°C and lightly grease a deep loaf tin. Line the base and two long sides with baking paper.

2   Combine all the ingredients except the tomato in a bowl and season to taste. Spoon into the prepared tin and top with the sliced tomato. Bake on a tray (in case of spillage) for 1 hour, until a skewer inserted in the centre comes out clean. Leave in the tin to cool slightly, then cut into thick slices.

Waste watcher

SAVING THE BACON   *How often have you opened a packet of bacon rashers for a recipe that calls for just half of them? The answer is to freeze the leftover rashers. Because of its high fat and salt content, bacon won't last as long in the freezer as other meats – 1 month at the most. But that is still plenty of time for you to find great ways to use it up.*

As soon as you open the packet, take out the extra for freezing and lay a small strip of baking paper between each rasher. Wrap into a parcel with waxed or baking paper and place in a snap-lock bag, being sure to label with the date and number of rashers. Cooked bacon can be frozen for a little longer – up to 6 weeks. You can also fry whole rashers or diced bacon, pack into a snap-lock bag and freeze, ready to add to your cooking at a later date.

Slice and pack the cooled bake into snap-lock bags and freeze —
it will keep for up to 1 month. Pack a slice in your lunchbox and by
lunch time it will be perfectly thawed. If you have a microwave at
work, pop it in on a medium setting for 20 seconds, and enjoy it warm.

Pastitsio

SERVES 6–8

This notch-above-a-pasta-bake Greek dish takes a bit of time to cook, but is so easy to put together and throw in the oven. We really recommend making two batches, as it's no more effort, and you can freeze the second batch for an easy meal another time. You can even freeze individual serves to take for lunches or to enjoy next time you have the house to yourself.

45 g butter
1 tablespoon olive oil
2 white or brown onions, finely chopped
750 g lean beef mince
1 × 400 g can chopped tomatoes
2 tablespoons tomato paste
sea salt and freshly ground black pepper
1 cup grated cheddar
400 g large tubular pasta, such as
   rigatoni or penne

CHEESE SAUCE

60 g butter
¼ cup flour
3 cups milk
1 egg, lightly beaten
½ cup grated cheddar

1   Melt the butter with the oil in a large frying pan with a lid over medium heat. Add the onion and cook, stirring, for 3–4 minutes until softened. Add the mince and cook for 5 minutes until browned. Add the chopped tomato and the tomato paste and season well. Turn the heat to low, partially cover with the lid and cook for 35–40 minutes, until the beef and tomatoes have formed a rich, thick sauce. Stir through the grated cheese.

2   Meanwhile, cook the pasta in a large pan of boiling salted water until al dente, then drain.

3   Preheat oven to 190°C and butter a large oval baking dish, ideally one about 5 cm deep.

4   Make the cheese sauce by melting the butter in a saucepan over low–medium heat. Add the flour and cook, stirring, for 2 minutes. Remove from the heat and gradually stir in the milk, then place over medium heat and cook for 5 minutes, stirring constantly, until the mixture thickens. Remove from the heat again and stir through the egg and cheese.

5   Place half of the cooked pasta into the prepared dish and spoon over half of the meat sauce. Add the remaining pasta and meat sauce. Spoon over the cheese sauce, then transfer the dish to the oven and bake for 30–40 minutes until golden and bubbling. Serve immediately, spooning out straight from the dish.

Freeze half

If you know you won't get through a batch of this within a couple of nights, divide the ingredients between two smaller dishes – that way you'll have one to cook now and one to freeze for later. Allow the spare batch to cool a little before freezing, then when you need it, thaw for an hour or so, and remember to bake it for just a bit longer than usual, until everything is bubbling and golden.

Instead of boiling the pumpkin, to retain more colour and flavour you can cook it in the microwave for about 12 minutes on the highest setting.

Maltese tuna, pumpkin and rice pie

SERVES 6

There are many versions of this traditional Maltese pie – this one comes from our friend Angela Muscat's mum. Angela is a gifted cook who prepares beautiful dishes, day in and day out, in her role as a home economist for books and magazines. Her family is from Malta, where this recipe has been popular for generations. Make this on the weekend and store it in an airtight container in the fridge so it doesn't dry out. It is even tastier a day or so after cooking.

1 butternut pumpkin, peeled and cut into chunks
⅓ cup long-grain rice
sea salt and freshly ground black pepper
1 × 425 g can tuna in oil, drained, reserving 2 tablespoons of the oil
2 golden shallots, finely chopped
55 g pitted kalamata olives, halved
2 tomatoes, diced
juice and finely grated zest of 1 lemon
3 sheets frozen puff pastry, thawed
20 g butter, melted

1 Preheat oven to 220°C and butter a 24 cm-diameter deep pie dish.

2 Cook the pumpkin in a pan of salted boiling water for 10–15 minutes until tender, adding the rice to the pan for the last 5 minutes. Drain, return the pumpkin and rice to the pan and mash together roughly. Season well and stir through the reserved tuna oil, the chopped shallots, olives, tomato, lemon zest and juice, then gently fold through the tuna.

3 Join two sheets of pastry by wetting one edge of each sheet and pressing them together to seal. Line the prepared dish with the pastry, letting the excess hang over the side. Fill with the tuna mixture and place the remaining pastry sheet on top. Press the edges together and trim away any excess pastry. Make a few slits in the top of the pastry with a knife.

4 Brush the pastry lid with the melted butter and bake for 1 hour. Leave to cool before packing in an airtight container. Cut into wedges to serve.

Save some for sandwiches

Meatballs are a lifesaver as last-minute sandwich fillers for school or work lunches. Just thaw, slice and add to your sandwich with salad greens or cheese. They're also great heated up and popped into a baguette with some of the leftover sauce – your own version of a meatball sub. (Warning: these are best eaten in private as the juices will drip messily down your chin!)

Italian meatballs with fresh tomato sauce

SERVES 4

This is a classic, please-everyone type of dish. Those with big appetites can have theirs with spaghetti, but a lighter, spaghetti-free version is still a satisfying meal (especially with a green salad). Make double the amount and save half for later. The meatballs can be frozen with the tomato sauce, but will keep for longer if frozen separately – just pop them into snap-lock bags once cooled and freeze straight away. They should be completely thawed in the fridge and heated right through before serving again. The sauce can be frozen in airtight containers.

1 cup milk
3 thick slices fresh bread,
   such as ciabatta
¼ cup chopped flat-leaf parsley
1 tablespoon chopped rosemary
¼ cup freshly grated parmesan
1 egg, lightly beaten
500 g lean beef or pork mince
   or 250 g of each
sea salt and freshly ground black pepper
30 g butter
2 tablespoons olive oil

125 g cooked spaghetti or pappardelle
   per person, to serve (optional)

FRESH TOMATO SAUCE
¼ cup olive oil
4 ripe tomatoes, roughly chopped
1 clove garlic, crushed with a little salt
handful basil or oregano leaves, roughly
   torn, with some smaller leaves
   reserved for garnishing
sea salt and freshly ground black pepper

1   Pour the milk into a bowl, add the bread and leave to soak for 5 minutes, then squeeze out any excess milk. Break the bread into small chunks and combine with the parsley, rosemary, parmesan and egg in a large bowl until well blended.

2   Add the mince to the bread mixture, season with salt and pepper and mix thoroughly with your hands to make the mixture light and fluffy. Chill in the fridge for at least an hour.

3   Roll the chilled meat mixture into small balls, rinsing your hands with cold water every now and then to prevent them getting too sticky. In a large, heavy-based frying pan, melt the butter with the oil. Add the meatballs, about 10 at a time, and fry, shaking the pan continually to ensure they cook evenly (or turn them regularly with tongs). They will take about 8 minutes to cook and should be golden brown on the outside. Transfer to a serving dish and keep them warm while you cook the rest.

4   To make the sauce, heat the oil over low–medium heat in a small saucepan, then add the tomato, cooking for about 5 minutes. Add the garlic and cook for a further 5 minutes. Stir in the torn basil or oregano leaves and season to taste with salt and pepper.

5   Serve the cooked meatballs smothered in the tomato sauce on a large platter, mixing through some cooked pasta, if using. Garnish with basil or oregano leaves.

Old-fashioned fish and potato pie

SERVES 4–6

This comforting pie is perfect for winter weekends spent indoors. The combination of smoked and white fish in a creamy sauce results in a really homely flavour, and the crispy and buttery potato topping is the *pièce de résistance*!

4 potatoes, quartered

1¾ cups hot milk

60 g butter

sea salt and freshly ground black pepper

250 g smoked hoki or cod

1 leek, trimmed and well washed, sliced

1 tablespoon plain flour

300 g white fish fillets (such as blue-eye or flathead), cubed

½ cup chopped flat-leaf parsley

4 hard-boiled eggs, peeled and quartered

1   Preheat oven to 220°C. Cook the potato in a large pan of boiling salted water until tender, then drain and mash well with ½ cup of the hot milk and 10 g of the butter. Season to taste.

2   Meanwhile, place the remaining milk in a shallow pan over low heat. Add the smoked fish, skin-side up, and poach for 3–4 minutes until cooked through and the skin lifts away easily. Remove the fish from the liquid and discard the skin. Strain the milk into a jug to cool.

3   Melt half of the remaining butter in a saucepan and cook the leek for 5 minutes over medium heat until soft. Stir in the flour and cook for 1 minute. Gradually add the cooled milk, stirring constantly until the sauce thickens.

4   Add the smoked fish, white fish and parsley to the sauce and gently fold together. Spoon the mixture into an 8-cup-capacity shallow ovenproof dish. Top with the egg and spoon over the mashed potato, spreading it evenly then roughing the surface with a fork to help create a crusty topping. Dot with the remaining butter and bake for 30 minutes until golden.

Smoked fish

There are two types of smoked fish: cold smoked and hot smoked. **Cold-smoked fish** is smoked at 32°C or below, and this is the most common way of smoking fish such as salmon and cod. Smoked salmon can be eaten as is, whereas cod and other cold-smoked fish usually need to be cooked before they are eaten. **Hot-smoked fish**, such as trout, ocean trout, mackerel, plus oysters and mussels, to name just a few, are smoked at temperatures above 150°C and can be eaten without further cooking. Smoked fish is a wonderful addition to all kinds of cooked dishes and salads, but its flavour can be quite strong so take care not to overdo it.

Waste watcher

The thrifty cook would use up some leftover cooked fish to make this pie, but it's essential that the leftovers have been handled and stored properly. After you've cooked the fish for the original meal, any leftovers should be cooled (and boned, if necessary) as quickly as possible, then popped into an airtight container and refrigerated straight away. The washing-up can wait — your number-one priority is seeing to the leftovers. Leftover cooked fish is perfect for saucy pies like this — just make sure you eat it up in one sitting: it mustn't be saved or reheated again.

Oven-braised lamb shanks

SERVES 4

* To trim or 'french' a lamb shank (or cutlet or rack) means to clean away excess gristle, fat and meat from the end of the shank and exposing the bone. You can ask your butcher to do this for you if you like.

Buying a house? Baby on the way? Starting your own business? Then you're probably seriously cash-strapped, and you'll need this dish in your repertoire. It's one of those recipes that seems luxurious and expensive, but really is very cheap to make. It's a great one to prepare in advance on the weekend (note the 2½ hour cooking time) if you're having guests over for a meal during the week, and you can easily double the quantities (or it freezes for up to 1 month). The lamb virtually falls off the bone, the fat melts and can be skimmed off the top, and you're left with the most succulent meat – perfect served with creamy mashed potato and a glass of red.

4–8 (depending on size) frenched lamb shanks, fat trimmed
¼ cup plain flour, seasoned with salt and pepper
2 tablespoons olive oil
1 brown onion, chopped
1 tablespoon balsamic vinegar
1 cup dry white wine
1 × 400 g can chopped tomatoes
4 anchovy fillets in oil, drained and finely chopped
3 carrots, quartered lengthways
1 stick celery, sliced
4 sprigs thyme
finely grated zest of 1 lemon

1 Preheat oven to 180°C. Dust the shanks with the flour, shaking off any excess.

2 Heat the oil over high heat in a large, flameproof baking dish. Brown the shanks in batches for a few minutes, turning to brown evenly, then remove and set aside. Reduce the heat to medium and cook the onion, stirring, for 5 minutes until softened.

3 Increase the heat, add the balsamic vinegar and boil briskly for a few seconds. Add the wine and bring back to a boil. Add the tomato and anchovies, then return the shanks to the dish with the carrot and celery. Scatter with the thyme, then cover with the lid or tightly with foil and transfer to the oven to cook for 1½–2 hours until the meat is falling-off-the-bone tender.

4 Remove the dish from the oven, uncover then return to the oven for a further 15 minutes. Serve immediately topped with the lemon zest.

Make a gremolata to sprinkle over the lamb shanks — simply combine chopped flat-leaf parsley and a little chopped garlic with the lemon zest.

Chicken with garlic purée

SERVES 4–6

Through intensive breeding practices, chicken has become one of the cheapest everyday foods. Our grandmothers used to call upon all the skill they could muster to transform a tough old boiler into a family meal. Now we find we need to use our skill and ingenuity to make the commonplace chicken seem interesting.

The famous French dish of chicken roasted with 40 cloves of garlic might set off alarm bells for some people, but garlic cooked this way is actually mild, sweet and delicious. This recipe is a variation of the classic – here the garlic is cooked to a soft purée and served as a sauce.

1 × 1.7 kg free-range chicken, trimmed of fat, washed and patted dry with paper towel
sea salt and freshly ground black pepper
few sprigs of thyme
⅓ cup olive oil
4 heads garlic, each wrapped in a square of foil with a drizzle of olive oil added
2 tablespoons cream (optional)
crusty bread and steamed green beans, to serve
2 tablespoons chopped flat-leaf parsley

1 Preheat oven to 200°C. Season the chicken all over, including the cavity, with salt and pepper. Pop a few thyme sprigs in the cavity and tie the chicken legs together with kitchen string if you like, to help give the chicken a good plump shape.

2 Heat half the olive oil in a deep flameproof casserole with a lid over medium heat and add the chicken, turning until golden-brown all over. Remove the casserole from the heat and set aside.

3 Place the parcels of garlic around the chicken and scatter with more thyme sprigs. Cover the casserole, transfer to the oven and cook for 1¼ hours.

4 Lift out the casserole and carefully remove the garlic parcels. Once cool enough to handle, unwrap and squeeze each clove between your thumb and index finger to extract the garlic (you can use a pair of thin rubber gloves to protect your fingers if you like). Transfer to a bowl and mash to a purée, using any oil or juices left in the parcels to moisten. Stir in the cream, if using.

5 Carve the chicken, scatter with parsley, and serve with crusty bread and some steamed green beans, with the garlic sauce to the side.

✱ To tie (or truss) a chicken aids even cooking if the bird is being stuffed, but even if not, it helps make a great-looking roast chicken. Cut a long piece of kitchen string and loop the centre under the tail end and around the ends of the drumsticks. Tie a knot to secure the legs. Run the string along both sides of the chicken towards the wings. Pull tightly around the wings and tie the ends together to pull the bird into a neat shape.

The week's meals, planned ahead

This recipe is worth making even just for two people, and if your budget can stretch to it, you could even cook two chickens so you have a whole one on hand for lunches during the week. The white meat is perfect for sandwiches (see page 39) and the dark meat can be thinly sliced and stirred through hot chicken stock with green onions, vegetables such as broccoli or snowpeas, and some grated ginger to make a delicious soup.

Garlicky mash

An equally splendid way of serving this chicken is with a creamy purée of potato and garlic. Cook the chicken and garlic as above. Meanwhile, boil 750 g peeled potatoes until tender, then drain and mash well, adding ½ cup hot milk. Add 1–2 tablespoons of the garlic purée to the mash and serve alongside the carved chicken. The remaining purée can be served separately for true garlic lovers.

Ragú alla bolognese

SERVES 8

The people of Bologna in Italy claim that a true ragú cannot be made anywhere else. This may be so, but here are a few tips to help you make the best ragú you've ever tasted even without moving to Bologna. Use a large, heavy-based pan and have the heat as low as possible while the sauce is simmering. Finely cubed lean beef, preferably chuck steak, or pork should be used rather than minced meat, as this gives a wonderfully succulent texture (it'll cost you a bit more but the results are worth it). Cream is also added at the end to give the sauce silkiness.

While ragú is traditionally served with spaghetti, other pasta such as tagliatelle, pappardelle or rigatoni can be used.

1 tablespoon olive oil

2 brown onions, finely chopped

2 sticks celery, diced

1 large carrot, diced

150 g pancetta, chopped

1 clove garlic, crushed

1 kg chuck steak or lean pork shoulder, trimmed and finely cubed

1 cup red wine

2 × 400 g cans chopped tomatoes

¼ cup cream

pinch of grated nutmeg

sea salt and freshly ground black pepper

125 g cooked spaghetti per person, to serve

freshly grated parmesan, to serve

1 Heat the oil over medium heat in a large heavy-based saucepan with a lid. Fry the onion for 3–5 minutes until soft. Add the celery, carrot, pancetta and garlic and continue to cook for another 5 minutes until the vegetables are soft.

2 Increase the heat to high and add the meat, cooking for 5 minutes or until browned. Add the wine and bring to a boil. Stir in the chopped tomato, reduce the heat to low and simmer, covered, for 1–2 hours (depending on how much time you have – the longer you cook this, the richer the flavour will be).

3 Remove the lid and simmer for another 20 minutes, until the sauce thickens and the meat is tender. Stir in the cream and nutmeg, then season to taste with salt and pepper.

4 Add the drained cooked spaghetti and toss over a low heat for 1 minute. Serve in individual bowls topped with the grated cheese.

***

* For an even heartier version, add 500 g trimmed and chopped chicken livers to the meat just before adding the wine.

Investment cooking

Ragú is a perfect dish to make in advance as the flavours really develop after cooking. Make it on the weekend, keep some for a weeknight meal and freeze the rest for another time. Remember to thaw any frozen portions in the fridge for a day or so and reheat gently for at least 15 minutes before using. It's also lovely served hot on toast for breakfast – that's at least three meals sorted for the family.

Sunday roast chicken with stuffing

SERVES 4–6 (OR 2, WITH LOTS OF LEFTOVERS)

If you're roasting a chicken and have a couple of extra guests, make it go further with a hearty stuffing (some prefer the stuffing to the chicken!). Best is a loose, light breadcrumb stuffing not bound by egg, as this can make it a little dry and dense – use some lemon juice, verjuice, stock or melted butter instead. The addition of fresh herbs, grated lemon or orange zest, nuts, some dried fruits or a sprinkling of spices like fennel seeds, cumin or paprika all help to give the stuffing a nice lift, and will help to keep the chicken meat moist and flavoursome.

1 cup fresh breadcrumbs (see page 128)

¾ cup chopped mixed herbs, such as thyme, flat-leaf parsley and chives

juice and finely grated zest of 1 lemon

sea salt and freshly ground black pepper

a little milk, verjuice, chicken or vegetable stock

1 × 1.7 kg free-range chicken, trimmed of excess fat, rinsed and
   patted dry with paper towel

2 tablespoons olive oil

6 potatoes, quartered

steamed vegetables and gravy, to serve

1   Preheat oven to 200°C. Combine the breadcrumbs, herbs and lemon zest and juice in a bowl. Season to taste and mix well, adding a little milk, verjuice or stock to bind if necessary. Push the stuffing into the cavity of the chicken.

2   Tie the chicken legs together with kitchen string to secure the stuffing (see page 123). Rub half the oil over the chicken and season. In a bowl, toss the remaining oil through the potatoes.

3   Place the chicken on a small rack in a roasting tin and scatter the potatoes around. Roast for 1¼ hours, turning the potatoes once, until the chicken is cooked through (test by inserting a skewer into the thickest part of the thigh – the juices should run clear) and the potatoes are tender. Serve with steamed vegetables and gravy.

Absolutely perfect gravy

While the French prefer thin, clear gravy, most of us Aussies love our gravy thick and rich. To make classic Aussie gravy, place a sliced onion under the meat before roasting to add colour and flavour to the juices. While the roast is resting, carefully pour off all but 2 tablespoons juices from the roasting tin, leaving any sediment undisturbed. Sprinkle 1 tablespoon plain flour into the tin and stir into the juices. Place over low heat, stirring until the mixture has browned. Slowly add 1–1½ cups cool stock (or cooled water leftover from steaming the vegetables), stirring and scraping the bottom of the tin until smooth. Bring to a boil, reduce the heat and simmer gently for 5 minutes. Season to taste, then serve piping hot.

✳ When roasting meat, use a rack to raise it off the base of the roasting tin and help the heat circulate around it. This ensures the meat browns evenly and will help give it an all-over crisp skin or crust. Without a rack, the base of the roast can tend to stew. Racks with wider-spaced rungs tend to give the best results.

French tarragon chicken

For a scrumptious, crispy finish, make a lemon herb butter to slip under the chicken skin. Blend 60 g butter with 1 tablespoon finely grated lemon zest. Gradually add 1 tablespoon lemon juice, mixing between each addition, 1–2 tablespoons freshly chopped tarragon, and salt and pepper. Starting at the neck end of the chicken and working towards the tail (including the tops of the drumsticks), carefully separate the skin from the meat with your fingers and push the butter in between, then pat the skin to smooth the butter into an even layer.

Melt-in-your-mouth beef casserole

SERVES 6

If you've got the time to marinate the beef in the red wine, garlic and herbs for a few hours, this dish will taste even better. Alternatively, you could cook the beef the day before you plan to eat it to allow time for the sauce to develop in flavour.

Transform the leftovers

Instead of eating the leftovers for this one as they are, why not transform them into a completely new dish? Place them in a deep pie dish and top with a sheet of thawed puff pastry. Brush the pastry with beaten egg or milk and bake at 220°C for about 35 minutes until the pastry has risen and turned golden.

Or make a fabulous saucy spaghetti – remove the beef from the cooled sauce and cut into smaller pieces. Do the same with the potatoes and carrots. Reheat the sauce, then cook some pasta and fold this through the heated beef and sauce.

Beef cheek is an economical cut of meat to use because there is very little waste. Unfortunately it can be hard to come by, in part because restaurants have caught on to this succulent meat and are snapping it all up. But it is great for making casserole such as this, and some butchers are starting to stock it due to increased demand (so keep asking!). Otherwise you can use chuck, gravy or shin, or even blade steak, which has a good flavour and becomes beautifully tender with long, slow cooking.

This can be made the day before and chilled, so the fat will set on the top and can be lifted away before reheating. It's not at all difficult to make, but be prepared – it takes time. You can just let it sit and bubble away on the stove, getting richer and softer and more melt-in-the-mouth as time passes. Think of it as the perfect weekend pastime that will reap rewards later in the week.

2 tablespoons olive oil

1 kg stewing beef, such as cheek, chuck, gravy or blade steak, cut into 3–4 cm cubes

8 small white or brown onions, peeled *or* 4 large white or brown onions, peeled and halved

2 tablespoons plain flour

2 cups red wine

2 cloves garlic, finely chopped

few sprigs thyme

1 bay leaf

sea salt and freshly ground black pepper

8 new potatoes

3 carrots, quartered *or* 1 bunch baby carrots, trimmed and scraped

1 punnet cherry tomatoes

¼ cup chopped flat-leaf parsley

crusty bread, to serve

1   Heat the oil in a heavy-based flameproof casserole over medium–high heat and brown the beef in batches for a few minutes, turning frequently. Remove and set aside.

2   Add the onions to the pan, reduce the heat to medium and fry until golden, then remove and set aside. Return the meat to the pan and sprinkle with the flour, then cook for 3 minutes, stirring, until browned.

3   Stir in the wine, garlic and herbs and season to taste with salt and pepper. Bring to a boil, then reduce the heat to low, cover and simmer for 50 minutes.

4   Meanwhile, drop the potatoes into a pan of boiling salted water and cook for 8 minutes until almost tender.

5   Add the potatoes, along with the carrots, tomatoes and browned onions, to the casserole, cover and cook for a further 20 minutes or until the beef and vegetables are tender. Scatter with the parsley and serve with crusty bread.

Waste watcher

USE UP YOUR STALE BREAD   *The thrifty cook doesn't throw out bread unless it's gone mouldy. If your bread is only a few days old, don't even think about getting rid of it – use it to make your own breadcrumbs. Lay the slices out on a baking tray and leave to dry, or place them in a low (150°C) oven for 15–20 minutes, then whiz them up in the food processor or chop finely with a large, heavy knife. Pack into snap-lock bags and freeze for up to 2 months.*

Best-ever meatloaf

Don't turn the page yet. We admit that the idea of a meatloaf is not exactly appealing to everyone, but having tried and tested, improved and re-tested the recipe, we're here to tell you that this is no ordinary meatloaf. It's soft and flavoursome, with a sticky, sweet glaze. Served with a rocket salad or some steamed green vegetables, it's a seriously delicious meal.

500 g lean beef mince

500 g sausage meat

1 cup fresh breadcrumbs (see opposite)

1 brown onion, finely chopped

1½ teaspoons curry powder

2 tablespoons chopped flat-leaf parsley

1 egg, lightly beaten

sea salt and freshly ground black pepper

½ cup milk

½ red onion, cut into wedges

bay leaves, to garnish

GLAZE

1 cup beef or vegetable stock

¼ cup tomato paste

2 tablespoons white vinegar

2 tablespoons honey

2 tablespoons Worcestershire sauce

½ teaspoon mustard powder

sea salt

1   Preheat oven to 200°C.

2   In a large bowl, combine the meat, breadcrumbs, onion, curry powder, parsley and egg and season well with salt and pepper. Add the milk and ¼ cup water and mix thoroughly with your hands. Shape into a 25 cm x 11 cm loaf and place in a large roasting tin. Top with the red onion and bay leaves and bake for 30 minutes.

3   Meanwhile, make the glaze by heating the stock in a saucepan with the tomato paste, vinegar, honey, Worcestershire sauce and mustard. Season with salt, bring to a boil and simmer for 10 minutes.

4   Remove the meatloaf from the oven and drain any fat from the tin. Spoon over half the glaze and return it to the oven, baking for a further 35–40 minutes until cooked through, basting with the remaining glaze once or twice more. Serve hot, warm or at room temperature, cut into thick slices.

Fiona's weekend cook-ups

ON SATURDAYS, Fiona and her two-year-old daughter Annie traipse around their local fruit and vegetable market in the Sydney suburb of Leichhardt. Invariably, out the front are trays of soft (verging on squishy) deep-red oxheart tomatoes or some other produce at bargain-basement prices. Fiona always stocks up on them: 'I'll make a big batch of pasta sauce for tonight, and freeze it in portions for when I haven't got the time or energy to pull a meal together at 4 o'clock in the afternoon.'

'When I find something on special, I build a meal around it,' says Fiona. As well as berries, which she preserves, meat for casseroles and bolognese, and overripe bananas to make banana bread, Fiona also buys bread on special (often at the end of the day just before the shops shut), slices it and freezes it. It can then be toasted from frozen – perfect for the morning rush.

Fiona's freezer is testament to her thrifty cooking skills: it's full of things like portion-sized tubs of bolognese sauce and slices of individually wrapped banana bread. The only barrier to her buying things on special, she says, is knowing the freezer is full. For example, she might buy two legs of lamb on special and freeze one, then use the other to make two meals for the coming week. She removes the meat from the bone in two large pieces, half of which she'll mince to make lamb meatballs (like the ones on page 41), and the rest she'll leave whole and marinate for a day or two in a little olive oil, grated lemon zest and juice, some fennel seeds, chopped garlic and a good grinding of pepper. She'll then have this on hand to throw on the barbecue one night during the week, to serve with a simple salad.

She likes to buy organic where possible for her kids, so she stocks up whenever she sees organic meat reduced. 'They often sell off the organic stuff. I buy it in bulk for the kids and freeze it. Then when I cook for them, I'll use that. Or I'll have a big cook-up and freeze it in portion sizes, then I have some good meals ready to go,' she says. While bolognese keeps very well in the freezer and tastes wonderful reheated, a leg of lamb and chicken pieces also store well. When she cooks these she uses long, slow cooking methods to tenderise the meat.

Fiona tries to keep simple ingredients on hand that she can use to create an easy meal. She buys pancetta vacuum-packed from her butcher and pops it in the freezer, and she'll grate a big block of good-quality parmesan to fill a few snap-lock bags to freeze. When she's run out of time to cook during the week, she can

Fiona makes a big casserole on the weekend to freeze for weeknight meals.

simply put some spaghetti on to boil and pull together a delicious carbonara sauce with these ingredients and a couple of eggs from the fridge. 'So I haven't actually made the meal ahead of time, but all the ingredients are there on hand.'

Look out for specials

Keep an eye on the clearance shelves at markets and greengrocers – where you might find anything from small containers of loose grapes, to some berries that will be perfect for jam, to a bag of carrots that are on their way out. Fiona says, 'If you're making a spag bol that night, it doesn't matter if they're not the world's crispest carrots or the basil is not at its freshest. I often start here before I go around the rest of the store.'

Easy vegetable chilli

SERVES 6–8

Packed with vegetables and full of flavour, this dish is a great one to cook in advance on the weekend as it's so easy to throw together and freezes beautifully. Just thaw and reheat it for dinner during the week. Serve with a bowl of grated cheese, some chopped green onion, sour cream and a few reduced-salt corn chips, and the kids will be over the moon.

½ cup olive oil
2 brown onions, roughly chopped
3 cloves garlic, finely chopped
2 red capsicum, white insides and seeds removed,
   cut into strips
2 zucchini, diced
1–2 teaspoons chilli powder (or more, to taste)
1 tablespoon ground cumin
2 x 400 g cans peeled chopped tomatoes
2 x 400 g cans red kidney beans, drained
sea salt and freshly ground black pepper
1 cup chopped flat-leaf parsley or coriander
2 tablespoons lemon juice

1   Heat the oil in a deep flameproof casserole over medium heat. Add the onion, garlic and capsicum and fry for about 3 minutes, then add the zucchini and fry for about 7 minutes.

2   Stir in the spices and fry, stirring, for 1 minute. Add the tomatoes and kidney beans, season well with salt and pepper, then cover and simmer for 15 minutes until the vegetables are tender.

3   Add the herbs and lemon juice and stir through, then serve.

CHAPTER 6

What to do with all those . . .

We were at the supermarket recently, loading our wares onto the conveyor belt at the checkout, when the woman behind us did a double-take. One by one we had piled up our lemons until we had a veritable mountain of them. The woman looked down at her own small pile of groceries: a flavoured yoghurt, a punnet of strawberries and two plastic-wrapped steaks, then back at the lemons, which were now rolling around everywhere, and gave a cautious smile. 'What *are* you going to do with all those?' she finally asked. Well, for a start, squeeze some juice into a cup of hot water every morning, but also preserve some, use some in a lemon delicious pudding, grate some zest over a pasta dish and whip up a batch of lemon curd to have on toast. After all, they were on special.

For those of us who cannot resist a bargain, gluts of certain ingredients are inevitable. Many supermarkets and greengrocers offer specials on in-season fruits and vegetables, when all sorts of produce, from eggplants and chillies to lemons, asparagus and even onions, can be bought by the bucketload relatively cheaply. Strike up a conversation with your greengrocer to find out what's in season, and stock up accordingly. (Just take care not to overdo it – the last thing you want is to be eating potatoes three ways, every meal, for a week because you couldn't resist buying two bags of dutch creams on special. Maybe one bag would have been enough…)

Some of us are lucky enough to be able to grow our own produce, be it a pot of basil on the windowsill, a few tomato plants in a sunny spot or a lemon tree in the back garden. And we often find ourselves with more than we need, all at once. This is how the great tradition of preserving food was born. Your grandmother probably always had a supply of homemade preserves on the go – back in her day, people would generally eat according to what was in season, and everything would be used up (even if that meant eating the same thing, day in and day out, to get through it all!). We're slowly re-discovering that we should be watching what we waste, and food is the best place to start. No more chucking out the entire contents of the fridge in the bin at the end of the week because we ended up getting takeaway most nights; no more throwing out apples because the kids just didn't get around to eating them: it's time to re-educate ourselves about how to eliminate food waste and make good use of every last morsel.

In this chapter, we've selected a few key ingredients that you might find yourself with too much of one day, and offer some inspiration for how to use them up. Don't shy away from making your own pickles, jams and chutneys – it's much easier than you think, and the result is generally so much better than the often preservative-laden bought alternative. Start washing and keeping your jam jars in preparation for a cook-up – you'll soon be enjoying your own homemade preserves and saving yourself lots of money to boot. This is also a chance to use ingredients in different ways. If you only ever eat apples raw on the go, it's time to try them cooked in a tarte Tatin or spread on toast in a jelly. Try preserving your own lemons to add a zing to any casserole, veggie dish or salad. There's endless ways that in-season fresh ingredients can be used. Here are just a few to get you started.

GROWING AND USING YOUR OWN HERBS

If you'd like to grow your own produce but don't think you have the time (or the space), then start with herbs. Fresh herbs are one of the best ways to enliven food with a minimum of effort, yet they must be one of the most frequent casualties of an unkempt fridge. Too often, a bunch is bought and only a few sprigs are used before it is thrown in the fridge and left to turn into a sodden mass. But it needn't be like this.

By growing your own herbs, you can have them fresh on hand to snip or pick whenever you need them. All you'll need to start are some seedlings, a bag of potting mix and a small pot or two. Choose two of your favourite herbs to start with, and take it from there. Speak to the staff at your local garden centre for watering and feeding tips to get you going. For herbs such as lemongrass, oregano, mint and thyme, you could take cuttings, or runners, from established plants (just ask your friends or neighbours before you cut!).

Don't be afraid to use lots of herbs in your cooking – a whole bunch of chopped flat-leaf parsley or coriander, along with a squeeze of lemon juice and a drizzle of olive oil, turns a bowl of freshly cooked lentils or beans into a magical dish. Or you could use up a bunch over a few days in random acts of garnishing to add a punch of flavour. A handful of freshly chopped flat-leaf

parsley gives a lift to grilled chops and chicken, as does a slice of herb-flavoured butter. A few sprigs of mint added to boiled or steamed new potatoes makes them just that bit more special, and the homely fragrance as they cook is a delight. A smattering of fresh coriander will enhance your stir-fries and curries, and some chopped mixed herbs can liven up the simplest of green salads.

Below is a list of the most commonly used herbs in cooking, but experiment with all types (try chervil and tarragon for their delicate aniseed flavour and pretty leaves, and dill for its feathery leaves and a fresh flavour that's wonderful with fish).

Parsley Fresh parsley should be used lavishly. Two common varieties of parsley are available: flat-leaf (continental) parsley and curly parsley. Flat-leaf parsley has the best flavour and is used in all kinds of dishes, whereas curly parsley is the best for fine chopping and garnishing. Parsley helps to temper the strong flavour of garlic dishes, and chewing the leaves can freshen your breath. The stalks tend to contain more flavour than the leaves.

Mint The round-leafed common or garden mint is one of the easiest herbs to grow. It thrives in sun or shade but needs plenty of water. Mint gives a freshness to everything – it's great with lamb, most fruits, peas, potatoes, lentils, tomatoes, eggplant, carrots and cucumber, and is lovely in an orange salad. It doesn't go particularly well with other herbs, parsley being an exception.

Basil A member of the mint family, basil has a hot, slightly clove-like flavour. Use it liberally in any tomato-based dishes: tomato salads, tomato sauce for pasta and tomato soup (in fact, basil is good in most vegetable soups). Sweet basil is the most commonly used variety; it has largish, shiny vivid green leaves, while bush basil has small leaves (there's also Thai basil, with small leaves and purple stems, which is fantastic in stir-fries). For more information on how to use basil, see page 140.

Freezing herbs

When the growing season is over, annual herbs like parsley, basil, dill and coriander can be preserved for later use in soups and stews by puréeing the leaves with a little olive oil and freezing in ice-cube trays. Stir into cooked dishes as you need them.

Rosemary The pungent flavour of rosemary has a great affinity with lamb, veal and pork. It also goes well with poultry and oily fish such as trout, mackerel, salmon or ocean trout. We love it with roasted vegetables. Combined with garlic, rosemary adds a fragrance to roast potatoes.

Sage An easy to grow, perennial herb with a strong, almost medicinal taste. For the best flavour, use fresh, young sage leaves sparingly. Sage is wonderful with pork, poultry and veal and is great chopped and added to hot oil or butter to make a simple sauce for pasta. It's loved by the English in a sage and onion stuffing for poultry, and by the Italians in dishes like saltimbocca (pan-fried veal steaks with prosciutto).

Thyme Whether fresh or dried, thyme is indispensable to the serious cook. It is one of the elements of a bouquet garni and a must in stocks and many sauces and stews. Try adding a few sprigs to vegetables or chicken pieces when roasting them. There are many varieties, but lemon thyme (with its citrussy flavour) and common thyme are the most used in the kitchen.

Coriander Coriander has a pungent aroma and flavour that people usually either love or hate. It is an essential flavouring in authentic Mexican and Asian cooking and has become popular here as well. Try using the chopped leaves and stems in a noodle salad, a stir-fry or a guacamole. The roots can be crushed and used to make curry pastes.

Waste watcher

To store herbs once picked, wash them well and wrap in paper towel, then place in an airtight container and pop in the fridge.

Apples

THE HUMBLE APPLE is such a versatile fruit, with each variety having its own particular strengths. Granny smiths, for example, are perfect cooked in a pie or puréed to make apple sauce to accompany roast pork. Golden delicious apples are great for tarts, while apples such as gala or pink lady are best eaten raw – crisp, juicy and noisy.

Whichever way you go, though, apples have to be fresh. Once they've shrivelled, or if they fell from the tree sometime last month, you're not going to be satisfied no matter how you eat them. Good, ripe apples are firm, crisp and deeply coloured, whether green, pink or red. You'll find apples continue to ripen after picking, even if kept chilled. Store them in perforated bags or well-ventilated containers in the fridge. Don't wash them until you are ready to eat them.

Buttered apples

SERVES 2–4

This is one of the best ways of cooking apples – perfect served warm with cream, yoghurt or ice cream for dessert.

    2–4 cooking apples (such as granny smiths or golden
       delicious), peeled, cored and sliced
    1 tablespoon brown sugar
    1 tablespoon unsalted butter, chopped into small pieces
    strip of lemon zest
    2 tablespoons chopped walnuts
    pinch of nutmeg and cinnamon
    cream, ice cream or yoghurt, to serve

1   Put the apple slices in a small, heavy-based saucepan, sprinkle with sugar, dot with butter and add the lemon zest. Cover and cook over low heat for 15 minutes or until the apple is tender, turning the slices gently from time to time.

2   Meanwhile, roast the walnuts in a dry frying pan over low heat until fragrant. Toss them in the spices and sprinkle over the cooked apple before serving.

Make your own apple sauce

For many, roast pork without apple sauce is unthinkable – and rightly so! The sweet fruit goes so well with the salty roast meat. To make your own while the meat is roasting, peel and quarter 3 golden delicious or granny smith apples. Place them in a small saucepan with ½ cup water, 1 tablespoon sugar and 1 strip of lemon zest, then cover and cook over low heat until soft. Remove from the heat and mash with a potato masher, or whiz with a handheld blender if you want your sauce really smooth. Return to the heat and cook over fairly high heat, stirring continuously until the sauce will just drop from the spoon, then serve hot. If you have plenty of apples to use up, make a big batch of this sauce and preserve it: carefully ladle the cooked sauce into warm sterilised jars (see page 152), seal and label.

Farmer's apple chutney

MAKES ABOUT 1 LITRE

Making chutney is one of the easiest ways to preserve ingredients, and a great way to dress up everyday meals. This chutney is spicy and can be made with granny smiths or other cooking apples. Like most chutneys, this improves with being stored for a while before use – after six months, the flavour really matures.

> 1.5 kg apples, peeled, cored and quartered
> 500 g white or brown onions,
>   cut into eighths
> ¾ cup seedless raisins
> 2 cloves garlic, halved
> 500 g brown sugar
> 1 cup cider or malt vinegar
> 2 teaspoons salt
> 1 tablespoon ground ginger
> 1 tablespoon mustard seeds
> good pinch of chilli powder

1   In two or three batches, blend the apple, onion, raisins and garlic in a food processor until roughly chopped. Transfer to a large heavy-based saucepan.

2   Add the rest of the ingredients and bring to a boil over medium heat, stirring. Reduce the heat to low and continue to cook, stirring from time to time, for about 40 minutes or until the mixture has thickened.

3   Ladle into warm sterilised jars (see page 152), then leave to cool, cover and seal. Store in a cool place, then keep in the fridge after opening.

Apple and rose-geranium jelly

Tart apples make a really good jelly, and this one is wonderful served with roast pork, duck or ham. If you're a keen gardener, you may already have a scented geranium growing in the back-yard, otherwise most nurseries will stock these plants.

> granny smith apples
> sugar
> rose geranium leaves (optional)

1   Cut out the stem and stalk ends of the apples, then slice cross-ways. Place in a heavy-based non-aluminium saucepan and add enough water to cover. Bring to a boil over low heat and simmer for about 1 hour until the apples are very tender.

2   Line a large sieve with several thicknesses of clean muslin and set over a large bowl. Transfer the apples and juice into the sieve and leave to drain for several hours or overnight.

3   Discard the pulp and pour the juice into a measuring jug. Allowing 1 cup of sugar for every 1½ cups of juice, measure out your sugar. Bring the juice to a boil in a large pan over high heat, then add the sugar and cook, stirring, for 20–25 minutes.

4   By now, the liquid should have thickened to a jelly – test by dropping a small spoonful on to a saucer and leaving it for 30 seconds. Push with your finger and if it crinkles at the edges and separates, the jelly is ready for bottling. If not, continue cooking, testing frequently.

5   Have ready warm sterilised jars (see page 152) each containing two geranium leaves, if using. Immediately pour the jelly into the jars until it reaches just below the rim. Close and seal the jars and store in a cool place. Refrigerate once opened.

* To maximise the juice extraction from the apples, don't discard the pulp the first time around. Instead, pop it back into a non-aluminium pan, cover with water and simmer for a further 20 minutes, then repeat the straining process – you'll get another batch of juice from the same apples. If, however, you want a clear jelly, use the first extraction only.

Apple tarte tatin

SERVES 8

This is an upside-down apple tart, apparently invented in the 19th century at the Hotel Tatin in France. The story goes that one of the two sisters who owned the hotel left some apples cooking too long in butter and sugar. She tried to remedy things by popping pastry on top and finishing it off in the oven, then turning it upside-down to serve. It proved very popular, hence this sticky, sweet dessert with a crisp pastry base was born.

You'll need an ovenproof frying pan or a shallow flameproof baking dish for this, or you could fry the apples in a frying pan then transfer them to an ovenproof dish before baking.

6 large granny smith or golden delicious apples, peeled, cored and thickly sliced
½–⅔ cup sugar (depending on the sweetness of the apples)
finely grated zest of 1 lemon *or* 1 teaspoon ground cinnamon
80 g unsalted butter, melted
whipped cream, to serve

SHORTCRUST PASTRY
1½ cups plain flour
good pinch of salt
100 g unsalted butter, cut into chunks
1 tablespoon sugar
¼ cup iced water

1 Start by making the pastry. Sift the flour and salt into a large bowl and add the butter. Using your fingertips, rub the butter into the flour until the mixture resembles breadcrumbs, then stir in the sugar. Make a well in the centre and add half the iced water, mixing it in quickly with a knife. Press together with your fingertips, then add the remaining water if necessary to make a smooth dough.

2 Turn the dough out onto a lightly floured bench and knead gently until smooth, then wrap in plastic film and chill in the fridge for 30 minutes.

3 Preheat oven to 200°C and butter your frying pan, saucepan or baking dish. Toss the apple slices in a bowl with one-third of the sugar and the lemon zest or cinnamon.

4 Sprinkle half the remaining sugar over the base of the pan or dish and arrange the apple over it. Drizzle over the melted butter and sprinkle with the remaining sugar. Place over a low–medium heat and cook for about 5 minutes. If you're not using an ovenproof pan, transfer the apple to a round buttered baking dish at this point.

5 Roll out the pastry to about a 5 mm thickness and cut into a round a little larger than the top of the pan or dish. Place the pastry over the apple, allowing the edges to fall against the inside edge of the pan or dish. Bake for 45 minutes–1 hour. Check that the tart is done by tilting the dish or pan slightly: this should reveal a thick, brown syrup underneath between the crust and the edge of the dish.

6 When cooked, immediately invert the tart onto a serving dish. The apple should be a rich amber colour; if not, brown the top by placing under a hot grill for a few minutes. Serve warm with a jug of whipped cream on the side.

More ways with apples

Still want more ideas for using apples? Look up these delicious recipes:

- Speedy apple breakfast (see page 4)
- Soft and crunchy muesli (see page 7)
- Apple and cinnamon breakfast muffins (see page 12)
- Apple and pine-nut cake (see page 188)
- Apple tarts (see page 191)
- Apple and fennel stuffing (see page 205)

Basil

BASIL, WITH ITS SLIGHTLY HOT, aniseed flavour, is the perfect herb. If you are growing your own, pick the leaves as you need them to toss through pasta, stir-fries or salads (especially tomato ones), use them to dress up boiled new potatoes or a grilled chop, or whiz them up with garlic, pine nuts, parmesan cheese and olive oil to make pesto. If you've bought a bunch and can't use it all in one hit, wash the leaves, wrap them in damp paper towel and store in a plastic bag or airtight container in the fridge. Just remember to use it up within 2–3 days.

Healthy and wise

If you're trying to cut down on your fat and salt intake, herbs are a fabulous alternative – they add tons of flavour while still being good for you.

Basil and vermouth cocktails

MAKES 2

KATE > Summery, dry and all too easy to drink, this little cocktail came together one hot New Year's Eve when Dan and I had friends around to watch the fireworks.

1 cup ice, plus more for serving
½ cup vermouth
2 tablespoons gin
⅓ cup fresh orange or grapefruit juice
¼ cup basil leaves, plus extra sprigs to garnish
tonic or soda water, to top up glasses
2 sticks cinnamon, to garnish

1   Put the ice, vermouth, gin, orange or grapefruit juice and basil in a cocktail shaker and mix well. Fill two large glasses with ice and strain in the mixture.

2   Top up the glasses with tonic or soda water and garnish with sprigs of basil and a cinnamon stick each.

Basil mayonnaise

MAKES 1½ CUPS

This mayonnaise is made in the food processor, and so it's incredibly quick and simple. It goes beautifully with poached fish or chicken. You can also use it in chicken sandwiches, or as a dip for steamed vegetables (like baby carrots, asparagus or snowpeas). It will keep for a couple of weeks in an airtight container in the fridge, so make double the quantity if you have enough basil, eggs and olive oil on hand.

2 cups firmly packed basil leaves
1 egg
1–2 tablespoons white-wine vinegar or lemon juice
1 cup olive oil
freshly ground black pepper

1   Blanch the basil leaves in boiling salted water for 30 seconds, then drain and squeeze any excess water from the leaves.

2   In a food processor, combine the basil and egg until the basil is finely chopped, then add half the vinegar or lemon juice and mix to combine.

3   With the motor running, add the olive oil in a thin, steady stream and mix until fully combined and thick. Add the remaining vinegar or lemon juice at the very end, then season with pepper and give it one last whiz to combine. Store in the fridge.

Homemade mayonnaise

Mayonnaise is delicious and really simple to make. Just omit the basil used here for a good all-purpose version, to which you can add all sorts of herbs to give different flavours. Try tarragon, dill or marjoram – just stir them through right at the end.

If you want to make this by hand, use 2 egg yolks in place of the egg, and use a whisk to blend all the ingredients together.

Basil and parsley pesto

MAKES 1½–2 CUPS

Traditional pesto is made with basil (see right), but here we've included a lighter version, substituting some of the basil with flat-leaf parsley (to make the classic version, use 6 cups basil and leave out the parsley). The pine nuts can be substituted with walnuts or pistachios, or even almonds. Whichever you prefer, it's worthwhile having a jar of pesto in the fridge, as it transforms everyday food into something special.

2 cloves garlic, chopped
4 cups basil leaves
2 cups flat-leaf parsley leaves
2 tablespoons pine nuts
½ cup freshly grated parmesan
sea salt and freshly ground black pepper
1 cup olive oil

1   Place the garlic, herbs, pine nuts, parmesan, salt and pepper in a food processor and mix until finely chopped, stopping to scrape down the sides of the bowl with a spatula once or twice.

2   With the motor still running, add the oil in a slow, steady stream and mix to a smooth paste.

3   Pack into jars and cover with a thin film of olive oil before sealing, then refrigerate.

Try these delicious variations:

- **Mint pesto** – Substitute the basil with 2 cups mint leaves and add an extra cup of flat-leaf parsley leaves.
- **Rocket pesto** – Substitute the basil with the same amount of rocket leaves.
- **Walnut pesto** – Substitute the pine nuts with the same amount of walnuts.

Pesto – the king of sauces

Pesto alla Genovese, the original version of pesto, is a traditional Italian sauce hailing from Genoa in the northern region of Italy. Perfect simply stirred through cooked pasta or gnocchi, we have also taken to smearing it on bruschetta or mini toasts for a quick appetiser, drizzling it over roasted or grilled meats and spooning it into soups.

Waste watcher

You can make a big batch of pesto and freeze some for later use – just pack into airtight containers, omitting the layer of oil. Add the layer of oil to the thawed pesto before use.

Thai chicken with chilli and basil

SERVES 4

KATE > This was one of my fiancé Dan's favourite meals when he was travelling around Thailand, so he brought back the recipe to cook it at home too. The Thais serve it steaming hot, accompanied by rice and a small bowl of chopped chillies in fish sauce. Thai basil is best for this dish, but it's also great with common sweet basil.

2 tablespoons rice bran oil
3 cloves garlic, finely chopped
2 long red chillies, finely chopped, seeds removed if you like
600 g lean chicken mince
2 teaspoons sugar
¼ cup fish sauce
1–2 bunches Thai basil, leaves picked
steamed jasmine or brown rice, to serve

1   Heat the oil in a wok over high heat. Fry the garlic and chilli until the garlic starts to turn golden, then add the chicken mince and break it up with a wooden spoon. Cook, stirring, until most of the juice has evaporated (2–3 minutes).

2   Add the sugar and fish sauce and cook for 1 minute, then add the basil and stir-fry for another minute or so. Serve with steamed rice.

Healthy and wise

To be sure the chicken mince you use is low in fat, mince it yourself — just buy some breast or thigh fillets, remove the fat, roughly chop the flesh and whiz in the food processor until minced. And if you need to cut down your salt intake, add 1–2 tablespoons of fish sauce instead of ¼ cup.

You can use Thai basil in any stir-fry — it adds a great aniseed flavour and goes very well with chilli.

Eggplant

EGGPLANT, OR AUBERGINE, gets a special mention in this book because it is so accessible and cheap – pretty exceptional, when you consider how versatile it is. It's one of the most esteemed vegetables in the world. From Italy, Greece, France, Turkey and all over the Middle East to China, Japan, South-east Asia and India, the eggplant is loved and used in a wealth of dishes. In fact, many of the world's cuisines would seem very poor without the eggplant's presence.

Eggplant is a great substitute for meat, and can add necessary bulk to a meal when your fridge is looking a bit bare. You can simply grill, fry or barbecue it, but there are also many other beautiful eggplant dishes that, with only a little more preparation, will reward with a succulent, silky treat.

You'll be familiar with the large deep-purple eggplant, which is the most common and versatile variety. Though you can buy it all year round, the peak season is late summer. This is the largest eggplant variety, weighing 400–700 g each, and is perfect for cutting into slices and chunks. Other varieties are also worth seeking out. You may be able to find the white or striped varieties, and there are also small eggplants known as ladies' fingers or Lebanese eggplants. Many Asian food stores sell tiny pea eggplants, which are great for stir-fries. These smaller varieties have tender flesh and seeds and don't need peeling (unless you're roasting and puréeing them for a dip). They also absorb less oil than the larger eggplants.

Look for firm eggplants with smooth, shiny skin (reject any with dimpled skin). The fruit should feel firm and spring back slightly when you touch it. Try to find an eggplant with a stem that looks thick and moist. A dull skin is a sign that the eggplant is too mature or was picked too early. It's best to use it when it's very fresh, but it will keep for two or three days in the crisper of the refrigerator.

PEELING

Large eggplants usually have tough skins, so peeling is a good idea. You can peel the whole eggplant, or peel it in stripes so you keep some of the skin for show.

SALTING

If your eggplant is young and fresh and not going to seed, salting is not necessary. But if it's showing signs of maturity (a thin

or withered stem usually indicates this), salting is a good idea as it helps to draw out the bitter juices. It can also help improve the texture. Because the flesh of large eggplants is especially sponge-like, it tends to soak up more oil than other varieties. The salt draws out the moisture and reduces the amount of oil the eggplant will absorb during cooking.

To salt an eggplant, peel it and then halve, slice, cube or quarter it, depending on the recipe. Sprinkle the pieces generously with salt and place them in a colander to drain for up to an hour (you'll see a lot of liquid beading on the surface). Rinse the eggplant in plenty of water to remove the salt, then take a few pieces at a time and squeeze firmly to extract as much moisture as you can. Pat dry with paper towel.

HOW TO COOK EGGPLANT

You can fry, grill, roast or steam your eggplant, but whichever method you choose, make sure you cook it thoroughly. Eggplant must be completely cooked through so that it's meltingly soft, smooth and creamy.

- **Frying or grilling**: probably the most common way to cook eggplant. You can salt the eggplant first (see opposite) to decrease the amount of oil it will absorb. Start with your oil very hot and put the slices in the pan in one layer to prevent the eggplant steaming and to help it cook evenly (if grilling, brush the eggplant slices with oil). Turn, adjusting the heat if necessary to avoid burning, and cook until the slices are a rich brown colour on both sides. Drain on paper towel. Fried eggplant is great as part of an antipasto or mezze selection, in sandwiches, layered in baked vegetable dishes or in dishes like moussaka or Lamb, eggplant and potato pie on page 102.
- **Stir-frying**: use large eggplant cut into cubes, halved Lebanese or whole pea eggplants. When the oil is very hot, toss the eggplant into the pan with a little salt and stir-fry until browned and soft. Great in all types of stir-fries and Thai curries.
- **Char-roasting**: this gives eggplant a deep, smoky flavour. Pierce the unpeeled eggplant with a skewer and cook it whole, directly over a gas flame or under the grill, turning regularly, for about 15 minutes, until the skin is blackened all over and the flesh is soft. This can get messy, so if you're doing this over an indoor gas flame, line the burner tray with foil first. Leave to cool slightly, cut in half and scoop out the flesh. Drain the flesh in a colander, let it cool completely then squeeze out all the moisture. This is great mashed or puréed for making baba ghanoush and other dips.
- **Oven-roasting**: pierce the unpeeled eggplant in several places and roast on a baking tray at 220°C for about 40 minutes until the eggplant is soft and starting to collapse. Leave to cool slightly, cut in half and scoop out the flesh. Mash or purée, season and serve instead of mashed potato, or add to a white sauce and serve with grilled, barbecued or roast lamb.
- **Steaming**: cut the eggplant into long, thick strips and arrange on a heatproof plate or in the top of a steamer. Cook, covered, over simmering water for 6–8 minutes or until the flesh is just tender when pierced with the tip of a sharp knife. Serve with some soy sauce seasoned with a few drops of sesame oil, a dash of malt vinegar and sugar to taste.

Eggplant caviar

SERVES 6

This dip or spread appears in several guises throughout the Middle East. It's great served with toasted pita bread when entertaining.

2 eggplants, halved
½ cup chopped flat-leaf parsley
2 cloves garlic, crushed
1 teaspoon salt
½ teaspoon freshly ground black pepper
½ cup natural yoghurt
2 tablespoons tahini paste
1 tablespoon lemon juice
olive oil and 1 black olive, to garnish
toasted pita bread, to serve

1 Preheat oven to 180°C. Roast eggplant for 1 hour or until soft.

2 Remove the skin and purée the eggplant flesh in a blender or food processor. Add the remaining ingredients except for the oil, olive and bread, and mix well, then leave to stand at room temperature for a few hours.

3 Transfer the 'caviar' to a shallow bowl. Make a small depression in the centre and pour in a little olive oil, then garnish with a black olive and serve with toasted pita bread.

Healthy and wise

Here's a chance to do away with butter on your sandwiches or toast: eggplant caviar is as good as mayo or hummus at replacing what may be your favourite (but highly saturated) fat. If you want to avoid dairy products, omit the yoghurt by all means — this scrumptious dip will still be wonderfully creamy.

Eggplant Sichuan-style

SERVES 4

Typically, the food from Sichuan province in China is hot, hot, hot! For this famous eggplant dish, they use a variety of spices, lots of chilli, plenty of vegetables and minced pork, in the process stretching just a small amount of meat to make a substantial meal. You can double the quantities here for a larger crowd, but make sure you cook the eggplant in batches so it fries rather than steams.

8 small Lebanese eggplants *or* 2 medium-sized
   regular eggplants
oil, for frying
1 teaspoon rice wine or dry sherry
1 tablespoon soy sauce
1 teaspoon malt or wine vinegar
1 teaspoon sugar
1 teaspoon finely chopped garlic
½–1 red chilli, finely sliced (or more to taste, if you like)
½ leek, trimmed and well washed, finely sliced
1 teaspoon finely chopped ginger
125 g lean pork or chicken mince
½ cup coriander leaves
steamed rice, to serve

1   If using small eggplants, cut lengthways into 4 or 6 slices. If using medium-sized eggplants, quarter crossways and lengthways so you end up with 8 pieces of each, then cut each eighth into wedges (or simply cut them into chunks if you like).

2   Heat 2 tablespoons of oil in a wok and fry the eggplant in batches until lightly browned and just tender, adding more oil as necessary. Remove and set aside to drain on paper towel. Mix the rice wine or sherry, soy sauce, vinegar and sugar together, then set aside.

3   Heat another 2 tablespoons of oil in the wok and stir-fry the garlic, chilli, leek and ginger until the leek has softened. Add the pork or chicken mince and stir-fry over high heat for about 5 minutes, breaking up any lumps of meat.

4   Sprinkle over the rice wine mixture, then add the eggplant. Stir-fry until everything is nicely glazed with the sauce. Stir through the coriander and serve immediately with steamed rice.

Eggplant parmigiana

SERVES 8

An Italian classic, oozing with tomato and cheese, this layered eggplant dish is more than satisfying as a meal on its own.

4 eggplants, thickly sliced lengthways
½ cup plain flour, seasoned with freshly ground black pepper
½ cup olive oil
3 cloves garlic, crushed
3 × 400 g cans diced tomatoes
¼ cup shredded basil, plus extra basil leaves to serve
½ cup freshly grated mozzarella
½ cup freshly grated parmesan

1   Preheat oven to 190°C and butter a deep ovenproof dish.

2   If using mature eggplant, sprinkle generously with salt and place them in a colander for 30 minutes. Rinse under cold water, squeeze to extract any excess moisture, then drain on paper towel.

3   Place the seasoned flour in a shallow dish. Dust the eggplant slices in flour, shaking off any excess.

4   Heat ⅓ cup of the oil over high heat in a large frying pan and fry the eggplant in batches, turning once, until golden, then remove from the pan and set aside to drain on paper towel. You may need to add more oil as you go if the pan dries out.

5   In the same pan, heat 1 tablespoon of the oil and fry the garlic for 1 minute without letting it brown. Add the tomato and simmer for 10 minutes, then stir in the basil.

6   Spoon one-third of the tomato sauce into the prepared dish. Top with half of the eggplant slices. Repeat with the remaining tomato sauce and eggplant, finishing with a layer of sauce.

7   Mix the cheeses together, then sprinkle over the tomato sauce and bake for 15 minutes until the cheese is bubbling. Remove from the oven and leave to stand for 15 minutes. Top with extra basil leaves and serve.

More ways with eggplants

Still want more ideas for using eggplants? Look up these
delicious recipes:

- Falafel pockets with eggplant (see page 42)
- Lamb, eggplant and potato pie (see page 102)
- Eggplant and feta salad with chilli and mint (see page 201)

IF YOU HAVE A SUNNY GARDEN or courtyard, you should plant a lemon tree, whether straight in the ground or in a large pot. You could easily use a lemon in the kitchen every day, whether to squeeze over fish, grilled meats or salads, to add to soups or sauces, or even just to give a glass of water a nice zing. There are also some great ways to preserve lemons to make interesting condiments and spreads that you will enjoy using regularly.

Spiced lemon pickle

MAKES 2 LITRES

This pickle goes well with curries, cold meats and grilled poultry and meats. Stored in a cool, dark place, it will keep indefinitely.

    1 tablespoon allspice berries
    2 teaspoons cardamom seeds
    1 teaspoon coriander seeds
    1 kg lemons, sliced
    2 large or 4 small green chillies, seeds removed,
       finely chopped
    60 g young ginger, peeled and grated
    500 g white onions, halved and thinly sliced
    2½ cups white-wine vinegar
    3 cups sugar

1 Wrap the spices in a piece of clean muslin and tie with kitchen string to secure. Place all the ingredients except the sugar in a ceramic or stainless-steel bowl and leave overnight.

2 Next day, tip the lemon mixture into a non-aluminium saucepan and gently simmer over low heat until the lemon slices are tender, about 1½ hours. Remove the spice bag, add the sugar and stir until dissolved. Boil over high heat for 20 minutes or until thick and syrupy, then spoon into warm sterilised jars (see page 152) and seal. Label and leave for at least a month before using.

Lemon barley water

MAKES 4 CUPS

This very refreshing drink, popular in Victorian times, is enjoying a revival today. Dilute with chilled water before drinking.

    ¼ cup pearl barley
    juice and thinly peeled zest of 2 lemons
    sugar, to taste

1 Place barley, lemon zest and 4 cups water in a saucepan and bring to a boil. Turn the heat to low and simmer, covered, for 2 hours.

2 Strain into a large jug and add lemon juice and sugar to taste. Leave to cool, then chill in the fridge.

Preserved lemons

MAKES 2 LITRES

A fundamental ingredient in Moroccan cooking, preserved lemons have a mild, salty flavour, a little like capers but tangier. Fresh lemons cannot be substituted for preserved; the taste and texture are quite different. Besides, preserved lemons are super-easy to make.

10 lemons (the smaller the better)
1½ cups coarse salt
5 red chillies (optional)
2 tablespoons black peppercorns or coriander seeds
handful of bay leaves
½ cup lemon juice, plus more if needed
olive oil, to cover

1 Cut the lemons into quarters, almost to the base but not right through, and spread the segments out. Gently press a handful or so of salt into each of the lemons to fill, then 'close' the lemons. Alternatively, cut the lemons into quarters and rub each piece all over with salt.

2 Pack the lemons into warm sterilised jars (see page 152), pressing down firmly as you go to get the juices flowing. Add the chillies, if using, the peppercorns and the bay leaves. Spoon any remaining salt into the jars, and top up with lemon juice, ensuring the lemons are covered.

3 Make sure the rims of the jars are free from salt or juice, and seal. Leave to stand at room temperature, away from direct light, for 7 days, turning the jar each day to redistribute the salt and lemon juice.

4 After 7 days, open the jars and add enough olive oil to cover the lemons. Reseal and store in a dark cupboard. The lemons will ripen within a month, and can be stored for up to 6 months.

5 To use, fork out a wedge, rinse the rind under the tap if it is too salty, and cut into dice or slivers.

* Opinions differ on whether to use the flesh as well as the rind of preserved lemons. Rather than waste anything, we say use the flesh as well, but sparingly – it's intensely salty.

Try this delicious variation:

Add cloves or pieces of cinnamon stick for a different flavour. Alternatively, keep the flavours simple and use just salt and lemon juice.

Other uses for preserved lemons

Preserved lemons are not just for using in Moroccan dishes. You'll find they make a great addition to many fish, meat and poultry dishes, marinades, casseroles, couscous and rice dishes, salads and stuffings. When using preserved lemons in casseroles and tagines, add them towards the end of the cooking time so they keep a nice bright, lemony flavour. Here are some more ways you can use them.

- Try adding some diced preserved lemon to a **cold lamb, beef or chicken sandwich**.
- Finely dice some preserved lemon and mix with soft butter to **smear over roast chicken, or when grilling fish or chops**.
- Finely dice some preserved lemon and heat together with **steamed vegetables such as beans or carrots** and a little butter or olive oil, until glazed.
- Add preserved lemon to **roast potatoes** and other vegetables to give them a lift.

Lemon curd

MAKES ABOUT 2 CUPS

This delicious lemon curd is wonderful for spreading on bread or toast, spooning over ice cream, folding through whipped cream to use as a filling for sponge cakes or pavlova or filling pastry cases.

125 g butter
1 cup sugar
juice and finely grated zest of 3 lemons
3 eggs

1   Place the butter, sugar and lemon zest and juice in a medium-sized bowl over a pan of gently simmering water over low–medium heat. Stir continuously until the sugar has dissolved and the butter has melted.

2   Beat the eggs then slowly add them to the hot lemon mixture, stirring continuously over a low heat until the mixture thickens (do not allow it to boil or it will curdle).

3   When it is thick enough to coat the back of a spoon, the lemon curd is ready. Pour into warm sterilised jars (see page 152) and seal. Label and store in the fridge for up to 2 weeks.

To make this in the microwave

Melt the butter in a microwave-proof bowl on the highest setting for about 1½ minutes. In another bowl, beat together the sugar, lemon zest and juice, and the eggs. Stir into the melted butter, mixing well. Cook on high for about 3 minutes, or until the mixture coats the back of a spoon, stopping the microwave and stirring the mixture every 30 seconds or so to keep it smooth. Store as above.

Chilled lemon sago

SERVES 4–6

This is an easy-peasy dessert: soft and fresh and just perfect served with cream or custard on a hot summer's evening. The sago has an incredibly soft texture – little caviar-like balls that hold bursts of lemon flavour. We're only using three lemons here, but you can easily make double the amount and keep the second batch for an easy dessert during the week.

1 cup sago
juice and finely grated zest of 2 lemons, plus the juice
    from 1 extra lemon
2 tablespoons golden syrup
⅓ cup sugar

1   Soak the sago in 3 cups water for 30 minutes, then add the remaining ingredients and pour into a saucepan. Bring to a boil over medium heat then simmer, stirring, for 8–10 minutes until the mixture is quite thick and the sago is tender.

2   Pour into individual dessert bowls, then chill until set. Serve with cream or custard.

Buying and storing lemons

You don't need your own lemon tree to get a good supply of lemons. If you buy between April and October, you can usually get lemons at a good price. Look for lemons that feel heavy for their size as these will be juicier, and keep in mind that smooth-skinned lemons are generally juicier than rough-skinned ones. Lemons, as with all citrus fruits, are best kept in the refrigerator.

More ways with lemons

Still want more ideas for using lemons? Look up these delicious recipes:

- Squid with capsicum and lemon (see page 67)
- Lemon and mushroom chicken pie (see page 96)
- Lemon syrup ricotta cake (see page 187)
- Tuna and lemon dip (see page 195)
- Sardines with lemon and herbs (see page 197)
- Lemon delicious pudding (see page 216)

Stone fruit

ALAS, THE STONE FRUIT SEASON is all too short. Your grandmother would have 'put down' jars of peaches, nectarines, apricots and plums while they were plentiful so she could afford the luxury of enjoying these choice fruits out of season. While you may not have acres of your own fruit trees (we wish we did!), every now and then you can pick up a tray of in-season stone fruit for a pittance. It's fairly easy to preserve your own fruit, and so satisfying to have rows of sparkling jars of fruit lined up on your pantry shelf to call on in the depths of winter for pies or desserts, or just to eat as they are with cereal or cream. No need to buy canned fruit again!

You can preserve almost any fruit, but stone fruits are especially suitable because of their short season. Choose only the best specimens – bruises and dents won't improve with age. The fruit needs to be prepared as you would for stewing or poaching. Apricots, nectarines, plums or peaches are halved (or left whole if the fruit is small) and the stones removed. Make sure you won't be disturbed during the bottling process, as it's important to work quickly and efficiently for best results.

Successful fruit preserving depends on efficient sterilisation of jars or bottles, so that any bacteria that could cause the fruit to ferment or turn mouldy is eradicated.

You can buy special jars for preserving foods, or you can use your leftover assortment of jam and chutney jars, as long as the inside of the lids (if they are metal) are coated with plastic; this will prevent any reaction with acids. If you are buying preserving jars, there are two types to choose from: those with rubber seals and clip lids, and those with an inner lid (which is either flat or slightly domed) and an outer screw band. All these jars seal in the same way – by the creation of a vacuum. When a jar is filled with hot ingredients and the lid is closed, the contents will cool, contract, and form a vacuum which causes the lid to seal. The lids will 'pop' as they are sucked down by the vacuum, so you are able to tell if your preserves have been successfully sealed. You'll find preserving jars at kitchenware shops or hardware stores.

Try to find preserving jars with wide mouths to make life easier when it comes to packing the fruit, and take care of your jars – don't probe them unduly with sharp knives as any chip will render the jars useless. Once you've bottled your ingredients, remember to label and date them before you store them away.

Sterilising jars

To sterilise preserving jars, wash them thoroughly in hot, soapy water then rinse in hot water and dry in the oven on the lowest heat. Rubber seals should be firm and a little elastic – soak them in hot water for a few minutes just before use.

Preserved fruit

MAKES 1 LITRE

In this simple method, the fruit is packed in sterilised preserving jars before being cooked in the oven. Then a sugar syrup is poured over the fruit and the jars are sealed and stored in a cool place. This method is suitable for preserving small quantities of fruit.

You won't need as much syrup to fill the jars as you might imagine because the fruit takes up most of the space. Make one lot of syrup and if you find you need more, you can quickly whip up another batch. The ratio of sugar to water in this syrup will suit most fruits, but if you like a lighter syrup, use just 1 cup sugar.

2 kg stone fruit (peaches, nectarines, apricots, plums),
    well washed, halved (or left whole if very small) and
    stones removed
2 cups sugar

1 Preheat oven to 120°C. Arrange the fruit in warm sterilised jars (see opposite) and stand them on a baking tray, spaced apart so they are not touching each other. Put on the lids but do not seal, then place the jars on a low shelf in the oven and leave for about 45 minutes.

2 About 10 minutes before the end of the cooking time, make the sugar syrup. In a saucepan, bring the sugar and 3 cups water to a boil over medium heat, then simmer for 4–5 minutes.

3 Carefully remove the jars of cooked fruit from the oven and stand them on some folded newspaper. Very carefully pour the boiling syrup into each jar until it reaches just below the rim. Close and seal the lids and leave to cool overnight.

4 The next day, test the seals. Take each jar and pop it in the sink. Release the clip or unscrew the lid and lift the jar up by the lid – if the lid stays closed, your jars are airtight. If not, use the fruit in the next day or two. The fruit is ready to eat straight away – store each jar in the fridge once opened.

✳ To remove the skins from peaches, plunge the fruit into boiling water, slowly count to 10, then remove them and cool immediately in iced water. Use a small paring knife to cut a small slit at the stalk-end of each peach to enable you to easily slip off the skins.

Brandied fruit

There are two ways of preserving fruits in brandy. The first, and simplest, is to lightly prick the fruit and pack it into preserving jars in layers, sprinkling with a small amount of sugar as you go, then fill the jars up with brandy and seal. Leave for at least 1 month before using.

The second method is to prepare and pack the fruit as for Preserved fruit (see left), but only fill the jars three-quarters full with syrup then top up with brandy before sealing. This gives a thicker juice, which is more suitable for desserts.

Chilli plum sauce

MAKES 3 CUPS

This is a gutsy, almost-sweet chilli sauce that is fabulous with fish, chicken or turkey, or even a simple stir-fry, as well as being perfect as a dipping sauce with any fried titbit.

It can be as thick or as runny as you like – just simmer the sauce until it is the consistency you prefer. Make two batches of this and you're set for the year (as are your lucky neighbours!).

1.5 kg plums, halved, half the stones reserved
1½ cups sugar
2 cups white vinegar
1 small bird's eye chilli, chopped
1 teaspoon coarse cooking salt
1 teaspoon ground ginger
½ teaspoon cayenne pepper
6 cloves
1 stick cinnamon

1 Combine the plums with the reserved stones and the remaining ingredients in a large saucepan. Stir over a low heat for 5 minutes, without boiling, until the sugar has dissolved.

2 Increase the heat to medium and bring to a boil, then reduce the heat to a simmer and cook uncovered, stirring occasionally, for 30–40 minutes or until the mixture is pulpy. Rub through a coarse sieve and pluck out the whole spices.

3 Return the mixture to the pan and bring to a boil. Reduce the heat to a simmer and cook, uncovered, for another 10 minutes or until the mixture has thickened slightly. Pour into warm sterilised jars (see page 152) and seal. The sauce is ready to eat straight away – store in the fridge once opened.

Waste watcher

Ever noticed how often condiments go to waste – how much gets washed off the plate at the end of a meal? Encourage people to take a small amount at first, then more if they really like it. Condiments are tiny punches of flavour, after all, and are not meant to be consumed as if they were the main part of the meal.

Peach chutney

MAKES ABOUT 3 CUPS

When peaches are in their prime, we tend to buy loads of them to eat fresh. But suddenly they all ripen at once and you're eating them for every meal just to avoid the waste, or forcing them on friends when they drop in. It needn't be like that. Use a glut of peaches to make this spicy chutney, which is perfect with grilled meat, cold meat or a potato salad. You won't be giving jars of this away in a hurry.

1 kg firm peaches, peeled (see page 153)
½ cup white wine
⅓ cup sugar
⅓ cup white-wine vinegar
2 tablespoons Chilli plum sauce (see left) or bought
   Chinese plum sauce
1 small red chilli
2 star anise
1 stick cinnamon
¼ cup sultanas

1 Halve the peaches, remove the stones and dice the flesh, then set aside.

2 In a large saucepan, combine the wine, sugar, vinegar, plum sauce, whole chilli, star anise and cinnamon stick. Place over low–medium heat and bring to a boil, then cook for 5 minutes until the liquid has reduced a little.

3 Add the peaches and sultanas, bring back to a boil, then cook, stirring occasionally, for about 15 minutes until the fruit is very tender and the liquid is thick and syrupy.

4 Remove the star anise, cinnamon stick and whole chilli before spooning the chutney into warm sterilised jars (see page 152) and sealing. Keep for at least a week before using. Store in the fridge once opened.

Fresh peach and plum compote

SERVES 6–8

Clingstone peaches and those little plums that never seem to ripen are perfect for poaching to make a compote. The French flavour their poaching syrup with a vanilla bean, whereas Italians like to use the rind of a lemon or orange – you can take your pick. Serve this compote with Crème anglaise (see right), pouring cream or ice cream.

If you like, you can omit the white wine and increase the quantity of water to 3 cups.

1 cup sugar
1 cup white wine
1 vanilla bean *or* the zest of 1 lemon or 1 orange
4 peaches, peeled (see page 153) or nectarines
4 plums or apricots

1 Place the sugar, wine, vanilla bean or citrus zest and 2 cups water into a medium-sized saucepan. Dissolve the sugar over low heat. Increase the heat a little, then simmer for 5 minutes to make a syrup.

2 Lower the fruit into the syrup and poach over low heat for 5–10 minutes, until tender (the time will depend on the ripeness of the fruit). While poaching, frequently spoon the syrup over the fruit and carefully turn it over in the syrup using two spoons.

3 Remove the fruit from the syrup and set aside. Increase the heat to medium–high and boil the syrup until it has reduced by about one-third. Leave to cool slightly, then pour over the fruit. Serve at room temperature or chilled.

Crème anglaise

MAKES 2 CUPS

If you're going to be preserving or poaching fruit, you'll also need to know how to make proper English egg custard, or crème anglaise. It's gorgeous dribbled over the fruit, swirling with the juices to create a sweet and creamy sauce. Pour some custard over a bowl of poached fruit in front of your guests and listen to the sounds of glee as the custard and deep-pink syrup of the fruit marble together.

2 cups milk
1 vanilla bean *or* ½ teaspoon vanilla extract
¼ cup caster sugar
4 egg yolks
1 tablespoon cornflour

1 Place the milk in a saucepan with the vanilla bean, if using, and bring slowly to scalding point (just before boiling point).

2 Beat the sugar, egg yolks and cornflour together in a large bowl until light in colour. Remove the vanilla bean and stir the scalded milk thoroughly into the egg mixture.

3 Transfer the custard to the saucepan and cook over low heat until it just comes to a boil, stirring continuously. If you are using vanilla extract, add it to the custard now. Pour the custard into a jug or bowl, cover the surface with plastic film and leave to cool before spooning over preserved or poached fruit.

What else can you do with crème anglaise?

There are plenty of delicious uses for a classic crème anglaise. Here are our favourites:

- **Make a trifle** – Dip pieces of leftover plain cake or sponge fingers in sweet sherry or marsala, then layer with fresh sliced fruits and top with a thick layer of crème anglaise.
- **Use it in a fool** – Purée fresh strawberries, raspberries, peaches and cooked apple and fold through equal quantities of crème anglaise and whipped cream.
- **Transform it into a chocolate sauce** – Stir through a little melted dark chocolate and spoon over poached pears or fresh sliced bananas.

Baked peach pancake

SERVES 4–6

This is a great way to use up ripe stone fruits before it's too late. We love it served for a late weekend breakfast with a big dollop of yoghurt, but you can also serve it as a dessert with mascarpone or crème fraîche.

¾ cup plain flour
¼ teaspoon salt
¼ cup sugar
3 eggs, lightly beaten
¾ cup pouring cream or milk
unsalted butter, for cooking
4 peaches, stones removed, flesh sliced
¼ cup brown sugar
1 teaspoon ground cinnamon

1   Preheat oven to 200°C. In a large bowl, whisk together the flour, salt, sugar, eggs and cream or milk.

2   Melt some butter in a large 25 cm-diameter ovenproof frying pan over medium–high heat. When hot, pour the batter into the pan to form a large pancake and cook just until set and lightly browned on the bottom.

3   Remove the pan from the heat and arrange the sliced peaches on top of the pancake. Sprinkle over the brown sugar and the cinnamon and bake in the oven for 15–20 minutes, or until golden brown on top and cooked through. Serve warm, cut into wedges.

*   You can omit the cinnamon if you find its flavour too strong. You could also substitute plums or apricots for the peaches.

Tomatoes

WHAT DO YOU DO WITH those sweet, plump tomatoes you've grown yourself that have suddenly all ripened at once? Or when you've noticed them in the greengrocers at a bargain price, just begging to be bought? Here are a few ideas.

- Make a few batches of **tomato soup** to freeze (see opposite).
- Make a **tomato relish** that will add a zing to sausages, chops or hamburgers right through the year (see right).
- Make **bruschetta** by toasting slices of ciabatta or sourdough, then rubbing them with a cut garlic clove before topping with diced tomato tossed in extra virgin olive oil and basil.
- Make a **fresh salsa** by mixing chopped tomato with chopped coriander, finely chopped red onion, a good pinch of ground cumin, a squeeze of lemon or lime juice, a dash of Tabasco and a drizzle of olive oil.
- Make a **tomato bake** by layering sliced tomato with sliced red onion in an oiled ovenproof dish, then top with a cup of fresh breadcrumbs mixed with a little melted butter or oil, some chopped parsley and crushed garlic and bake for 30 minutes, to serve with roast lamb or chicken.

Tomato relish

MAKES 6–7 CUPS

We all love a good dollop of tomato relish on a hamburger or grilled chop, yet most of us never seem to take the time to make our own these days (leaving it mostly to the CWA). So, in the spirit of keeping the tradition alive, get cracking and make your own when you get your hands on a boxful of ripe tomatoes.

1.5 kg very ripe tomatoes, peeled (see page 65)
2 brown onions, chopped
2 cups sugar
2½ cups malt vinegar
1 tablespoon plain flour
1 tablespoon curry powder
pinch of cayenne pepper
1 tablespoon mustard powder
1 tablespoon salt

1 Roughly chop the tomatoes, placing them in a colander set over a bowl as you go to collect the drained juice. Reserve ¾ cup of this juice.

2 Put the remaining juice, along with the chopped tomato, onion, sugar and vinegar, in a large heavy-based saucepan. Simmer over medium–high heat, stirring every now and then, for about 15 minutes or until the mixture has thickened.

3 Mix the remaining ingredients with the reserved tomato juice and stir through the simmering tomato until boiling, then simmer for another 5 minutes.

4 Spoon into sterilised jars (see page 152) and seal when cool.

Cream of tomato soup

SERVES 4–6

This is the kind of tomato soup everyone loves: comforting and familiar. While it has a satiny, creamy consistency, it doesn't contain cream, though you can add a little swirl to enrich the soup just before serving. Make this meal with some toasted cheese sandwiches on the side. This one's great for kids – familiar and easy to eat.

1 kg ripe tomatoes, roughly chopped
1 white or brown onion, finely chopped
3 cups chicken stock, vegetable stock or water
1 small bay leaf
2 tablespoons chopped mixed herbs, such as flat-leaf
   parsley, basil or marjoram
pinch of sugar
45 g butter
2 tablespoons plain flour
sea salt and freshly ground black pepper
cream, for swirling (optional)

1 Place the tomato in a saucepan with the onion, stock or water, bay leaf and chopped herbs. Add sugar and cook over low heat for 15–20 minutes. Remove from the heat and leave to cool for a few minutes, then push the mixture through a coarse sieve into a large jug.

2 Wipe out the saucepan, then melt the butter in it over a low heat. Remove the pan from the heat and add the flour, then return to the heat, stirring for a minute or so. Add the strained tomato liquid, increase the heat to medium and bring to a boil, then simmer for about 5 minutes, adding more stock or water depending on the consistency you like. Season with salt and pepper and serve with a swirl of cream, if desired.

Roasted tomato and basil soup

SERVES 4–6

Roasting tomatoes gives them an extra intensity, so it's worthwhile doing if you've already got the oven on for something else.

1 kg ripe tomatoes, preferably roma, halved
2 tablespoons olive oil
2 cloves garlic, finely chopped
⅓ cup chopped basil, plus leaves to garnish
4 cups chicken stock or water

1 Preheat oven to 180°C and lightly butter a baking tray. Place the tomato halves, cut-side down, on the tray and roast for 20 minutes, then remove from the oven. Leave them to cool slightly, then, while still warm, carefully slip off their skins. Chop the flesh finely, reserving the juice.

2 Heat the oil in a large saucepan and add the tomato flesh, along with the garlic and chopped basil, and simmer for about 5 minutes. Add the chicken stock or water and reserved tomato juice and cook for a further 5 minutes.

3 Serve immediately with a sprinkling of basil to garnish.

Quick tomato chutney

Heat 1 tablespoon oil over medium heat in a saucepan. Add 1 chopped brown onion and a crushed clove of garlic and cook for a few minutes until the onion has softened. Stir in a 400 g can chopped tomatoes, ½ cup brown sugar and ½ cup malt vinegar. Bring to a boil, stirring, then reduce the heat to low and cook for 30 minutes until thick and syrupy. Season to taste with a little cayenne pepper, salt and pepper, then transfer to a warm sterilised jar (see page 152) and seal when cool.

Salsa di pomodoro

As a general rule, we always say its best to cook from scratch rather than use packaged foods, but as with any rule there are some exceptions. Frozen green peas can be as tasty as fresh ones. And dried pastas are often so good there is little reason to make your own unless you're really in the mood for it and have all the necessary equipment. Salsa di pomodoro (Italian tomato sauce), however, is another story entirely. You'd be hard-pressed to find a commercial version as good as a homemade one.

There are many versions of salsa di pomodoro, originating from different regions of Italy. A simple version from Naples contains little more than tomatoes, garlic, olive oil and herbs. A more complex one, as they might make in Rome, uses a *soffrito* (a base of diced onion, carrot, celery and aromatics cooked in olive oil or butter over low heat) before adding the tomato. If you want to turn the salsa into a *sugo*, you can add a little meat, usually pancetta, which releases flavour as it cooks and transforms the blend into a flavoursome, deliciously complex sauce. Once you've made your basic sauce you can give it a punch by simmering it with chilli flakes to make an arrabbiata. Or add capers, finely chopped anchovies, olives, chillies and more garlic to make a puttanesca (see page 65).

Here's a basic recipe for salsa di pomodoro plus two variations, all of which can be easily doubled for storing and using later. Use any one of them as a base for a sauce to go with spaghetti or other pasta, the starting point for a homemade soup, for cooking mussels or other seafood, or for making an eggplant parmigiana. Stockpiling jars of this versatile sauce means you'll have some on hand all through the year.

A great gift for food-lovers

Make up a basket of your favourite pasta (dried or fresh), a wedge of parmesan cheese, a little pot of basil, a small bottle of olive oil and one or two jars of your very own salsa di pomodoro. Tied with raffia, this makes for a really special, and practical, gift.

Salsa di pomodoro

MAKES 1 LITRE

1 kg ripe tomatoes, chopped *or* 2 × 400 g cans
    chopped tomatoes
80 g butter
1 onion, peeled and halved
sea salt and freshly ground black pepper

1   Put all the ingredients into a large saucepan and simmer, uncovered, on a low heat for about 45–60 minutes, stirring from time to time and breaking up any large bits of tomato with a spoon.

2   Remove from the heat and push the sauce through a coarse sieve, discarding any solids. Finish with salt and pepper to taste.

Salsa di pomodoro with herbs and garlic

MAKES 1 LITRE

2 large cloves garlic
⅓ cup olive oil
1 kg ripe tomatoes, chopped *or* 2 × 400 g cans
  chopped tomatoes
2 sprigs basil
2 sprigs flat-leaf parsley
sea salt and freshly ground black pepper
½ tablespoon chopped oregano

1 Press down on the garlic with the flat side of a knife to bruise, then slip off the skins. Heat the oil in a saucepan over medium heat and fry the garlic until it starts to turn golden. Remove the garlic cloves and discard, retaining the oil.

2 Add the tomato, basil and parsley to the oil with some salt and pepper to taste. Reduce the heat to low and cook, partially covered, for 30–40 minutes, until the sauce is thick and pulpy.

3 Remove the pan from the heat and push the sauce through a coarse sieve, discarding any solids. Reheat the sauce gently, stirring through the oregano.

Salsa di pomodoro with pancetta

MAKES 1 LITRE

1 kg ripe tomatoes, peeled (see page 65) *or*
  2 × 400 g cans peeled and chopped tomatoes
¼–½ cup olive oil
1 onion, diced
1 carrot, diced
1 stick celery, diced
2–3 slices pancetta, finely diced
2 cloves garlic, crushed
sea salt and freshly ground black pepper
chopped oregano, basil or mint (optional)

1 Purée the tomatoes in a blender or food processor.

2 Heat the oil in a large saucepan over medium heat and fry the onion, carrot and celery for 5 minutes, until softened. Add the pancetta and garlic and cook for another 2 minutes.

3 Add the tomato purée and some salt and pepper to taste, then partially cover and simmer for 30–40 minutes, until the sauce is thick and pulpy. Stir through the herbs, if using.

Waste watcher

Salsa di pomodoro can be used straight away, but if you want to preserve it for using later, carefully ladle the sauce into warm sterilised jars (see page 152), seal and label. If you've done this properly and the jars and lids are very clean and absolutely dry, the seal should form a vacuum after an hour or so as the sauce cools. You might hear a little click as this happens, and if you tap the lid with your fingertips, it should sound solid rather than hollow. If, after several hours, this hasn't happened, you will need to heat the sauce and try again. An alternative is to freeze the sauce. Let it cool, ladle into snap-lock bags and freeze for 2–3 months. Whichever way you store your sauce, be sure to label and date it. You'd be surprised how quickly you can forget these details!

More ways with tomatoes

Still want more ideas for using tomatoes? Look up these delicious recipes:

- Fettuccine with chicken and tomato cream (see page 100)
- Lamb, eggplant and potato pie (see page 102)
- Turkish bean salad (see page 111)
- Tomato and zucchini bake (see page 112)
- Maltese tuna, pumpkin and rice pie (see page 117)
- Italian meatballs with fresh tomato sauce (see page 118)

Roman stuffed tomatoes

SERVES 4–6

This is a great way to use up big, juicy tomatoes, as well as any cooked rice you have left over. Kids love these, and the anchovy fillets add a nice richness, without being overbearingly fishy (or you can omit these for a vegetarian option).

6 large tomatoes

1½ cups cooked long-grain rice (equivalent to ⅔ cup uncooked)

2 tablespoons each chopped basil and flat-leaf parsley

¼ cup olive oil, plus extra for cooking

4 anchovy fillets in oil, drained and chopped

2 cloves garlic, crushed

sea salt and freshly ground black pepper

1 Preheat oven to 190°C. Slice the tops off the tomatoes and reserve.

2 Use a teaspoon to scoop some of the flesh out of each tomato, leaving a thick shell. Roughly chop the scooped-out tomato flesh and combine with the remaining ingredients in a large bowl, seasoning well.

3 Stand the tomato shells in an oiled shallow ovenproof dish. Fill the shells with the rice mixture and cover with the tomato tops.

4 Bake for 15 minutes, basting with the cooking juices every now and then. Serve hot or at room temperature.

* This dish is also great for using up leftover risotto or rice pilaf (omitting the other flavourings suggested here, though remember to add a fresh element, such as chopped herbs).

Healthy and wise

You really don't need to have 'meat and three veg' every night – in fact, we are told we only need two or three servings of meat a week. So what do you have the other nights? One of our favourite vegetarian dishes is these tomatoes, done as the Italians love them – filled simply with rice, made full of flavour with herbs, anchovies and garlic, and baked so they're melt-in-the-mouth delicious! There's plenty of other delicious options to choose from: why not try Quick minestrone (see page 95), Eggplant parmigiana (see page 146) or a veggie curry or stir-fry?

CHAPTER 7

Baking

If you're trying to sell your house, a sure way to impress at the open inspection is to pop a chocolate cake in the oven before the hordes arrive. It's a simple but effective way to persuade people that this is just the home they've been looking for – we're all suckers for the smell of a freshly baked cake.

Sadly, baking is becoming a lost art in many homes, with many preferring to buy a frozen chocolate Bavarian, a packet of biscuits or a sugary muffin on the way home from work instead. Lack of time is a factor, sure, but when you weigh up the rewards, we think home baking is a skill worth acquiring, and one that should be preserved for future generations.

Some steer clear of baking because they think special skills are required – it's all well and good to make a roast tarragon chicken with a potato gratin, but a tray of scones? Too hard! Sure, the finest croissants and most delicate pastries can be a challenge, but there are plenty of easier options that are more than accessible for even the novice cook.

In fact, baking can be a great introduction to cooking, as it is often as simple as measuring the quantities accurately, choosing the right size baking tin and setting the oven at the correct temperature. And the best thing is that once you have mastered a basic muffin or teacake recipe, you can start to experiment with other flavourings and toppings according to your taste and what you have in the pantry.

What draws a lot of people to baking is the way it illustrates the science of cooking (see Baking for beginners, opposite). Often it's someone who's not necessarily that interested in cooking the weekday meal who will take on the responsibility of baking some bread or making the dough for pizzas, simply because of a fascination with the science of it. Kate's fiancé, Dan, recently took up the challenge of making pizzas from scratch with enthusiasm, insisting on doing everything himself, and found a real sense of satisfaction with the process (see page 212 for the results!). The moral of the story is that even those of us without training can pick up the skills of baking very quickly and easily.

For kids, baking is a great way to learn about the transformative process of cooking: the impact beating has on eggs, the way you can turn a lump of butter into a creamy mixture and then a cake. Though perhaps first lured in by the promise of licking a wooden spoon coated in cake mix, children can be taught the basic elements of cooking very quickly by watching the process of baking, and they'll also learn that cookies and cakes don't just come in bright packets from the supermarket (indeed, sometimes we grown-ups have to remind ourselves of that fact).

Nothing lifts the spirits quite like baking – it can be therapeutic and reassuring. And when times are tight, baking is a really easy and satisfying way to save money on your weekly food bill. Once you have the basic equipment (most of which you can buy cheaply from the supermarket) and a good stock of basic ingredients, you can make a whole array of goodies to dip into all week. So instead of purchasing that extravagant chocolate-mousse cake from the local patisserie, roll up your sleeves, get the apron on and get baking!

Some hints for baking success

- **Always use eggs at room temperature,** as they whip better than cold eggs taken straight from the fridge.
- **To test whether a sponge or butter cake is cooked,** gently press the centre of the cake with your finger – if it springs back, it's done.
- **To separate eggs,** you'll need two small bowls. Tap the egg on the side of one bowl, pull the two halves apart and let the eggwhite fall into the bowl. Gently transfer the yolk from one eggshell to the other, letting the remaining eggwhite drip into the bowl. Place the yolk into the other bowl. If the yolk breaks into the eggwhite, or if a little bit of shell falls in, use a half-shell to scoop it out. Eggwhites containing traces of yolk will not beat as well.
- **Stir the flour into the mixture until just incorporated** (too much mixing and you'll get a tough result).
- **Store butter in the freezer** if you don't use it regularly – and just let it soften as you need it.
- When baking things like sweet pastries, pie bases and cakes, **use unsalted butter**. It gives a better flavour, and helps reduce your overall salt intake.

Baking for beginners

KATE > Neither Mum nor I were particularly brilliant at science at school, but when it comes to science in the kitchen, Mum (who trained as a pastry chef) is a veritable baking Einstein. So, sit down and pay attention – this is what I've learned from the expert herself:

- **Baking soda**, also known as sodium bicarbonate or bicarbonate of soda, is a chemical leavener which has various uses. In cooking, when combined with liquid and an acid (such as lemon juice or buttermilk, or cream of tartar) in a batter or non-elastic dough, it releases bubbles of carbon dioxide that cause the batter or dough to 'rise' once cooked. It's also very good for getting stains off the carpet, but that's for another book . . .
- **Baking powder** is the more common ingredient used in baking. It's essentially baking soda with an acid already added (usually cream of tartar). When combined with liquid, it works in the same way as baking soda.
- **Plain flour will keep for longer than self-raising**, so if you don't use self-raising flour very often, you can make your own – just add 2 teaspoons baking powder to every cup of plain flour needed before sifting.
- **Yeast** is a tiny living organism that grows best in damp, warm conditions. Excess heat will kill it, which is what happens when you bake dough in the oven. Sachets of dried instant yeast (available in 7 g quantities) keep very well and are easy to use, nowadays largely replacing the once-common block of fresh compressed yeast.

The essence of vanilla extract

Vanilla extract is real vanilla, usually incorporating the tiny seeds from a vanilla pod. The flavour is stronger and the quality generally much better than the more common vanilla essence. The essence often contains very little (if any) actual vanilla, and is more of a hint of flavour than the real thing, but it is much cheaper. Go for extract if you can afford it, and just use less. In some dishes – a vanilla panna cotta, for instance – it's important to use extract as the flavour is going to make or break the dish, but if you're making a chocolate sponge, essence will do just fine.

Sweet as sugar

There are myriad types of sugar to be found in the baking aisle of your supermarket, all of which have their own particular uses.

- **Granulated sugar**, also called white sugar, is the refined sugar usually found in the sugar bowl. As well as an everyday sweetener, it is best for making jams, syrups and caramel.
- **Caster sugar** is finer than granulated and is ideal for using in cakes, pastries, biscuits and puddings.
- **Icing sugar** is a very finely ground sugar used for making delicate cakes, biscuits and icings, as well as for dusting. Icing sugar mixture is icing sugar mixed with a little cornflour to prevent lumps forming.
- **Demerara sugar** is light-brown with large, slightly sticky crystals. A good sweetener for tea or coffee, it is also added to biscuits, cakes and desserts before baking to form a delicious crunchy topping.
- **Raw sugar** is natural, golden granulated sugar with a light flavour of honey. It is especially good in biscuits and cakes made with oatmeal and wholemeal flours.
- **Brown sugar** is soft, moist and compact, and is made by adding molasses to refined white sugar in varying proportions (light brown sugar contains less molasses than dark). Use in cakes, puddings and biscuits, or for sprinkling on desserts.

No-knead bread

MAKES 1 × 1 KG LOAF

Bread improver helps give bread a good texture and crust. Only 1 teaspoon is needed for every 4 cups of flour used. Most supermarkets stock the Lowan brand.

There are few foods as wonderful as homemade bread. It offers a burst of subtle and complex flavours that are extremely satisfying and bear little resemblance to their refined, additive-laden store-bought counterparts.

This no-knead bread is a bit revolutionary. It's been adapted and simplified from a recipe by Jim Lahey of the Sullivan Street Bakery in New York, and is based on the principle that kneading can be done away with by using very little yeast to create a soft, slack dough, giving it a long rising time and then baking it in a preheated pan with a lid. The rising time, over 20 or so hours, is a substitute for the intensive kneading – it brings the gluten molecules into alignment to cause them to bind to each other and produce a strong elasticity. It is best not to double the quantities to make 2 loaves because it can become too unwieldy.

4 cups plain flour (or you can use a mixture of white and wholemeal flour
    if you like – see page 170)
1 teaspoon bread improver
¼ teaspoon instant yeast
1½ teaspoons salt
2¼ cups warm water
plain flour, cornmeal or wheat bran, for dusting and topping

1 In a large bowl combine the flour, bread improver, yeast and salt. Add the warm water and stir with a plastic or silicone spatula until combined. Cover the bowl with plastic film, then a clean tea towel. Set aside at room temperature for 10–12 hours, until lots of bubbles appear on the surface.

2 Uncover the dough, use the spatula to scrape any dough from the sides of the bowl and fold it over on itself three or four times. Cover again with the plastic film and a tea towel and leave for another 6–8 hours, until the dough has doubled in volume.

3 Meanwhile, 15 minutes before you're ready to bake, preheat oven to 240°C and place in it a heavy cast-iron, ceramic or enamel casserole with a lid. When the dough is ready, carefully remove the pan from the oven and put it on a heatproof trivet. Sprinkle the base of the pan with a thick dusting of flour.

4 Take the bowl containing the dough and, with your hand under the bowl, invert the dough into the heated pan. Shake the pan very lightly to distribute the dough evenly. Sprinkle on the plain flour, cornmeal or wheat bran, then cover and bake for 40 minutes.

5 Remove the lid and bake for a further 20 minutes, until the bread is browned and crusty. The bread is cooked if it sounds hollow when the underside is knocked with the knuckles. If not, return it to the oven for a few more minutes.

6 Turn the bread out of the pan as soon as it comes out of the oven, and cool on a wire rack.

Customising your no-knead bread

Here are a few ways you can vary your homemade bread.

- For a **crisper crust on top**, you can reduce the length of time the pan is covered to 30 minutes, and then bake for a further 30 minutes uncovered.
- For a **crisper crust all over**, take the bread out of the pan and bake directly on the oven rack for the last 10 minutes of the cooking time.
- For a **golden, shiny crust**, brush with a little beaten egg; for a **cottage loaf**, dust the bread lightly with flour; and for a **rich dark crust**, brush with melted butter.
- Want to bake your bread **freeform**? It's easy . . . use just 2 cups warm water instead of 2¼ and proceed with Steps 1 and 2 on the previous page (the rising stage may take a few more hours because less liquid is used). Preheat oven to 240°C and turn the dough out of the bowl onto a lightly floured bench. Without handling the dough too much, pat and push it into whatever shape you want to end up with. Cover with a clean tea towel and leave for 15 minutes (**this is called semi-proving**). Next, using lightly floured hands, pat the dough out a little, pushing down on any air pockets to dispel you previously chose. Place on a lightly floured baking tray, cover with a tea towel and leave for an hour or so (**this is the proving stage**). When ready, slash the top in two or three places and bake for about 35 minutes, until golden and crusty.
- You can add **seeds and grains** to the bread to make it extra healthy and interesting. Experiment with cornmeal, polenta, rolled oats, wheatgerm or oat bran, which can be kneaded through the dough before cooking or sprinkled over the bread before baking to create a crusty, nutty top. Sunflower seeds, linseeds, quinoa and burghul are all good also but need to be soaked for a few hours before being mixed with the flour.
- Coarse salt, poppy, sesame or caraway seeds or coarse wheat can also be sprinkled over the bread before baking to **add even more flavour**.

✳ Dough will take longer to rise in cold weather than in warm weather. Be sure to keep it out of draughts and, in the winter, pop it in a sunny spot, well covered with perhaps two tea towels.

The word on yeast

Whether it's compressed, dried, or in the form of a mother culture or sourdough starter, yeast is essential to bread making. It is a single-cell organism that feeds on sugar and, as it feeds, it produces alcohol and carbon dioxide – the gas that makes the bread rise. Cooking destroys the alcohol and kills the yeast, and the bubbles of air that are left behind give bread its texture. Yeast cells are more active when it's warm (but too warm and the cells will die) and less active when kept cool. The general rule is that the longer the yeast cells are left to work, the more maltose and alcohol they produce and the more flavoursome the bread will be. High-quality compressed yeast has a shelf life of up to four weeks and has to be kept refrigerated. Either compressed fresh yeast or instant dried yeast can be used, though the fresh can be hard to find – health food stores are your best bet.

Which flour?

The best flour for baking bread is bread flour, made from whole wheat. It has a pleasant nutty taste, starch to give the bread colour, bulk to feed the yeast, gluten to help the bread stretch and rise, germ for essential oils and bran to help our digestive systems. The downside is that wheat is not suitable for people with gluten intolerance. Other flours such as barley, rye and oat all have very low gluten content but tend to make less palatable, heavier bread. For our no-knead recipe, you really need the high-gluten variety. You can use all wholemeal or white flour but a mixture of both is best. Bread made completely from wholemeal can be a bit heavy for some tastes, while just white flour is a bit light. Experiment for yourself, but a ratio of 50–50 is a good place to start. There is no need to sift the flour – just place it in a bowl and run your fingers through it. Remember though that wholemeal flour soaks up more water than white, so you may need to add more or less water, depending on the ratio you use.

Fortunately, most supermarkets stock a good selection of bread flours and you'll find an even greater choice in wholefood shops and organic stores. However, if you're going to make your own bread regularly it is much better to buy your flour in bulk from a flour mill. Look in the Yellow Pages or search the web to find local millers who will supply you with a range of flours at very reasonable prices. Remember that flours do deteriorate, so only buy what you can use in a couple of months – just store it in a plastic storage bin with a properly sealed lid.

Banana and raspberry bread

SERVES 6–8

Virtually every coffee shop in our suburb seems to sell this moist, fruity bread – it's popular with commuters to go with their morning caffeine hit. But so often it's incredibly expensive to buy, considering it's basically just a slice of bread. Plus, it's the luck of the draw in terms of how many raspberries you get – too often you get a big chunk of bread with an unfair fruit shortcoming (almost as disappointing as a bad coffee). This version can be made ahead of time, sliced and frozen, then popped in the microwave for a morning treat. And the bonus is you can cut the slices as thick as you like.

2 eggwhites, lightly beaten
2 large ripe bananas, mashed
¾ cup brown sugar
¼ cup vegetable oil
1½ cups plain flour
1¼ teaspoons baking powder
1 teaspoon ground cinnamon
½ teaspoon bicarbonate of soda
1¼ cups frozen raspberries
butter, to serve

1   Preheat oven to 160°C and butter a 21 cm × 14 cm loaf tin. Line the base and long sides with baking paper.

2   Combine the eggwhites, mashed banana, sugar and oil in a bowl. Sift in the flour, baking powder, cinnamon and bicarbonate of soda, and fold together until just combined. Fold through the raspberries, then spoon the mixture into the prepared pan.

3   Bake for 1¼ hours, until a skewer inserted in the centre comes out clean. Leave to cool in the pan for 5 minutes or so before turning out onto a wire rack to cool completely. Slice, toast and serve with butter.

Spicy date pillows

MAKES ABOUT 36

These Middle Eastern date pastries will take you on a magic carpet ride, if not to heaven, then certainly to a place you'd like to be. With a cup of tea or coffee, the trip is complete.

1½ cups plain flour
125 g unsalted butter
¼ cup caster sugar
1 tablespoon orange flower water, orange juice or sherry,
   mixed with 2 tablespoons water
icing sugar, to sprinkle (optional)

DATE FILLING

45 g butter
250 g pitted dates, roughly chopped
½ teaspoon mixed spice

1 Sift the flour into a bowl and rub in the butter with your fingers until the mixture resembles breadcrumbs. Stir in the sugar. Sprinkle over the orange flower water mixture and combine to form a firm dough. Knead lightly, then wrap in plastic film and set aside for 30 minutes at room temperature.

2 Preheat oven to 180°C and lightly butter a baking tray.

3 To make the date filling, melt the butter in a small saucepan, then add the dates, mixed spice and ¼ cup water. Stir over low heat for about 5 minutes to soften the dates. Remove from the heat and leave to cool.

4 Cut the dough into quarters. On a lightly floured bench, roll one quarter into a long rectangle about 30 cm × 8 cm. Turn the dough over and, with a spoon, spread a quarter of the cooled date mixture into an even log along the centre of the dough. Pick up one long side of the dough and fold it over to join the other side, making a long sausage. Continue to roll the sausage backwards and forwards to make it longer and thinner (you want it about 36 cm long). Slice this into 9 pieces, each about 4 cm long, and arrange on the baking tray. Repeat this process using the remaining dough and date mixture.

5 Bake for 30–35 minutes or until pale golden, then remove from the oven and leave to cool. Sprinkle with sifted icing sugar, if using. Store in an airtight container.

Orange flower water

If you're lucky enough to have an orange tree you'll be familiar with the beautiful fragrance of orange blossoms. Orange flower water (or orange blossom water) is a much-loved ingredient in French and Middle Eastern cuisines, especially in desserts. Look for it in small bottles in specialty food stores, delicatessens and some health food stores.

Scottish oatcakes

MAKES 16

Sorry, Prince Charles, but we think these are every bit as good as your Duchy Originals. Ours are a homemade-but-by-no-means-ordinary version of the pricey imported ones. Essentially a savoury biscuit, there's nothing nicer with a piece of cheese and a wee dram.

1 cup rolled oats
½ cup wholemeal flour
⅓ cup plain flour
1 teaspoon caster sugar
¼ teaspoon bicarbonate of soda
½ teaspoon salt
90 g unsalted butter, diced
2 eggwhites

1   Preheat oven to 200°C.

2   In a food processor, blend the oats until fine. Add the wholemeal and plain flours, sugar, bicarbonate soda and salt, then mix briefly and, with the motor still running, add the butter and process until the mixture resembles breadcrumbs. Add the eggwhites and process until the mixture forms a ball.

3   Halve the mixture and, on a square of floured baking paper, roll out one half into a 20 cm-diameter round. Transfer to a baking tray, then repeat with the other half.

4   Cut each round into 8–12 wedges and, keeping them in the round, bake for 20 minutes until light golden. Transfer the cooked oatcakes to wire racks to cool, then store them in an airtight container.

* These are also great with a bowl of soup, or even with a cup of tea. And they're perfect to give to your kids as a wholesome alternative to a sugary snack.

Waste watcher

THINK ABOUT RECYCLING   *Always be conscious of the consumable products you're using in the kitchen. Foil, for instance, is not environmentally friendly, so use it sparingly and only when nothing else will do. Baking paper is better, but you still don't want to go using it like there's no tomorrow. The baking paper is helpful in this recipe because it makes the dough easier to roll and transfer to the baking trays. You could roll the dough out directly onto the floured baking tray, but if the tray has a lip this could be awkward. So, to make up for this, and since the baking paper comes away clean from the cooked biscuits, let it cool, then wipe it with a dry cloth and put it away to use again. You can re-use baking paper many times.*

Meringues

IT ALL BEGAN, APPARENTLY, when a Swiss pastry cook from the town of Meiringen was expecting a visit from Napoleon, for whom he had made a confection using nuts, sugar and egg yolks. Not wanting to waste the whites, he whipped them together with sugar and shaped them into mounds, which he baked until crisp and served with cream. Napoleon supposedly preferred the latter dessert, and named the clever invention after the town.

Any recipe that asks you to beat eggs until they are a gleaming, satiny mass is bound to be pretty good. Meringues are a must to master, not least because they are so easy to make, so versatile and so crispy, chewy and light. The cost is virtually negligible, as they are a great way to use up leftover eggwhites from yolk-only recipes (just pop them in an airtight container, label with the date and amount and freeze them; they'll keep for up to 3 months). Then all you need is some sugar and cream of tartar on hand to be ready to make meringues at the drop of a hat.

Timing is everything when it comes to making meringues. You need to work quickly once you've added the sugar to the eggwhites or the meringue will wilt. Avoid making them on rainy days, in damp, humid weather or, most importantly, when you're cooking other things – the moisture in the air will make the meringues weep (and you'll cry too when they're ruined). If cooked meringues absorb any moisture, they can be made fresh again by drying them in the oven at 100°C for 15 minutes or so. Clean, dry utensils are also essential, as the residue of water, fats, oils and grease or even the slightest bit of egg yolk will reduce the volume of your meringue (some cooks even wipe around the inside of their mixing bowl with the cut-side of a lemon half to help cut any grease). You'll also need to have the eggwhites at room temperature to maximise the air they will absorb during beating.

You can shape your meringues into shells, clouds, discs, squares or all manner of fancy or plain designs. As soon as they have cooled after baking, they should be packed in a clean, airtight container, where they'll keep for weeks, even months, ready at any time to use. Fill them with cream, berries or any other soft fruits and finish with a fruit sauce or coulis, or fill with a fluff of chocolate, coffee or chestnut cream.

Meringue fingers

Put on your flapper dress, curl your hair, draw a single line down the back of your legs to suggest you're wearing silk stockings – these smart little meringue fingers are just perfect to serve at an elegant cocktail party. Put the meringue mixture into a piping bag fitted with a plain nozzle and pipe out small finger-lengths. Bake as described opposite until crisp and dry. To make these even fancier, melt some chocolate in a heatproof bowl that fits snugly over a pan of boiling water, and finely chop some nuts and put in another bowl. Dip either one or both ends of the meringue fingers into the chocolate, then sprinkle lightly with the nuts. Return them to the rack to allow the chocolate to set.

Plain meringues

MAKES ABOUT 24

eggwhites from 3 large eggs, at room temperature
small pinch of cream of tartar
1 cup caster sugar

1 Preheat oven to 120°C and line 2 large baking trays with baking paper.

2 Using an electric mixer or a bowl and a balloon whisk, beat the eggwhites, slowly at first, until frothy. Add the cream of tartar and beat quickly by hand or on the highest speed in the mixer, until the peaks hold their shape without flopping over but still look a little wet.

3 Gradually beat in 2 tablespoons of the sugar and continue beating for 2–3 minutes – the eggwhites should now be very stiff. Add all the remaining sugar and use a large metal spoon or spatula to fold it in lightly and quickly, gently cutting down through the mixture and lifting some mixture up and over until the eggwhites and sugar are lightly mixed. It is not necessary to mix thoroughly; if the mixture is overworked, the meringue will wilt.

4 Spoon or pipe the meringue mixture (see right) onto the prepared trays, leaving a space of at least 2 cm between each. Bake for 1½ hours, swapping the position of the baking trays halfway through the cooking time.

5 Remove the trays from the oven and ease the meringues from the trays. Turn them over and lightly push the centre of the bases with an index finger to make a slight indentation (this ensures they can hold a good dollop of whipped cream, and that the two halves will stay together when sandwiched), then return them to the oven placed on their sides for a further 30 minutes, or until crisp, dry and a delicate beige colour. Remove from the oven and leave to cool completely, then store in an airtight container.

Demerara meringues

MAKES 12

Moist, brown demerara sugar adds a crunchy dimension to a plain meringue. These are especially good filled with chocolate cream and topped with glacé ginger (see page 176).

125 g demerara sugar, plus extra to sprinkle
eggwhites from 2 large eggs, at room temperature

1 Preheat oven to 100°C. Spread the sugar out on a large baking tray and place in the oven for 1 hour to dry out. Leave to cool, then place in a blender or food processor and grind fairly finely.

2 Increase the oven temperature to 120°C and line 2 baking trays with baking paper. Beat the eggwhites until they form soft peaks, then beat in half the sugar until the mixture is thick and shiny. Using a large metal spoon, gently fold in the remaining sugar.

3 Spoon or pipe the meringue mixture (see below) onto the prepared trays. Sprinkle the tops with a little extra sugar and bake for 1½–2 hours or until crisp and dry. Turn the oven off and leave them there to dry out completely.

To spoon or to pipe?

You don't need to go for the perfect look every time – meringues shaped with spoons can look just as gorgeous as the piped variety. You will need two dessertspoons, a metal spatula and a jug or bowl of iced water. Dip one spoon in the iced water and fill with meringue mixture. Dip the spatula in the iced water and quickly smooth the mixture, piling it up in the centre and pointing the two ends. Dip the second spoon in iced water and use it to scoop the meringue out onto the prepared trays, then bake.

Having said all that, piped meringues do have a lovely pomp and ceremony about them (imagine them on a platter dressed with doilies at a country fair). You can make them big or small, depending on what you plan to use them for. Put the meringue mixture into a piping bag with a plain nozzle and pipe out rounds, each one wider at the base then spiralling to a peak, then bake.

Chocolate cream and ginger meringues

SERVES 6

This decadent chocolate cream is an easy way to transform your meringues into a luscious dessert. The addition of ginger adds a warm spiciness.

60 g dark chocolate
1 cup cream, whipped
12 Demerara meringues (see page 175)
thick cream, for serving (optional)
60 g glacé ginger, roughly chopped
shaved dark chocolate, for sprinkling

1   Melt the chocolate in a heatproof bowl that fits snugly over a pan of boiling water, then set aside to cool completely. As soon as it cools but before it has time to harden, fold through the whipped cream.

2   Dollop a good scoop of this chocolate cream onto the base of a meringue, then top with another meringue. Repeat with the remaining meringues and cream, place on a plate and set aside in a cool place or chill in the fridge for an hour.

3   Serve one meringue 'sandwich' per person and spoon a dollop of thick cream alongside, if desired. Scatter with the glacé ginger and top with the shaved chocolate.

Passionfruit sauce

Like peaches go with cream, sweet, crumbly meringues are perfect teamed with a tart, smooth passionfruit sauce. Halve 6 passionfruit and scoop the pulp out into a small bowl. Heat 2 tablespoons sugar mixed with ¼ cup water in a small saucepan over low heat until the sugar has dissolved and the sauce has thickened to a syrup. Stir through the passionfruit pulp and drizzle over meringues sandwiched together with whipped cream. A lighter alternative to the chocolate cream, these are perfect for entertaining or as a romantic dessert for two.

Pavlova

SERVES 8–10

Summer just wouldn't be the same without this quintessential Australian dessert. With its crisp outer shell and delicate marshmallow-like insides, and piled high with whipped cream and tart passionfruit, pavlova has become Australia's national dessert. New Zealanders may tell you differently, but this famous contribution to the culinary world is said to have been created by the chef of Perth's Hotel Esplanade in the 1920s, and named after the great ballerina Anna Pavlova. The chef's aim, or so says Australian folklore, had been to improve on a 'meringue cake' that was at the time well-known in New Zealand. The meringue puffed up, white and light as a feather, looking just like Pavlova's tutu.

4 eggwhites, at room temperature
pinch of salt
1½ cups caster sugar
1 teaspoon vinegar
1 teaspoon vanilla extract
300 ml cream, whipped
3 passionfruit, halved, pulp scooped into a small bowl

1 Preheat oven to either 200–210°C (electric) or 150°C (gas). Place a piece of baking paper on a baking tray and trace a 20 cm-diameter circle.

2 Using an electric mixer, beat the eggwhites with the salt on the highest setting until stiff peaks form. With the motor running on high speed, gradually sprinkle in the sugar, 1 tablespoon at a time, until all the sugar has been added. Lastly, fold in the vinegar and vanilla with a spatula. Spoon large dollops of the mixture onto the round of baking paper and smooth the top lightly.

3 If using an electric oven, place the pavlova in and immediately reduce the temperature to 150°C, cook for 1 hour, then switch off the heat and leave the pavlova in the oven until completely cooled.

4 If using a gas oven, cook the pavlova at 150°C for 1 hour, then reduce the heat to 120°C for a further 30 minutes. Switch the oven off and leave the pavlova in the oven until completely cooled.

5 When the pavlova has cooled, slide it onto a large cake platter, removing the baking paper. Don't worry if it collapses slightly or cracks on the surface. Spoon the whipped cream over and drizzle the passionfruit pulp on top.

Make Eton mess

Strawberries and cream, as we know, is a divine pairing. But the English perfected this dessert by crumbling in some meringue. Boys at English private school Eton apparently used to mush up their pudding of cream, berries and meringue together, creating a downright Eton mess. We don't care if it's true – it tastes great! Top hats off to you, boys. This is a great way to use up broken or leftover meringues, and you can swap raspberries (frozen are good for this) for strawberries if you like. To serve 6, roughly crumble 4 meringues into 700 ml gently whipped cream and 700 g crushed strawberries and fold lightly together. Leave for an hour or so before dolloping into individual glasses (martini glasses or champagne saucers are perfect), then top with a few more juicy berries, and let some of the red juices dribble down the sides of the glass.

Tutti-frutti

Passionfruit is everyone's favourite topping for a pav, but you don't need to stop there. Passionfruit and sliced strawberries are a good combination, or try sliced firm bananas, peaches, blueberries, mango or raspberries (and you could even make a raspberry coulis by whizzing frozen raspberries in a food processor with a little lemon juice and sugar, then leaving it to thaw before drizzling over).

Jam finger-holes

MAKES 40

These are so much better than the jammy biscuits you buy in packets – try these chewy homemade versions once and you'll be sold. Plus, it's a great way to use up any jam you have on hand.

2½ cups plain flour
½ teaspoon salt
250 g unsalted butter, softened
1 cup caster sugar
1 large egg
1 teaspoon vanilla extract
2 cups walnuts, very finely chopped (optional)
½ cup raspberry, fig, apricot or strawberry jam, warmed

1 Line 2 large baking trays with baking paper. Sift the flour with the salt and set aside.

2 Using an electric mixer, cream the butter and sugar on high speed until light and fluffy. Add the egg and vanilla extract and beat until combined.

3 Add the flour and mix on low speed until the dough comes together to form a ball. Remove the dough from the mixer, divide in half and pat each half into a thick round. Wrap in plastic film and chill in the fridge for 1 hour.

4 Pinch off tablespoonfuls of dough and roll into balls. If you want a nutty coating, roll the balls of dough through the chopped walnuts. Arrange the dough balls on the prepared trays about 5 cm apart, then use your thumb or the end of the handle of a wooden spoon to make an indentation in the centre of each ball. Chill in the fridge for 20 minutes. Preheat oven to 190°C.

5 Bake in batches for 15–20 minutes or until very lightly golden. Remove from the oven and use the end of a wooden spoon to redefine the indent. Fill each centre with some warm jam and leave to cool on a wire rack. Cool completely before storing in an airtight container.

✱ Keep in mind that the unfilled biscuits will keep for a few weeks in an airtight container, but once they're filled, they will become soft after a day or so. You may want to make up the filled biscuits as you need them.

Passionfruit yoyos

MAKES 20

Along with a lemon tree, a passionfruit vine is one of the best things to grow in your garden if you have the space. Passionfruit are quite expensive to buy (unless you manage to find them cheap at a good market) but so easy to grow. During the summer months, a 'Nelly Kelly' vine will supply fresh passionfruit daily. Use them to make these sweet morsels.

3 passionfruit, halved, pulp scooped into a small bowl
125 g unsalted butter, softened
½ cup caster sugar
1 egg
1 cup plain flour
½ cup self-raising flour

PASSIONFRUIT FILLING

80 g butter, softened
⅔ cup icing sugar
1 tablespoon reserved passionfruit juice

1 Preheat oven to 180°C and line 2 large baking trays with baking paper. Strain the passionfruit pulp, reserving 1 tablespoon juice for the filling.

2 Using an electric mixer, cream the butter and sugar until light and fluffy, then beat in the egg. Sift in the flours, add the passionfruit pulp and fold through.

3 Lightly flour your hands and roll 2 level teaspoonfuls of mixture into a ball. Place on the prepared trays and flatten slightly with the palm of your hand. Repeat with the remaining mixture – you should get about 40. Bake for 10 minutes, then leave to cool completely on the trays. Once cooled, lift the biscuits carefully off the trays with a metal spatula.

4 Meanwhile, make the passionfruit filling. Using an electric mixer, cream the butter and icing sugar together, then mix in the reserved passionfruit juice. Spoon the filling onto the underside of a cooled biscuit then sandwich another biscuit on top, repeating until all the biscuits are filled.

Some like it hot

For best results, always preheat the oven when making biscuits. The placement of the trays in the oven during baking is also important. Heat should circulate around the trays, so don't crowd them by putting the oven shelves too close together. Turn the trays halfway through the cooking time and swap their positions in the oven to compensate for uneven heat distribution.

Using the food processor for Cheese and walnut biscuits

Start with the butter well-chilled. Fit the metal blade in the food processor, then put the flour, paprika and salt into the bowl. Cut the butter into small pieces and add to the flour mixture with the cheeses. Process for about 20 seconds or until the dough just clings together, adding the chopped walnuts right at the end. Turn the dough out on to a board and pull together into a rough ball, then lightly knead to form a smooth dough. Wrap in foil or plastic film and chill for 1 hour before rolling out and baking as above.

Crispy oat, coconut and sultana biscuits

MAKES ABOUT 15

It's hard to avoid the ever-expanding biscuit aisle at the supermarket, filled with endless choices of delicious-sounding treats. If you're the sort of person who likes something sweet with their cup of tea, the cost of shop-bought biscuits can really escalate. These biscuits are simple to make and they're fresh, light and crispy. Have them on hand for your next cuppa.

250 g unsalted butter, softened
⅔ cup brown sugar
1 egg
2 tablespoons treacle
1 cup bran
¾ cup wholemeal flour
1 cup desiccated coconut
½ cup rolled oats
½ cup sultanas
½ cup walnuts, chopped
1 teaspoon baking powder
1 cup plain flour

1 Preheat oven to 180°C and line 2 large baking trays with baking paper.

2 Using an electric mixer, cream the butter, gradually adding the sugar until the mixture is light and fluffy. Beat in the egg and, when thoroughly incorporated, beat in the treacle.

3 Fold in the remaining ingredients except the plain flour. Tip the plain flour onto a clean bench and turn out the biscuit mixture. Knead to form a smooth dough, adding more plain flour if it gets too moist to handle.

4 Divide the dough in half. Wrap one half in plastic film and set aside. Form the remaining mixture into a 1 cm-thick rectangle (again, using extra flour if needed). With a sharp knife, cut the dough into 7 cm squares and arrange on the baking tray. Unwrap the other half of the dough and repeat the process.

5 Prick the biscuits a few times with a fork and bake for about 20 minutes until a rich, golden brown. Transfer to wire racks to cool, then store in an airtight container.

Cheese and walnut biscuits

MAKES ABOUT 36

Save yourself a small fortune by making your own little cheese biscuits the next time you're expecting friends for drinks. Crisp and moreish, these take no time at all, especially when made in a food processor (see opposite).

185 g butter, softened
1½ cups freshly grated cheddar
⅓ cup freshly grated parmesan
1½ cups plain flour
1 teaspoon paprika
1 teaspoon salt
2 tablespoons chopped walnuts

1 Preheat oven to 180°C and line 2 large baking trays with baking paper.

2 Cream the butter with the cheeses. In a large bowl, sift the flour, paprika and salt together. Add this to the creamed mixture with the chopped walnuts. Mix well until combined and then bring together with your hands to make a firm dough.

3 Cut the dough in half, then turn out onto a lightly floured bench and shape each half into 2 long rolls, 4 cm in diameter. Wrap the logs in foil or plastic film and refrigerate for 1 hour.

4 Using a sharp knife, cut the dough into 5 mm-thick rounds. Place on the prepared baking trays, sprinkle over the extra parmesan and bake for 12–15 minutes until light golden. Leave to cool, then store in an airtight container.

Five-minute cardamom tea cake

SERVES 8

Try using other spices – this tea cake is great with a tablespoon of caraway seeds added in place of the cardamom, or you can use another ground spice such as cinnamon or mixed spice.

This is so easy to make and worth remembering for all those times when you need a cake but can't really spare the time fiddling around with mixers and creaming butter. And the oil works beautifully. Seriously, in 5 minutes you'll have a cake in the oven.

2 cups self-raising flour
pinch of salt
1–2 teaspoons ground cardamom
1 cup caster sugar
3 eggs, well beaten
½ cup milk
1 cup olive or rice bran oil
icing sugar, for dusting (optional)

1   Preheat oven to 180°C, butter a ring tin or a 22 cm-diameter round cake tin and dust lightly with extra caster sugar.

2   Sift the flour, salt and ground cardamom into a large bowl. Stir in the sugar. Using a wooden spoon, gradually beat in the eggs, milk and olive oil, mixing until well combined.

3   Pour the mixture into the prepared tin and bake for 1½ hours or until a skewer inserted in the centre comes out clean. Serve dusted with icing sugar, if using.

Waste watcher

As this is such an easy cake to prepare, it's a great one to pop in the oven straight after you've cooked the evening meal. A lot of energy is used in preheating the oven so this is a good way to make the most of it. Here are some other cooking tips to help make your kitchen as energy-efficient as possible.

- ***Steam foods in a stackable steamer:*** *it has to be the most energy-efficient way to cook. This way you can cook a whole meal by steaming different ingredients in the baskets at the same time (for example, fish in one steamer, thinly sliced zucchini and carrot in another and some Asian greens in a third, and dinner is done).*
- ***Choose the correct-sized gas ring or electric plate on the stove*** *for the pan you're using. If the ring or plate is too small you'll need to cook the dish for longer, and if it's too big you'll be wasting energy.*
- *When you're boiling water for pasta or rice or reheating meals on the stovetop,* ***always cover the pan with a lid*** *to reduce the wasted heat.*

Dutch ginger shortcake

SERVES 8–10

As soon as the cake cools, keep it in an airtight container and it will easily last a week, maybe more. You don't have to score the top – it still looks beautiful simply glazed with the egg. Or, if you like, you can sprinkle the top with chopped walnuts before it goes in the oven. If you like lots of ginger, add a bit more each time you make it until you're entirely satisfied.

You're going to love this buttery ginger shortcake, the recipe for which took a fair bit of effort to get. Having first tasted one made by a friend, who was grudgingly given the recipe by a Dutch friend of hers (reluctant to share an old family treasure), we've worked on it, finding inspiration from our own testing and tastings. What's a little research when you love good food?

1½ cups plain flour
1 teaspoon ground ginger
good pinch of salt
200 g unsalted butter, cubed
1 cup caster sugar
125 g crystallised ginger, chopped
1 teaspoon vanilla extract
1 egg, lightly beaten

1 Preheat oven to 180°C and butter and line the base of a 23 cm-diameter sandwich cake tin.

2 Sift the flour, ground ginger and salt into a large bowl. Add the butter and use your finger-tips to rub it into the flour until the mixture resembles fine breadcrumbs. Stir in the sugar, then add the chopped ginger, vanilla extract and half the beaten egg and mix to a firm dough.

3 Turn the dough out onto a clean bench and knead lightly with floured hands until smooth. Press the dough into the prepared tin using the heel of your hand and smooth over with a spatula. Brush the top with the remaining beaten egg, then use a fork to score the top, first one way in diagonal lines, then the other way to form a lattice pattern.

4 Bake for 40–45 minutes, until the cake is firm, shiny and golden. Cool on a rack and cut into wedges to serve, preferably with a good cup of coffee.

You can use the food processor to pulse the flour and butter together, but you'll need to tip the mixture into a bowl before adding the ginger and mix by hand or it will be too finely chopped.

Plum tea cake

SERVES 8–10

This cake takes it name from whatever seasonal fruit you use: it could be plums, cherries, apples or pears. Happily, it can be a raspberry tea cake any time of the year, thanks to the excellent frozen raspberries now available from the supermarket. Or you could omit the fruit altogether and make a simple cinnamon tea cake. Serve with tea or coffee, or warm with cream or ice cream as an easy dessert.

1 egg, separated
½ cup caster sugar
½ cup milk mixed with ½ teaspoon vanilla extract
1 cup self-raising flour, sifted
30 g unsalted butter, melted
4–6 plums, halved

TOPPING

20 g butter, melted
½ teaspoon cinnamon mixed with 1 tablespoon sugar

1 Preheat oven to 190°C, butter a 20 cm-diameter sandwich cake tin and line the base with baking paper.

2 Using an electric mixer, beat the eggwhite until stiff peaks form, then mix in the egg yolk. Gradually add the sugar, beating well after each addition, then the milk mixture, beating well after each addition. Gently stir in the flour and melted butter.

3 Pour the mixture into the prepared tin and top with the fruit, cut-side down. Bake for 35–40 minutes, until a skewer inserted in the centre comes out clean.

4 Remove from the oven and, while still hot, brush the top with melted butter and sprinkle over the cinnamon and sugar mixture. Serve warm or at room temperature.

* This cake will be best on the day you make it – because of the small amount of butter used it's not really suitable for making the day before. It's so quick to make, however, that you can whip it up in no time on the day you need it.

Lemon syrup ricotta cake

SERVES 10

Surprisingly soft, lemony and moist, this cake is a cinch to make. Sweet lemon syrup is drizzled over the cake at the end, giving it a fabulous tart flavour.

1 cup self-raising flour
1 teaspoon baking powder
175 g unsalted butter, softened
⅔ cup caster sugar, plus 2 tablespoons extra
juice and finely grated zest of 2 lemons
3 eggs, separated
1¼ cups ricotta

1 Preheat oven to 180°C and butter and flour a 20 cm-diameter springform cake tin. Sift the flour and baking powder into a bowl and set aside.

2 Cream the butter and sugar until light and fluffy, then beat in the lemon zest, egg yolks and ricotta. Whisk the eggwhites until stiff peaks form, then gently fold them into the ricotta mixture with a metal spoon.

3 Fold in the sifted ingredients and half the lemon juice, then spoon the mixture into the prepared tin. Bake for 1 hour until the cake is golden and a skewer inserted in the centre comes out clean.

4 Combine the remaining lemon juice with the extra sugar and drizzle over the hot cake. Leave to cool for 1 hour in the tin before transferring to a wire rack to cool completely.

Healthy and wise

Literally meaning 're-cooked', ricotta is made from the whey leftover after making cheese. You can get both full-cream and low-fat varieties. If you want to eat it just as it is (in salads or on toast, for example), full-cream ricotta is wonderful stuff – rich, smooth and so creamy. If, on the other hand, you want to bake with it or use it in pancakes, the low-fat variety still provides a lovely light texture and a great flavour.

Apple and pine-nut cake

SERVES 8

This is the sort of cake you should bake when you're trying to sell your house – the gentle smell of baking apple fills the kitchen with a reassuring homeliness. It's amazing served while still a little warm, with cream.

1 cup plain flour
1 teaspoon baking powder
½ cup caster sugar
2 large eggs, lightly beaten
125 g unsalted butter, melted
4 golden delicious apples, cored and thinly sliced
½ cup pine nuts
finely grated zest of 1 lemon
icing sugar, to dust
whipped or pouring cream (optional), to serve

1 Preheat oven to 180°C and butter and flour a 20 cm-diameter springform tin.

2 Sift the flour with the baking powder into a bowl, then stir in the sugar. Make a well in the centre and add the beaten egg and butter. Stir the wet ingredients together, gradually incorporating the surrounding dry ingredients to make a thick batter.

3 Fold in half the apple, half the pine nuts and all the lemon zest and spoon into the prepared tin, smoothing the top evenly. Top with the remaining apple and pine nuts and bake for about 65 minutes, until a skewer inserted in the centre comes out clean (cover the cake with baking paper or foil if the top is browning too much).

4 Remove from the oven, leave to cool in the tin for about 10 minutes, then transfer to a serving plate to cool completely. Dust with icing sugar and serve as is, or with cream.

Waste watcher

You've made this for the family on the weekend and there's plenty left over. Don't let it go stale; this is the time to freeze it for another day. Wrap up the leftovers carefully in plastic film and pop into an airtight container, then freeze them for up to 4 weeks. Thaw at room temperature, or warm gently in the microwave on medium power, then serve with ice cream or custard for a pudding on a night when the sweet-tooth gremlin drops in.

Apple tarts

SERVES 6–8

Every country, every family, every cook seems to have their own version of apple tart. From using shortcrust pastry to puff pastry or filo (like we've used here), to turning it upside-down like the sticky Apple tarte tatin (see page 138), the wonderful apple tart always stays in fashion in the best restaurants as well as on our own dining tables. These little tarts look fabulous and are just the thing if you're wanting a dessert that is big on flavour but low in fat and kilojoules.

6–8 sheets filo pastry
45 g unsalted butter, melted
3 golden delicious apples, cored and thinly sliced
⅓ cup flaked almonds
1–2 tablespoons white, raw or demerara sugar
icing sugar, for dusting
ice cream, yoghurt or cream, to serve (optional)

1   Preheat oven to 190°C and lightly oil 2 baking trays.

2   Unwrap the filo pastry and peel off a sheet. Brush one half with some of the melted butter, then fold the other half over and brush the surface with more butter (keep the rest of the pastry covered with a clean damp tea towel while you are doing this). Crumple the sheet loosely into a rough round, gathering it inwards as you work. Transfer to one of the prepared baking trays and repeat with the remaining pastry sheets.

3   Arrange the apple slices among the folds of filo so that each tart is filled, then scatter with almonds and sugar. Bake for about 20 minutes until golden.

4   Dust with icing sugar and serve warm with ice cream, yoghurt or cream, if using.

* Keep some store-bought filo pastry on hand for tarts such as these – it can be stored in the freezer for months. Then you can turn out these tarts if you have a few apples that need to be used up, or when friends pop over unexpectedly.

CHAPTER 8

Entertaining on a budget

When you're having friends over or entertaining relatives, it seems like the time to pull out all the stops: bringing out entrées, mains, a sorbet taster perhaps, then dessert followed by cheese, coffee and chocolate. But this sort of entertaining can be an expensive business. Your guests will no doubt be impressed, but they'll have to loosen their belts on the drive home, and you'll have to tighten the budget for the next few weeks. Some families are forced to adopt rigid policies like 'family members hold-back' when having friends over, just to make sure there is enough to go around. This is all way too fussy and restraining, not to mention unnecessary if you choose the right things to cook.

When the purse strings are tight, don't despair at the demise of the three-course meal for entertaining. In fact, the single-course meal is *de rigueur* in even the finest food institutions when the economy tightens. You can cut your costs, but that doesn't mean you have to cut down on the feeling of luxury when entertaining – there are plenty of ways to wow your guests without going overboard. A shoulder of lamb can be an impressive feast when slow-roasted with potatoes, anchovies and garlic. A roasted and stuffed belly of pork is not exactly everyday eating, yet it is far from expensive to put together.

You can up the ante in other ways when entertaining. On more formal occasions, a beautifully set table can establish the tone of the meal. Ironing even a simple tablecloth and serviettes and picking a few flowers for the table will show everyone that you've made an effort. Tea-light candles or small bowls of water holding freshly picked gardenias or similar will give the room a lovely atmosphere and ensure a sense of occasion.

When selecting wine for a meal or party, consider the clean-skin bottles that are now readily available. Buy by the case to save yourself about 10 percent, and shop around for the best deals on the wines you like. Organisations like The Wine Society do excellent selections of own-brand and local wines at a fraction of the cost. You have to fork out a small initial sum to join, but that's soon tempered by the savings you make, especially when ordering by the dozen. Most people will take a bottle of something when going somewhere for dinner, which also helps offset the costs of drinks. After all, you're doing more than enough at the food end.

> **KATE>** When Dan and I have friends over for a meal, instead of serving expensive champagne or wine, we often have Italian prosecco with a drizzle of peach nectar added to each glass. It's a variation on the famous bellini, and a little goes a long way.

Making your own beer is another way, albeit a sometimes messy one, to save money on alcohol, or instead of serving a *digestif* after the meal, brew a big pot of tea with some dried lemon verbena leaves or mint added – the fresh, clean brew makes a soothing end to a meal. And everyone will be grateful the next day when they don't have a hangover!

Throwing a party for friends and family should be a joy, not a chore. Make it informal, relaxed and expressive of your own style and personality. That way you will enjoy yourself, and so will your guests.

Last-minute entertaining lifesavers

No need for any more apologies about the spread you're offering guests – try these fast and fabulous party ideas.

- For a quick canapé, **blanch 500 g shelled broad beans** (the frozen variety, which you should keep on hand for just such situations), then purée to a coarse paste with the finely grated zest of a small lemon and ¼ cup olive oil. Season to taste and serve on crostini (slices of toast cut into quarters or thin slices of toasted baguette) topped with parmesan shavings.

- **Mash an avocado** and add some lemon or lime juice, Tabasco, chopped chilli and chopped coriander to taste. Season and serve on thin slices of toasted baguette.

- For an instant dip, **purée a can of drained and rinsed white beans (or chickpeas)** along with 1 clove crushed garlic, the grated zest of ½ a lemon and 2 tablespoons flat-leaf parsley. Season to taste and drizzle with olive oil, then serve scattered with extra chopped flat-leaf parsley.

- For more hearty fare, **couscous is a great option** (it has saved many a host faced with an onslaught of unexpected guests). Prepare the couscous according to the instructions on the packet and leave to stand until fluffy. Stir through some chopped mint and coriander leaves, a sprinkling of ground cumin and coriander and a squeeze of orange juice. Drizzle with olive oil and serve with spicy sausages.

- The barbecue can help calm your entertaining fears. **Barbecue some squid and chorizo**, chop into bite-sized pieces and toss through drained and rinsed canned chickpeas or white beans. Add a handful of torn flat-leaf parsley and mint leaves and some thinly sliced red onion, then drizzle over some olive oil and a good squeeze of lemon juice and serve on a big platter for people to help themselves.

- **For a refreshing drink**, mix together some coarsely torn mint leaves, coarsely chopped lemon or lime and some caster sugar in the bottom of a sturdy jug. You can either add a couple of shots of vodka or gin and top up with any juice you have on hand, or just keep it simple and fill the jug with tap water and lots of ice.

Entertaining quick fixes

DON'T FANCY ANOTHER spread of supermarket-bought antipasto? If the idea of entertaining throws you into a panic, these simple ideas will help keep you cool under the collar. Serve these all up together on a platter to feed the hordes.

Hot cheese and bacon bites

125 g cheddar
Dijon mustard, to taste
2 rashers bacon, rind removed, cut into strips

1 Cut the cheese into 2.5 cm cubes and smear a little mustard over each. Wrap a strip of bacon around each cheese cube, securing with a wooden toothpick.

2 Grill, turning once, until the bacon is crisp and the cheese is starting to melt, then serve immediately.

Rumaki (Chicken liver and bacon bites)

1 tablespoon peanut or vegetable oil
250 g chicken livers, sinew removed
1 teaspoon grated ginger
1 small clove garlic, crushed
¼ cup soy sauce
1 tablespoon Chinese rice wine or dry sherry
1 teaspoon sesame oil
100 g water chestnuts, thickly sliced
125 g bacon rashers, rind removed, each rasher
    cut into three pieces

1 Heat the oil in a frying pan over high heat and fry the chicken livers for a few minutes until lightly browned.

2 Combine the ginger, garlic, soy sauce, wine or sherry and sesame oil and toss through the chicken livers. Cover and marinate in the fridge for 30 minutes, or longer if possible.

3 Drain the chicken livers, then wrap each one with a slice of water chestnut in a piece of bacon and secure with a toothpick. Place under a preheated grill for about 5 minutes until the bacon is crisp and the chicken livers are cooked through. Serve hot.

Ham and garlicky ricotta rolls

250 g ricotta or cream cheese
1 clove garlic, crushed
2 tablespoons each snipped chives and chopped
    flat-leaf parsley
1 teaspoon chopped marjoram or oregano
250 g sliced ham

1 Mash the ricotta or cream cheese with the garlic and herbs. Spread a large spoonful of the mixture over each slice of ham, roll up to a fat cigarette-shape and transfer to a plate. Cover with plastic film until ready to serve.

2 Cut each roll crossways into halves or thirds and serve.

Tuna and lemon dip

1 × 200 g can tuna in oil, well drained
⅓ cup mayonnaise
finely grated zest of 1 lemon
1 clove garlic, finely chopped
½–1 teaspoon curry powder or drained and mashed canned
    green peppercorns (optional)
2 tablespoons olive oil
1 tablespoon snipped chives, plus 1 tablespoon
    extra to garnish
sea salt and freshly ground black pepper

1 Place the tuna in a food processor. Add the remaining ingredients and process until smooth. Transfer to a serving bowl.

2 Garnish with the remaining chives and chill in the fridge.

Crostini con fegatini di pollo
(Toasts with chicken livers)

SERVES 6

* The sinews of chicken livers are easily removed with scissors or by cutting the livers in half and cutting the sinew away from each piece.

So sixties, so retro, so delicious. Little pieces of toast topped with just about anything are pretty popular now, but since chicken livers are so cheap, and these are so easy to make, we're bringing this one back. Don't tell the kids they're eating chicken livers, and you might find they like them too. Groovy.

Snap up some brandy

It's worth getting a decent-quality bottle of brandy to use for cooking. You're not exactly going to use it all in one go, and it's great to have on hand for French-inspired dishes.

Sage advice

Sage is such a versatile herb and is used in a lot of Italian cooking. Wrap a chicken breast in prosciutto and pat a sage leaf on each side before grilling or barbecuing, or use sage leaves in a stuffing for roast chicken.

2 tablespoons extra virgin olive oil
60 g butter
1 small brown or white onion, finely chopped
6 sage leaves, roughly chopped
400–500 g chicken livers, sinew removed
2 anchovy fillets in oil, drained and chopped
1 tablespoon capers, rinsed, plus extra to garnish
¼ cup dry white wine
1 tablespoon brandy
¼ cup chicken stock
18 thin slices ciabatta, toasted and quartered
chopped flat-leaf parsley, to garnish

1 Heat the oil and half the butter over low heat in a large frying pan. Add the onion and sage and cook for 5 minutes until softened.

2 Increase the heat to medium, add the chicken livers, anchovies and capers and fry for a few minutes until the livers are lightly browned. Add the wine and brandy and continue cooking for another 3–5 minutes until the liquid has evaporated. Add the chicken stock and cook for 2–3 minutes, then remove the pan from the heat and leave to cool for 5 minutes.

3 Remove the mixture from the pan and chop finely or process briefly in a food processor in one or two batches, returning each batch to the pan as you work. Add the remaining butter and reheat gently over low heat.

4 Spread the warm mixture on toasts and arrange on a serving platter. Garnish with extra capers and chopped flat-leaf parsley.

Where to buy chicken livers

Chicken livers are available from most supermarket butchers, but you may need to ask for them if they are not on display. Otherwise, just visit your local butcher who will have some without doubt, even if frozen out the back. If you buy frozen chicken livers, just thaw them in the fridge for a day or so before use, and don't re-freeze them. Use them soon after purchase – they don't keep well.

Sardines with lemon and herbs

SERVES 6

Don't turn your nose up at sardines – these lovely little fish deserve a second chance. They're too often ignored by those who happen not to like the canned variety, but the fresh ones are delicate, sweet and soft, and very reasonably priced. Get them at fish markets or your local fishmonger. This makes a great entrée.

500 g fresh sardines
1 teaspoon chopped fresh oregano *or* ¼ teaspoon dried oregano
2 teaspoons chopped fresh thyme
2 teaspoons chopped flat-leaf parsley
juice of 1 lemon
plain flour seasoned with salt and pepper, for dusting
¼ cup olive oil
crusty bread, to serve

1   Rub the soft scales off the fish with a dry cloth. Cut the heads off from the start of the backbone. Open up the fish enough to pull out the guts and backbone, cutting the backbone free with scissors close to the tail (leave the tail on). Rinse the fish and pat dry, reforming them to their original shape.

2   Place the fish in a shallow dish. Mix the herbs together in a small bowl. Pour the lemon juice over the fish, add half the mixed herbs and marinate for 10 minutes, turning the fish over once or twice.

3   Drain the fish, dust with the flour and brush with some oil. Heat a chargrill pan over high heat, brush the pan with oil, and arrange the fish in one layer. Cook for 2 minutes, then turn the fish and cook for a further 2 minutes until the flesh is opaque. Sprinkle over the remaining herbs and serve with crusty bread.

* A friend of ours loves to cook sardines Greek-style: roasted whole over hot coals and then transferred to a bed of chopped parsley, doused in lemon juice and left to stand, covered, for 20 minutes. Serve at room temperature and enjoy the amazing flavours.

What else can you do with mussels?

- They are **delicious with spaghetti or any kind of pasta**. Steam them as in Step 1 and reserve the cooking liquid to add to the water in which the pasta will be cooked. When cool enough, remove the mussels from their shells, reserving a few in shells for a garnish if you like. Put the pasta on to cook. In a separate pan, melt some butter and fry a little chopped garlic. Add a splash of white wine and bring to a boil, cooking for a few minutes to reduce. Add the mussels and warm them over low heat. Drain the pasta and mix through the mussels and sauce, stirring in a good handful of chopped flat-leaf parsley and plenty of freshly ground black pepper.

- If you've never tried **mussel fritters**, you're missing out on a treat. Steam 1 kg mussels and remove them from their shells. Chop roughly and set aside. In a bowl, beat 2 eggs, then whisk in ½ cup flour sifted with 1 tablespoon baking powder. Stir in the mussels, ¼ cup chopped flat-leaf parsley, 1 tablespoon chopped basil and season to taste. Form large tablespoonfuls of the mixture into patties and fry in sizzling butter or oil for 1–2 minutes each side until golden. Serve with lemon wedges.

Mussel and parsley soup

SERVES 6

Some of the best cooking experiences are action-packed, and making mussel soup is definitely one of them. Organise it so that everyone has a job – making breadcrumbs, scrubbing mussels, chopping onions and picking the parsley, keeping the dog or cat out of the kitchen and pouring the cook a glass of wine. There's nothing like the atmosphere of everyone working together, united by a common goal, and then settling down to a good meal together.

Mussels have everything going for them. They are cheap compared to most other seafood, delicious, versatile, easy and quick to prepare – and not nearly as tedious to clean as you might imagine. It is worth the trip to the fish markets to get your mussels, but you have to be choosy. Try to find fairly small ones that feel heavy for their size, preferably the Australian cultivated ones – the large green New Zealand mussels arrive frozen and can be too strong and tough.

Here's a stunning mussel soup for a fun and relaxed feast. To make a creamy version, add 1 cup cream with the stock or water to the cooking liquid when making it up to 6 cups.

2 kg mussels
fish stock or water, for cooking
¼ cup olive oil
2 white onions, chopped
1 cup dry white wine

2 cups fresh sourdough breadcrumbs
 (see page 128)
½ cup chopped flat-leaf parsley
freshly ground black pepper

1 Fill the sink with cold water and tip the mussels in, scrubbing them well and tugging off their beards along with any seaweed. Change the water and scrub them again, then rinse thoroughly. Place them in a large, wide saucepan over medium–high heat and cover. Steam with the lid on, shaking the pan occasionally, for 4–6 minutes, or until the shells have opened. Drain in a colander set over a bowl, reserving the liquid from the mussels.

2 Strain the reserved liquid through a fine sieve into a large measuring jug. Add enough fish stock or water to make up to 6 cups liquid. Remove the mussels from the shells, leaving a few in their shells for garnish. Discard the empty shells and set the mussels aside.

3 In a large, heavy-based pan, heat the oil and fry the onion for 5 minutes, stirring until softened. Add the reserved mussel liquid and wine and bring to a boil over low heat. Add the breadcrumbs and simmer gently for about 10 minutes. Add the parsley and pepper to taste and continue to simmer for another minute or so, without letting the soup boil. Stir in the mussels to reheat and ladle into bowls.

Waste watcher

MUSSEL MYTHS   *There is much confusion around whether to discard mussels that don't open during cooking, but in fact they're not necessarily bad if they haven't opened. Try popping any unopened mussels back into the pot and giving them another stir over the heat. If they still do not open, you should be able to prise them open by sliding a knife very carefully between the two shells. You'll know pretty quickly if you've struck a bad one – the smell will tell you.*

Three flashy salads to impress your guests

SUZANNE > In France, they really know how to make an awesome salad, bringing together seasonal ingredients to make something crunchy, soft, salty and sweet, sometimes all in the one dish. Make sure you use good-quality extra virgin olive oil – it's an essential ingredient and can make or break a salad. Here are some simple recipes, but think about experimenting with different ingredients you find at the greengrocer.

It's really important not to let the salad dressing take over from the other ingredients; sprinkle rather than soak your salad with dressing. When I attended the Cordon Bleu cookery school in London, how a salad was dressed was of utmost importance. When marking a student's salad, the head chef or teacher would literally lift the salad ingredients out of the bowl – if there was any dressing left in the bowl, the salad was a failure. You can make a basic vinaigrette and keep it in the fridge for a week's worth of salads, but practise making your own dressing regularly and you won't even have to refer to a recipe – you'll be doing it fresh on the day with ease.

Mixed greens, walnut and pear salad

SERVES 4

¼ cup roughly chopped walnuts
1 radicchio, trimmed and cut into strips
1 endive, trimmed and cut into strips
100 g baby spinach leaves
2 firm ripe pears, cored and thinly sliced
⅓ cup shaved parmesan

DRESSING

2 tablespoons white- or red-wine vinegar
2 tablespoons olive oil
⅓ cup walnut oil
1 teaspoon Dijon mustard
sea salt and freshly ground black pepper

1   In a small dry frying pan, roast the chopped walnuts over high heat for a minute or so, then set aside.

2   Whisk together all the dressing ingredients in a large bowl. Toss the radicchio, endive, spinach leaves and pear through the dressing. Pile on to a serving platter and scatter with the roasted walnuts and parmesan shavings.

* Walnut oil may cost a little more than olive oil, but it adds a wonderful fragrance; remember though to store the bottle in the refrigerator, as it turns rancid fairly quickly.

Which oils for salad?

For most salad leaf-based salads, you should use extra virgin olive oil. Invest in a good-quality one, and go for a 4-litre can rather than the small fancy bottles, as it will be much more economical in the long run. For a really special flavour, walnut oil is a good one to try (see above), and if you are making an Asian salad, you might want to use rice bran, peanut or sesame oil.

Eggplant and feta salad with chilli and mint

SERVES 6 AS AN ENTRÉE OR SIDE DISH

2 eggplants, sliced lengthways
olive oil, for brushing
2 red onions, chopped
⅓ cup olive oil
3 cloves garlic, chopped
2 red chillies, halved, seeds removed, sliced
juice of 1 lemon
100 g feta, crumbled
⅓ cup Greek yoghurt
½ cup mint leaves, roughly torn
extra virgin olive oil, for drizzling
freshly ground black pepper

1   Brush each eggplant slice with a little olive oil, then chargrill on both sides on a barbecue until golden and tender.

2   In a large, heavy-based pan, fry the onion in the olive oil until soft. Add the garlic and chilli and cook for 2 minutes.

3   Arrange the eggplant slices on a serving platter and drizzle over the lemon juice. Sprinkle the onion mixture over and then top with the feta and dollops of Greek yoghurt. Scatter over the mint leaves and drizzle with some extra virgin olive oil. Season with pepper (there should be enough salt in the feta) and serve at room temperature.

Mussel, fennel and potato salad

SERVES 4–6

1 kg mussels, scrubbed and beards removed
splash of white wine
1 clove garlic, sliced
1 large bulb fennel, trimmed (stalks reserved)
   and thinly sliced
4–6 desiree or kipfler potatoes, quartered
½ bunch basil, leaves picked and roughly torn

VINAIGRETTE

1 clove garlic, peeled and bruised with the flat side of a knife
⅓ cup extra virgin olive oil
1 tablespoon red-wine vinegar
sea salt and freshly ground black pepper

1   Place the mussels in a wide pan with a tight-fitting lid. Add the white wine, garlic and fennel stalks, then close the lid and bring to a simmer over high heat, cooking for 3 minutes. Shake the pan and then remove the mussels as they open, cooking those still closed for a little longer with the lid on. Let them cool and then remove mussels from their shells. Strain the cooking juices through a fine sieve and reserve.

2   Cook the potato in boiling salted water for about 10 minutes or until you can easily insert a knife into the centres. Meanwhile, make the vinaigrette by putting all the ingredients into a small jar and shaking until combined.

3   While the potato is still hot, transfer to a bowl and pour half the vinaigrette over. Add the fennel slices, half the basil, the mussels and the remaining vinaigrette to taste. Serve scattered with the remaining basil.

Ricotta gnocchi with browned butter and sage sauce

SERVES 4

These ricotta gnocchi are so easy and yet so impressive – and the magic is you can make them well ahead of time, then just drop them into boiling water and add sauce to serve. Your friends will be bowled over, we promise. Go for a full-fat ricotta if you're allowed.

250 g ricotta
⅓ cup freshly grated parmesan, plus a little extra to serve (optional)
1 egg
1 teaspoon salt
1 cup plain flour, sifted

BROWNED BUTTER AND SAGE SAUCE

60–90 g butter
12 sage leaves
sea salt and freshly ground black pepper

Healthy and wise

A light, fresh tomato sauce is a nice change from the richness of a butter and sage sauce. Heat 1 teaspoon olive oil over low heat and add 2 cloves finely chopped garlic, cooking until fragrant but not browned. Add 1 punnet chopped cherry tomatoes and about 10 basil leaves and bring to a boil. Reduce the heat to low and simmer for 8 minutes. Season with salt and pepper and add a pinch of sugar. Garnish with extra basil leaves and serve with freshly cooked gnocchi.

1 Lightly flour a large baking tray. Place the ricotta, grated cheese, egg and salt in a bowl, then gradually add the flour and lightly mix between additions (add only as much flour as you need to create a firm dough, and do not overmix).

2 Divide the dough into quarters, and roll each into a log roughly 2 cm in diameter. Cut each log into 2 cm pieces. With the back of a fork, press down lightly on top of each gnocchi to create indents where the sauce will cling. Place the gnocchi on the baking tray as you go and, if not using immediately, store in the fridge for up to 24 hours.

3 Meanwhile, make the sauce by melting the butter in a small saucepan over medium heat, swirling the pan frequently until the butter turns a deep-brown colour and smells sweet and nutty – watch it carefully so it doesn't burn. Add the sage and cook for 30 seconds or until the leaves crisp up a little. Add salt and pepper to taste and set aside.

4 To cook the gnocchi, bring a large pan of lightly salted water to a boil. Drop in the gnocchi (in batches so as not to crowd the pan) and cook for 1–2 minutes until they float to the top. Place the cooked gnocchi in a warmed serving bowl, top with the brown butter sauce and gently toss to mix. Serve with a little extra parmesan sprinkled on top, if you like.

If time allows, drain the ricotta well before using by placing it in a strainer over a bowl and leaving in the refrigerator for at least 30 minutes.

What's the secret to wonderfully smooth gravy?

Lumpy gravy will be a thing of the past once you understand the basic principle of making sauces and gravies: hot added to hot equals lumps. So, if your roux (the mixture of fat and flour) is already hot, as it is with gravy, then the liquid added to it should be cool (and if the roux is cool, the liquid added should be warm). The trick is to have cool stock at the ready when you make gravy, and to keep stirring the mixture until it starts to thicken. If the gravy threatens to go lumpy, use a small whisk to smooth it out.

Roast belly of pork with apple and fennel stuffing

SERVES 8

There was a time when a roast leg of pork was a fairly common meal in Australia, but it's rare to see a pork leg in the butchers these days. More often, you'll see a loin of pork, which is, of course, also wonderful roasted. Still, even a roast pork loin can be a costly meal. Coming to the rescue of all those who love a pork roast is the economical pork belly, which can be stuffed and roasted to a crispy finish.

Choose a piece of pork belly with a good proportion of lean to fat, as they can really vary. The lean pork mince used in the stuffing helps to increase the proportion of lean to fat.

sea salt and freshly ground black pepper
1 × 1.5 kg piece pork belly, boned and
   scored (ask your butcher to do this
   for you)
2 tablespoons plain flour
2 cups chicken or vegetable stock
roast potatoes, to serve

APPLE AND FENNEL STUFFING

1 cup fresh breadcrumbs (see page 128)
200 g lean pork mince
1 cooking apple, grated
2 cloves garlic, crushed
¼ cup chopped flat-leaf parsley
⅓ cup freshly grated parmesan
1 teaspoon fennel seeds
1 large egg, lightly beaten
sea salt and freshly ground black pepper

Potatoes with the roast

As soon as you've put the pork in the oven, drop some peeled and quartered potatoes into a saucepan of boiling salted water to cook for 3 minutes. Drain, cool a little and score lightly with a fork. Add them to the roasting tin 30 minutes into the cooking time and roast, turning several times, for about 45 minutes until cooked through.

Can't get your crackling crisp?

No need to be disappointed if the crackling hasn't turned out nice and crispy like you imagined. While the meat is resting, slice the crackling away from the joint in two or three large pieces and pop under the grill. Watch it like a hawk – it will soon crisp up and start to 'bubble', so take care not to let it catch and burn. It won't be long before you have lovely crisp crackling.

1   Rub salt all over the skin of the pork belly and leave for 30 minutes to draw out some of the moisture. Preheat oven to 230°C and lightly butter a flameproof roasting tin large enough to hold the pork belly lying flat.

2   To make the stuffing, combine all the ingredients in a bowl. With a sharp knife, starting from one short end, carefully cut a slit lengthways through the centre of the pork towards the middle. Turn the pork and make a cut towards the middle from the other short end, leaving the sides intact, to form a pocket for the stuffing. Fill the cavity with the stuffing and close each end with one or two small skewers.

3   Transfer the stuffed pork to the prepared roasting tin, skin-side up. Rub the skin with a little more salt, then bake for 25–30 minutes until the skin has blistered. Reduce the oven temperature to 190°C and cook for a further 45 minutes, until the meat is cooked through. Transfer to a warmed serving platter and leave to rest for 5–10 minutes.

4   Meanwhile, make the gravy by pouring 1½ tablespoons of juices from the roasting tin into a small saucepan. Add the flour and stir over medium heat until browned. Pour in the stock and cook, stirring and scraping the bottom of the tin, until the gravy has thickened and is smooth. Simmer for 1 minute, then season to taste and serve in a jug at the table.

5   Remove the crackling in sections to make carving easier, if you like. Cut the meat into thick slices and serve with a piece of crackling for each person, alongside plenty of roast potatoes.

Carbonnade of beef

SERVES 4–6

This is a traditional dish from Belgium with a rich, beer-based sauce and a crunchy topping. For a richer flavour, make the beef stew the day before and reheat the next day with the mustard-bread topping.

2 tablespoons olive oil
1 kg beef, such as chuck, shin or blade,
   cut into 3–4 cm cubes
2 white or brown onions, sliced
1 tablespoon plain flour
1 cup beer
1 cup hot beef stock
1 clove garlic, finely chopped
1 bouquet garni (a bay leaf, a few sprigs
   of parsley and thyme and a few black
   peppercorns, tied with kitchen string)

pinch of freshly grated nutmeg
½ teaspoon sugar
1 teaspoon white-wine vinegar
sea salt and freshly ground black pepper
8 thick slices baguette
Dijon mustard, for spreading
steamed green beans and baby carrots,
   to serve

* A bouquet garni adds depth of flavour to casseroles and stews. Place a few black peppercorns in a folded fresh bay leaf, take a few sprigs of parsley and thyme and secure the whole bundle together with kitchen string. Drop it into your casserole before cooking, and remember to remove it before serving.

1 Preheat oven to 160°C. In a flameproof casserole with a lid, heat the oil over medium heat and brown the meat in batches.

2 Return the meat to the pan, add the onion, then reduce the heat and cook for 2 minutes. Sprinkle over the flour, pour in the beer and stock and bring to a boil, stirring constantly. Add the garlic, bouquet garni, nutmeg, sugar and vinegar and season with salt and pepper.

3 Cover and transfer to the oven to cook for 1½–2 hours or until the meat is very tender. Remove the casserole from the oven and pluck out the bouquet garni.

4 Spread one side of the baguette slices thickly with mustard, then arrange on top of the meat, mustard-side up, pushing the bread down into the gravy (it will float back to the top as it cooks). Return to the oven and cook, uncovered, for a further 30 minutes or until the bread forms a nice brown crust. Serve with steamed green beans and baby carrots.

Chicken roasted with green olives

SERVES 6

Transport yourself to the Italian countryside with this simple rustic dish. Don't worry too much about over-cooking the chicken because the marylands won't dry out as easily as breast meat will. The idea is to caramelise all the ingredients nicely without letting them burn.

6 chicken marylands (leg and thigh portions)
1 head garlic, cloves peeled
12 golden shallots, peeled
1 cup extra virgin olive oil
30 green olives
6 potatoes, halved
3 sprigs rosemary
sea salt and freshly ground black pepper

1   Preheat oven to 200°C. Place all the ingredients in a large roasting tin and mix thoroughly, making sure that everything is well coated with oil, then cover with baking paper or foil.

2   Pierce the paper or foil a few times and bake for about 50 minutes, turning and basting the chicken and vegetables frequently. Remove the paper or foil and bake for a further 10 minutes uncovered to help caramelise the chicken and vegetables. Check that the chicken is cooked by piercing the thigh with a skewer – the juices should run clear.

3   Serve immediately or set aside to stand until you're ready to serve (the flavours will develop nicely). Follow with a tossed green salad.

A perfectly simple green salad

To make a really tasty green salad to go with a dish like this, you'll need about 200 g mixed salad leaves (choose from any varieties, such as mesclun, baby rocket, baby spinach, iceberg, cos or mignonette lettuce). Arrange the salad leaves in a bowl and add one, or a combination of, the following ingredients: thinly sliced fennel, sliced cucumber, sliced avocado, thinly sliced celery, parmesan shavings, toasted walnuts or hazelnuts, coarsely snipped chives, torn flat-leaf parsley leaves or torn mint leaves. Dress with a dash of balsamic and a slurp of extra virgin olive oil and toss together well before serving.

Slow-roasted lamb shoulder with potatoes, anchovies and garlic

SERVES 4–6

The secret to this recipe is the long, slow cooking time. After 3 hours the lamb is so tender that it almost falls away from the bone when you serve it. The juices from the roasting lamb also give a delicious flavour to the potatoes baking underneath, as does the splash of vinegar. It's a great dish to turn to when you're entertaining, as most of the work is done well ahead, and the smell just about knocks people out with anticipation as they arrive. All you need to go with it is a big bowl of steamed beans or a green salad to follow.

1.5–2 kg lamb shoulder, trimmed of excess fat
sea salt and freshly ground black pepper
1 kg desiree potatoes, thinly sliced
2 red onions, thinly sliced
2–3 heads garlic, papery skin removed,
    cut in half crossways
4 anchovy fillets in oil, drained
1 tablespoon olive oil
30 g butter
1 sprig rosemary, broken into pieces
1½ tablespoons white-wine vinegar

1   Preheat oven to 180°C.

2   Rub the lamb all over with salt and pepper. Heat a flameproof heavy-based roasting tin over medium heat, then add the lamb and brown all over. Take the tin off the heat, then remove the lamb and set aside on a plate.

3   Spread the potato and onion slices in alternate layers in the roasting tin, and nestle the garlic halves in among the slices. Top with the anchovy fillets, olive oil and butter and season well with salt and pepper. Lay the browned lamb on top, sprinkle with rosemary and vinegar, and pour over 2 cups water.

4   Cover the tin tightly with foil and bake for 1½ hours. Reduce the oven temperature to 160°C and remove the foil, then continue to cook for another 1½ hours.

5   Cut off tender chunks of lamb and serve with the vegetables. Serve half a head of roasted garlic per person, and let your guests scoop out the sweet flesh.

Let's take a closer look at the ingredients

Lamb shoulder – Because this contains a lot of connective tissue, lamb shoulder is at its best when the bone is left in and it is cooked over a long period. For this dish, a leg of lamb just isn't the same.

Potatoes – Go for waxy potatoes such as desiree for this dish, although most other potatoes will do, except baby new potatoes which won't provide the wonderful creaminess needed.

Anchovy fillets – Using a fishy punch to perk up the flavour of meat is a trick known the world over. What would much of South East Asian food be without fish sauce or dried shrimp paste, and how would the Chinese fare without oyster sauce in their stir-fries? Even the French have *Tournedos morateur*, in which they serve anchovy butter atop a nice fillet steak.

Rosemary – The English have mint sauce with their lamb but for the French, rosemary is best. Add rosemary leaves to roast potatoes, and use whole sprigs in casseroles or stews so you can fish them out before serving.

Persian baked chicken and rice

SERVES 6

This is a rice cake layered with yoghurt and spicy marinated chicken: fragrant, soft in the middle with a crunchy, golden crust. Serve sliced into wedges to show off the golden layers inside, and your guests will feel like royalty. Note the cooking time – yes, it does take 2 hours to cook, but that just means you'll have extra time to be super-organised for your visitors!

1½ cups Greek-style yoghurt
⅓ cup olive oil
3 egg yolks
1 teaspoon ground cinnamon
1 teaspoon ground allspice
sea salt and freshly ground black pepper
500 g chicken thigh fillets, cut into strips
2 cups basmati rice
green salad, to serve

1   Combine the yoghurt, oil, egg yolks and spices with 2 tablespoons water in a shallow dish and season with salt and pepper. Add the chicken strips, tossing through to coat, then leave to marinate in the fridge for 2 hours.

2   Preheat oven to 180°C and lightly butter a 23 cm-diameter heavy-based baking dish with a lid. Cook the rice in a large saucepan of boiling salted water for 5–6 minutes, until just starting to soften but still firm in the centre. Drain the rice, rinse under cold water and drain again.

3   Remove the chicken from the marinade. Spread two-thirds of the marinade over the base and sides of the prepared dish. Arrange one-third of the cooked rice in the dish, then half of the chicken. Level the mixture out and arrange another third of the rice and the remaining chicken on top. Finish with the remaining rice, pressing down with the back of a spoon so that the rice and chicken stick together. Sprinkle over ¼ cup water. Pour the remaining marinade around the edges. Poke a few holes through the rice with a skewer, cover, then transfer to the oven to cook for 1 hour.

4   Reduce the oven temperature to 150°C and bake for 1 hour more. Remove the dish from the oven and leave to stand, covered, for a few minutes, then turn out onto a serving platter. Cut into wedges and serve with a green salad.

Healthy and wise

You could use ordinary long-grain rice here, but basmati is better for you because it has a lower glycemic index (GI) rating than other types of rice. GI is a rating (between 0 and 100) that indicates how quickly a food releases glucose into the blood. Foods with a lower GI rating break down into the bloodstream slowly, leaving you feeling fuller for longer. GI ratings for packaged foods are now often included with the nutritional information on the packet.

Dan's barbecued pizza

'**WHEN I FIRST STARTED WORKING** full-time back home in England, I confess I used to buy frozen pizza bases from my local supermarket. I'd top them with tomato sauce from a jar, some pre-cut slices of salami, then I'd scatter the lot with frozen mozzarella – and be pretty pleased with my "home-cooked" meal. Failing that, I'd call up my local pizza place and order a takeaway "Inferno" with extra chilli.

Then when I moved to Australia, I embraced the barbecue. Surrounded as I was by good cooks, and with a desire to eat good food, my repertoire soon expanded to include dishes like Portuguese chicken and lemon-and-chilli-marinated steaks. Pizzas went out the window, as did the extra London weight I had been carrying around. But soon I hankered for proper pizza: not the store-bought variety but something I could create myself using the basic *pomodoro* sauce I had mastered, and all the excellent fresh produce available here.

My first instinct was to try cooking pizza on the barbecue – a marriage of my two great food loves. If I could get a pizza stone like the ones they use in Italy to fit into the Weber, I thought I might be on to something. I was. I found a flat terracotta paving stone at a friend's house, which was a perfect fit for my barbecue. I got Margaret Fulton to teach me how to make the base (okay, so not everyone is as fortunate as I was to learn from the best, but we do, after all, have a couple of things in common: a love of whisky, and a fondness for Kate, Margaret's granddaughter and my fiancée).

Soon I was ready to test my basic Margherita pizza out on Kate. It was chewy and crisp and tasted like a real pizza – success! The barbecue suddenly had a new purpose, and I had my new speciality. I experimented with topping after topping, from a tomato base topped with three types of mushrooms to a plain base with thinly sliced potato, rosemary and garlic. I tweaked the dough recipe slightly to make it perfect for barbecue cooking (you want it stretchy and malleable so it doesn't stick to the tile). Soon I was ready for the ultimate test: I cooked barbecue pizzas for Margaret's birthday. I'm happy to report that everything, including my signature "Inferno", was a raging success.'

Dan adding the final touch to his homemade pizza.

Turn up the heat

Here's the recipe for Dan's 'Inferno' pizza – it's extremely simple and if you like things spicy, you'll love this. You can temper the heat by adding less pepperoni or using a mild variety but, as the name suggests, this is supposed to be hot. You'll need to get some good-quality Italian pepperoni from a delicatessen. (It's worth spending a little more and using a bit less as the quality is really important. Don't be afraid to ask to try a couple of different varieties to test the heat level before you buy.) Spread a thin layer of Basic tomato sauce (see opposite) evenly over the prepared pizza base, then sprinkle over about 5 torn basil leaves and top with 6–10 slices pepperoni. Scatter a good handful of roasted capsicum strips over and cook in a preheated 230°C oven or a covered barbecue (see opposite) for 10–15 minutes until crisp and golden. Drizzle generously with extra virgin olive oil or homemade chilli oil (see opposite) before serving.

Basic pizza dough

MAKES 2

2¼ cups plain flour (or fine Italian '00' flour, if you can get it)
1 teaspoon salt
½ teaspoon sugar
1 × 7 g sachet instant yeast
¾ cup lukewarm water
¼ cup olive oil, plus extra for oiling

1 Sift the flour into a large bowl with the salt and stir in the sugar and yeast. Make a well in the centre and add the water and oil. Using a wooden spoon first and then your hands, mix to a dough and turn out onto a well-floured bench.

2 Knead lightly for 4–5 minutes until the dough is smooth and elastic. Transfer dough to an oiled bowl, turn it to coat with the oil and cover with a clean tea towel. Set aside in a warm place for about 1 hour to rise; it should double in volume.

3 Preheat oven to 230°C or prepare the barbecue (see below). Turn the dough out onto a floured bench, divide in half and roll out thinly to fit the pizza trays. Top as desired and bake for 10–15 minutes until crisp and golden.

✱ To barbecue your pizza, Dan-style, you'll need a covered barbecue and a pizza stone or large terracotta tile that will fit in the barbecue. Assemble the pizza on a cutting board or baking tray, then transfer it to the stone or tile just before baking in the preheated barbie.

Homemade chilli oil

To make your own chilli oil to spice up a pizza, fry 3 finely chopped bird's eye chillies (seeds and all) in ¼ cup olive oil over low heat for about 10 minutes. Cool, then strain and mix with some extra virgin olive oil to taste.

Basic tomato sauce

MAKES 2 CUPS

¼ cup olive oil
1 × 400 g can chopped tomatoes
5 basil leaves *or* a few sprigs oregano
sea salt and freshly ground black pepper

1 Heat the oil in a large, heavy-based pan, then add the tomatoes and the basil or oregano. Simmer for 10–15 minutes, stirring from time to time, until the sauce has thickened.

2 Remove the herbs and season well with salt and pepper.

Funghi pizza

MAKES 2

1 quantity Basic pizza dough (see page 213)
2 tablespoons olive oil
100 g fresh flat mushrooms, thinly sliced
3 cloves garlic, chopped
1 golden shallot, chopped
1 red chilli, seeded and chopped
150 g button mushrooms, thinly sliced
50 g grated mozzarella
30 g pecorino or parmesan

1 Preheat oven to 230°C or prepare the barbecue (see page 213).

2 Prepare the pizza dough, place on trays and set aside.

3 Heat 1 tablespoon of the oil in a heavy-based frying pan over medium–high heat. Add the flat mushrooms, garlic, shallot and chilli and toss for 8 minutes until golden, then scatter over the prepared pizza base.

4 Top with the button mushrooms and mozzarella, then bake for 10–15 minutes until crisp and golden. While the pizza is still hot, shave the pecorino or parmesan over and season well. Drizzle with the remaining olive oil and serve.

Shaved prosciutto, bocconcini and baby rocket pizza

MAKES 2

1 quantity Basic pizza dough (see page 213)
1 quantity Basic tomato sauce (see page 213)
¼ cup basil leaves
⅓ cup olive oil
sea salt and freshly ground black pepper
150 g finely sliced prosciutto
1–2 balls bocconcini, sliced
50 g baby rocket leaves

1 Preheat oven to 230°C or prepare the barbecue (see page 213).

2 Prepare the pizza dough, place on trays and spread evenly with tomato sauce.

3 Scatter the basil over the pizzas and drizzle with half the oil. Season with salt and pepper, then bake for 10–15 minutes until crisp and golden.

4 Top with the prosciutto, bocconcini and baby rocket, drizzle with the remaining oil and serve.

Less is more

It started out centuries ago in Naples as a simple, cheap peasant dish, and look how far the pizza has come. Come to think of it, so have we – no longer do we feel the need to pile our pizzas high with sliced meat, tinned pineapple and way too many vegetables. A thin spread of fresh tomato sauce, a few slices of prosciutto, a handful of rocket, some shavings of fresh mozzarella or parmesan and a drizzle of good-quality olive oil is more than enough. And because we're using better-quality ingredients, and fewer of them, we're actually tasting the pizza dough.

The following ideas should find Italian favour, but these are just a start and, as you get into the spirit of it, you will enjoy dreaming up your own combinations. Remember, less is more when topping a pizza: three or four ingredients max should suffice.
- Halved cherry tomatoes, roasted capsicum and grated parmesan.
- Pitted black olives and anchovy fillets.
- Cooked seafood, such as mussels, prawns or squid.
- Slices of mozzarella and a sprinkling of grated parmesan.
- Sliced ham, sliced mozzarella and sliced button mushrooms.

These pizzas can also be baked in the oven, of course — just preheat it to 230°C beforehand and bake them for 10—15 minutes or until crisp and golden.

Lemon delicious pudding

SERVES 4–6

Whether you call it a lemon delicious or lemon surprise, this refreshing yet creamy pudding is a family favourite. It's also an essential for any thrifty cook's repertoire, because it barely costs a thing to make – all you need are a couple of eggs, some flour, milk, sugar and (hopefully) a lemon tree in the back garden. The charming surprise underneath the sponge topping is a creamy lemon sauce. Just delicious.

> 60 g unsalted butter, softened
> juice and finely grated zest of 1 lemon
> ⅔ cup caster sugar
> 2 large eggs, separated
> ⅓ cup self-raising flour, sifted
> 1¼ cups milk
> cream or custard, to serve

1 Preheat oven to 190°C and butter a shallow ovenproof dish.

2 In an electric mixer, beat the butter with the lemon zest and sugar until creamy, then beat in the egg yolks. Stir in the flour alternately with the milk, beating well between additions.

3 Beat the eggwhites until stiff peaks form, then use a metal spoon to fold them lightly but thoroughly into the butter mixture along with the lemon juice. Pour the mixture into the prepared dish and bake for about 45 minutes (see below). Serve with cream or custard.

* Try this traditional winter pud with a spring twist – a splash of refreshing lime juice. Just add the juice of 1 lime along with the juice of half a lemon, instead of the juice from a whole lemon.

Where's the sauce?

The lemon sauce will only make an appearance if the pudding is cooked just right – too long, and the sauce will become firm; not long enough, and there won't be sufficient sponge topping. Check your pud after 45 minutes and if there doesn't seem to be enough sponge (there should be a nice, thick layer visible when you insert a small sharp knife), return it to the oven for a little longer.

Blueberry and raspberry clafoutis

SERVES 4

These take no time at all to put together, and always impress with their creamy silken texture. They looks gorgeous brought to the table – positively bursting with berries. The raspberries add tartness to the dish, while blueberries are reliably sweet, and together they make the perfect couple. Use some halved figs in place of the blueberries if you like.

> 1 punnet fresh blueberries or 1 cup frozen blueberries
> 1 cup fresh or frozen raspberries
> ¼ cup blanched whole almonds
> 2 tablespoons plain flour
> ¾ cup milk
> ½ cup caster sugar
> 2 large eggs
> 1 tablespoon port
> ¼ teaspoon salt
> 2 tablespoons cold unsalted butter, chopped
> whipped cream, to serve (optional)

1 Preheat oven to 200°C and butter four 2 cm-deep flan dishes.

2 Tip the blueberries into the prepared dishes and sprinkle the raspberries on top.

3 In a blender or food processor, grind the almonds to a meal. Add the flour, milk, ⅓ cup of the sugar, eggs, port and salt and blend well (stopping and scraping down the sides every now and then until you have a smooth batter).

4 Pour the batter over the fruit, then dot with the butter and sprinkle with the remaining sugar. Place the dishes on a baking tray and bake in the middle of the oven for 30–40 minutes, or until the tops are golden and the batter has set.

5 Transfer to a wire rack and cool for a few minutes, then serve warm, with whipped cream, if you like.

You can try this pud with just about any fruity addition: sultanas, raspberries or even some slices of banana. If you like, you can also add some dark chocolate or preserved ginger. The upshot is to be creative, using what you have in the fridge, what's in season and what's on sale.

Rhubarb bread and butter pudding

SERVES 6

A delicious, homely pudding with the wonderful tang of rhubarb. The best thing about this pudding, apart from how it tastes, is that it is so easy. You can make it ahead of time and put it in the oven when your guests arrive or as you're sitting down to your meal – you'll be eating it about an hour later, so just work out the timing on that basis. This version, *sans* whisky, is a good choice for family meals, but you can always serve a wee dram on the side if you can't imagine bread and butter pud without it.

8 slices white bread, crusts removed, thickly buttered on one side
  and cut into triangles
1 small bunch rhubarb, cut into chunks (about 2 cups)
½ cup caster sugar, plus extra for sprinkling
½ teaspoon ground cinnamon
4 eggs
2½ cups milk
½ cup pouring cream
2 teaspoons vanilla extract (optional)
¼ teaspoon grated nutmeg
butter, for dotting

1   Preheat oven to 190°C and butter a shallow ovenproof dish. Arrange half the bread triangles in the base of the dish, buttered-side up, top with the rhubarb and sprinkle with half the sugar and the cinnamon. Cover with the remaining bread triangles.

2   In a large mixing bowl, beat the eggs until frothy, then mix in the remaining sugar and the milk, cream, vanilla extract, if using, and nutmeg. Pour this mixture evenly over the bread and leave to stand for 15 minutes. Dot generously with butter and sprinkle with a little extra sugar. Cover with a piece of buttered baking paper and bake for about 25 minutes.

3   Remove the paper and cook for 30 minutes more until the top is golden brown and crisp. Serve hot straight from the dish.

Off the shelf

You can use stale bread to make bread and butter pud – it's a traditional way of using up bread that's on its way out. Your guests will love this dessert (and they'll appreciate your thrifty ways). This and the Lemon delicious pudding (see page 216) are just like mother used to make – and now you can too.

How to grow rhubarb

Look for rhubarb roots in garden centres in the winter months – you want the crowns (sections of root that have been cut away from another plant). Rhubarb is quite a thirsty plant, but it won't survive in boggy conditions. It prefers plenty of sun, and if you're planting it in a pot, it needs more water and care than if in the ground. Use blood and bone or compost and plant the crown about 5 cm below the ground among other plants that need regular watering. When the time comes to harvest, pull the largest stalks cleanly downwards and away from the rest of the plant, always leaving at least four stems on the plant. Rhubarb is a hardy plant that can live for many years and so is well worth the effort. Just remember though that rhubarb leaves are highly poisonous, so don't feed them to chickens or rabbits, if you have them.

Lucy's chocolate puddings

MAKES 6

Our friend Lucy makes double quantities of these, freezes them and then has a great sweet treat on hand for any occasion. They are, without doubt, the softest, most chocolatey puddings you'll ever have.

olive oil, for brushing
130 g dark chocolate (70% cocoa), broken into pieces
90 g unsalted butter, chopped
2 tablespoons ground almonds
2 tablespoons plain flour
1½ tablespoons caster sugar
¼ teaspoon ground cinnamon
3 eggwhites
vanilla ice cream, to serve (optional)

1 Lightly brush six ½ cup-capacity ramekins with oil (or use decorative ovenproof cups, as we have here).

2 Melt the chocolate and butter in a heatproof bowl that fits snugly over a saucepan of simmering water. Stir in the ground almonds, flour, sugar and cinnamon until combined.

3 Using an electric mixer, beat the eggwhites until stiff peaks form, then gently fold through the chocolate mixture. Spoon this into the prepared ramekins or cups and freeze for at least 30 minutes (if freezing for longer, cover each one with plastic film).

4 When ready to cook, preheat oven to 220°C. Remove the ramekins or cups from the freezer and place them in a baking dish, filling the dish with enough warm water to come two-thirds of the way up the sides of the ramekins or cups. Leave them in this water bath for 10–15 minutes to thaw slightly.

5 Bake the puddings for 10–15 minutes until they have risen a little and a soft crust has formed. Serve immediately, with a scoop of ice cream if desired.

* Chocolate can be expensive, but sometimes you'll find the 70% cocoa varieties on sale, or in two-for-one packs. Pick them up when you do; good-quality chocolate is always handy to have.

Waste watcher

STOCK UP ON EGG YOLKS *Don't throw out the surplus egg yolks – pop them into an air-tight container and freeze and they'll keep for up to 2 months. They will thaw well and, although they will have burst and lost their shape, they'll still be fine to use in a homemade mayonnaise (see page 140) or other recipes.*

Acknowledgements

The origins of this book date back far further than that fateful day when Lyn Amy, my literary agent, came to ask if my daughter Kate and I could write a book for 'the home economist'. The book was already in the making generations ago, when my grandmother, Isabella, and my mother-in-law, Marion (Kate's paternal grandmother), were growing up. One was in Scotland, the other in New Zealand, and although they never met, they were as one in their philosophy and the way they approached food, cooking and the world of the kitchen. These were women who grew most of what they ate, who gave to the fullest, and who prepared and shared with their families and loved ones the most wonderful, delicious, nourishing, comforting food that could be had anywhere. It might have been on a shoestring, yet watching them cook and sitting at their tables was always a celebration. Kate and I thank them both for giving us such a sound basis for life.

Then I learned from my mother, Margaret Fulton, and Kate learned from me, how to adapt and continue the heritage of these two women, so that we too can enrich the lives of the people around us through food.

We thank our publisher Julie Gibbs (the surname is just a coincidence, but we feel so akin to her that it may as well not be), for her unique ability to sense the genuine, and the tenor of the times. She knew *The Thrifty Kitchen* had to be written, and she also knew who should write it.

Thank you to Virginia Birch, who has been a dream of an editor, keeping us in line throughout countless emails and phone calls, until she coaxed the best out of us. Once again, Ingrid Ohlsson's calm resolve, and her gentle way of keeping the book on track, have given us great reassurance.

Thank you, Chris Chen, for the beautiful photographs, and for giving the book 'your all'. And Margot Braddon, we were over the moon to learn that we had snared you for the styling. Thanks also to Tracey Meharg, for preparing the beautiful food for the photographs, and overseeing the presentation of each dish with an exacting eye; and to Megan Pigott, for coordinating the photoshoot.

Through their fresh and accessible design, Debra Billson and Kirby Armstrong have successfully captured the lively, practical tone we wanted to convey. Our thanks also go to the rest of the team at Penguin, including production controller Elena Cementon and editorial assistant Bethan Waterhouse.

It's been quite a journey, but a rewarding one, and one that we hope will encourage future generations to spend time in the kitchen, and to think of the table as a place for sharing, nourishing and celebrating.

Index

A

Aïoli 91
almonds
  blanching 99
  flaked 99
  slivered 99
anchovies
  with meat 209
  Lamb chops with anchovy sauce and
    bean purée 75
  Slow-roasted lamb shoulder with potatoes,
    anchovies and garlic 209
  Spaghetti puttanesca 65
  Spanish-style toast 14
appetisers
  Crostini con fegatini di pollo (Toasts with
    chicken livers) 196
  Ham and garlicky ricotta rolls 195
  Hot cheese and bacon bites 195
  Rumaki (Chicken liver and bacon bites) 195
  Sardines with lemon and herbs 197
  Tuna and lemon dip 195
apples
  juice extraction 137
  more ways with 138
  storing xiv, 136

varieties 136
Apple and cinnamon breakfast muffins 12
Apple and fennel stuffing 205
Apple and pine-nut cake 188
Apple and rose-geranium jelly 137
Apple sauce 136
Apple tarte tatin 138
Apple tarts 191
Buttered apples 136
Farmer's apple chutney 137
Speedy apple breakfast 4
artichokes
  Tuna and artichoke sandwiches 39
Asparagus and salmon chowder 55
Asparagus soldiers 15
avocado
  to replace butter 38
  Ricotta and avocado toast topping 15

B

bacon
  freezing 112
  Bacon and corn muffins 30
  Bacon and egg roll 15
  Hot cheese and bacon bites 195

Rumaki (Chicken liver and bacon bites) 195
Baked peach pancake 157
baking
  for beginners 167
  for kids 166
  hints for success 166, 179
baking paper 173
baking powder 167
baking soda 167
bamboo shoots 68
Banana and raspberry bread 171
Basic pizza dough 213
Basic tomato sauce 213
basil
  classic pesto 141
  in stir-fries 140, 143
  storing 140
  Thai basil with chilli 143
  varieties 135
  Basil mayonnaise 140
  Basil and parsley pesto 141
  Basil and vermouth cocktails 140
  Roasted tomato and basil soup 159
  Thai chicken with chilli and basil 142
beans, canned and dried
  pantry essentials xvi
  preparing 35
  what to do with dried kidney beans 111

beans, canned and dried (*continued*)

   Bean purée 75

   Chickpea, pea and bean salad with aïoli 91

   French vegetable soup with pistou 108

   Pasta and beans with pork ragù 71

   Quick minestrone 95

   Tuna and bean salad with pita crisps 35

   Turkish bean salad 111

beans, green

   Steamed fish and green-bean salad 53

beef

   buying mince xx, 118

   cuts xx

   for casseroles 126

   marinating 126

   Beef sausage rolls 32

   Beef stock 107

   Best-ever meatloaf 129

   Carbonnade of beef 206

   Comfort mince on toast 53

   Italian meatballs with fresh tomato sauce 118

   Melt-in-your-mouth beef casserole 126

   Pastitsio 114

   Ragù alla bolognese 124

   Red beef and pumpkin stir-fry 72

   The quickest Thai beef salad in the world 53

berries

   Banana and raspberry bread 171

   Bircher muesli with berries 7

   Blueberry and raspberry clafoutis 216

   Eton Mess 177

   Raspberry and coconut muffins 12

Best-ever meatloaf 129

Bircher muesli with berries 7

biscuits

   cooking 179

   storing 178

   Cheese and walnut biscuits 181

   Crispy oat, coconut and sultana biscuits 181

   Jam finger-holes 178

   Passionfruit yoyos 178

Blueberry and raspberry clafoutis 216

Bolognese toast topping 15

bouquet garni 135, 206

brandy for cooking 196

bread

   adding seeds and grains 170

   for bread and butter pudding 219

   for breadcrumbs 128

   stale 128, 219

   Banana and raspberry bread 171

   No-knead bread 168

   Rhubarb bread and butter pudding 219

   see also toasts

broad beans

   frozen xvi

   in hummus 28

broccoli

   Sausage and broccoli pasta 53

brown sugar 167

Browned butter and sage sauce 202

bruschetta

   toppings 14

   Bruschetta with ricotta, tomato and pesto 14

burgers

   They love babycinos, now here come baby-

     burgers 53

butter

   replacing with avocado 38

   replacing with hummus 28

   storing in freezer 166

   unsalted for baking 166

   Lemon herb butter 125

Buttered apples 136

buttermilk

   substitutes for 45

   Cinnamon, sultana and buttermilk

     muffins 45

C

cakes

   testing if cooked 166

   Apple and pine-nut cake 188

   Dutch ginger shortcake 184

   Five-minute cardamom tea cake 182

   Gingerbread cake 49

   Lemon syrup ricotta cake 187

   Plum tea cake 186

capers

   Tuna, lemon and caper pasta salad 36

capsicum

   preparing 31

   seeds for chickens 96

   using roasted capsicum 31

   Mozzarella and capsicum sandwiches 39

   Ranchers' eggs 21

   Rice-stuffed capsicum 96

   Roasted capsicum 31

   Squid with capsicum and lemon 67

   Summery cold gazpacho 53

Carbonara poached eggs 52

Carbonnade of beef 206

casseroles

   bouquet garni 206

   leftovers 126

   Melt-in-your-mouth beef casserole 126

caster sugar 167

cheese

   freezing 56

   shelf-life 56

   storing 70, 87

   Cheese and walnut biscuits 181

   Cheese sauce 114

   Eggplant parmigiana 146

   Hot cheese and bacon bites 195

   Mozzarella and capsicum sandwiches 39

   Pastitsio 114

   Shaved prosciutto, bocconcini and baby rocket

     pizza 214

   see also ricotta

chicken

   buying xx

   make-your-own mince 142

   roasting rack for 125

   storing xxiii

   trimming fat 72

   trussing 123

   Chicken and mayo sandwiches 39

   Chicken florentine 61

   Chicken roasted with green olives 207

   Chicken sausage rolls 32

   Chicken stock 107

   Chicken with garlic purée 123

   Crispy chicken parcels 52

   Easy, one-pan chicken 52

   Fettuccine with chicken and tomato

     cream 100

   French tarragon chicken 125

   Japanese chicken donburi 81

   Lemon and mushroom chicken pie 96

   Miso chicken soup 52

   Moroccan chicken couscous 53

   Perfect poached chicken 38

   Persian baked chicken and rice 211

   Roast chicken with tomato and fennel 76

   Sticky chicken 53

   Sunday roast chicken with stuffing 125

   Thai-can-do chicken curry 52

   Thai chicken with chilli and basil 142

   Thai green chicken curry 64

   They love babycinos, now here come baby-

     burgers 53

   Vietnamese chicken with vermicelli 68

chicken livers
removing sinews 196
storing 196
where to buy 196
Crostini con fegatini di pollo (Toasts with chicken livers) 196
Rumaki (Chicken liver and bacon bites) 195
chicken-keeping
capsicum seeds for 96
requirements and tips 3
rhubarb leaves poisonous 219
chickpeas
cooking 54
soaking 54
Chickpea, pea and bean salad with aïoli 91
Easy, last-minute hummus 28
Green-pea hummus 28
Italian chickpea and pasta soup 54
Lamb and chickpea balls 41
Tuna and bean salad with pita crisps 35
Chilled lemon sago 150
chilli
with Thai basil 143
Chilli plum sauce 154
Eggplant and feta salad with chilli and mint 201
Homemade chilli oil 213
Sardine and chilli spaghettini 62
Thai chicken with chilli and basil 142
chocolate
buying 221
Chocolate cream and ginger meringues 176
Lucy's chocolate puddings 221
chowder
Salmon, leek and potato chowder 55
chutney
Farmer's apple chutney 137
Peach chutney 154
Quick tomato chutney 159
Cinnamon, sultana and buttermilk muffins 45
clafoutis
Blueberry and raspberry clafoutis 216
cleaning
fridge 87
microwave xv
oven xv
products xv
coconut
Crispy oat, coconut and sultana biscuits 181
Raspberry and coconut muffins 12
coconut cream 64
coconut milk 64
Comfort mince on toast 53

compote
Fresh peach and plum compote 155
condiments
wastage 154
see also chutney; relish
coriander
preparing 73
uses 135
Coriander yoghurt 41
corn
baby 68
Bacon and corn muffins 30
Corn chowder 55
They love babycinos, now here come baby-burgers 53
couscous
Moroccan chicken couscous 53
Cream of tomato soup 159
Crème anglaise 155
Crispy chicken parcels 52
Crispy oat, coconut and sultana biscuits 181
Crostini con fegatini di pollo (Toasts with chicken livers) 196
Crunchy tuna and egg mornay 57
cucumber
Summery cold gazpacho 53
Tomato and cucumber salad 68
curry
leftover meat for 99
Sweetish colonial curry 99
Thai-can-do chicken curry 52
Thai green chicken curry 64
Very retro curried eggs 60
curry pastes xv, xvi
green vs. red 64
store-bought 64
storing 64, 94
custard
Crème anglaise 155

D

dairy products, light alternatives 101
dashi broth powder 81
dates
Spicy date pillows 172
Demerara meringues 175
Demerara sugar 167
dips
Aïoli 91

Easy, last-minute hummus 28
Eggplant caviar 145
Skordalia 88
Tuna and lemon dip 195
dressings
Vinaigrette 201
drinks
fruit juice packs 49
school lunchbox 48, 49
Basil and vermouth cocktails 140
Fluffy egg flip 4
Lemon barley water 148
Milky egg flip 4
Morning sunshine 4
Pineapple sunrise 4
duck-keeping 3
Dutch ginger shortcake 184

E

Easy, last-minute hummus 28
Easy, one-pan chicken 52
Easy vegetable chilli 131
Easy vegetable soup 53
eggplant
choosing 144
how to cook 144–5
more ways with 147
peeling 144
salting 144
varieties 144
Eggplant and feta salad with chilli and mint 201
Eggplant caviar 145
Eggplant parmigiana 146
Eggplant Sichuan-style 146
Falafel pockets with eggplant 42
Lamb, eggplant and potato pie 102
eggs
boiling tips 60
cleaning 2
freezing yolks 221
freshness (dip test) 2
frying pan for 21
hardboiled test 2
hardboiling 60
health benefits 18
home-grown 3
poaching 16
raw in drinks 2
room temperature 2, 166

eggs (*continued*)
  separating 166
  shelling 60
  storing 2, 86
  Asparagus soldiers 15
  Bacon and egg roll 15
  Carbonara poached eggs 52
  Crunchy tuna and egg mornay 57
  Egg fried rice 92
  Fluffy egg flip 4
  Frog in the hole 15
  Melt-in-the-mouth French toast 8
  Milky egg flip 4
  Morning sunshine 4
  Pineapple sunrise 4
  Poached eggs with rocket and prosciutto 16
  Ranchers' eggs 21
  Spaghetti carbonara 70
  Very retro curried eggs 60
energy efficiency in the kitchen 182
Entertaining
  last-minute lifesavers 194
  quick fixes 195
Eton Mess 177

F

Falafel pockets with eggplant 42
Farmer's apple chutney 137
fennel
  Apple and fennel stuffing 205
  Mussel, fennel and potato salad 201
  Pork chops with fennel and pear salad 52
  Roast chicken with tomato and fennel 76
feta
  Eggplant and feta salad with chilli and mint 201
  Potato, mint and feta rösti 22
Fettuccine with chicken and tomato cream 100
filo pastry, for tarts 191
fish
  environmental contaminants 78
  fishy whiffs 61
  smoked 119
  storing xxiii
  sustainable xxi
  using leftover 119
  Fish and risoni stew 78
  Fish florentine 61
  Fish stock 107
  Old-fashioned fish and potato pie 119

Slightly spicy salmon fish cakes 58
Steamed fish and green bean salad 53
see also anchovies; salmon; tuna
fish sauce 94
Five-minute cardamom tea cake 182
flour
  for baking 167, 170
  gluten content 170
  pantry essentials xvi
  plain 167
  self-raising 167
Fluffy egg flip 4
freezer
  stocking xvi
  storage times xxiii, 86
French tarragon chicken 125
French toast
  made with fruit loaf 8
  savoury 8
  Melt-in-the-mouth French toast 8
French vegetable soup with pistou 108
Fresh peach and plum compote 155
Fresh tomato sauce 118
fridge
  cleaning 87
  safe storage time-limits in 86
  zones 87
fried rice
  using leftover rice 92
  Egg fried rice 92
  Fried rice 92
  Thai-style fried rice 94
fritters
  Mussel fritters 198
Frog in the hole 15
fruit juice packs 49
Fruity muesli bars 46
frying, olive oil for 23
frying pan, seasoning 21
Funghi pizza 214

G

garlic
  Aïoli 91
  Chicken with garlic purée 123
  Garlicky mash 123
  Pistou 108
  Salsa di pomodoro with herbs and garlic 161
  Skordalia 88

Slow-roasted lamb shoulder with potatoes,
    anchovies and garlic 209
gazpacho 53
GI rating 211
ginger
  Chocolate cream and ginger meringues 176
  Dutch ginger shortcake 184
Gingerbread cake 49
gnocchi
  Ricotta gnocchi with browned butter and sage
      sauce 202
granulated sugar 167
Grated vegetable hash brown 95
gravy 125, 204
Greek-inspired lentil salad 52
Green-pea hummus 28
Gremolata 78, 121

H

Ham and garlicky ricotta rolls 195
Ham and pasta salad 36
hash browns
  Grated vegetable hash brown 95
herbs
  bouquet garni 206
  freezing 135
  growing and using 134–5
  storing 135
  Lemon herb butter 125
  Salsa di pomodoro with herbs and garlic 161
  see also basil; coriander; mint; parsley; rosemary;
      sage
honey
  Speedy apple breakfast 4
Hot cheese and bacon bites 195
hummus
  to replace butter 28
  with broad beans 28
  Easy, last-minute hummus 28
  Green-pea hummus 28

I

icing sugar xvi, 167
Italian chickpea and pasta soup 54
Italian meatballs with fresh tomato sauce 118

J

Jam finger-holes 178
Japanese chicken donburi 81
jelly
    Apple and rose-geranium jelly 137

K

kecap manis xvi, 72
kidney beans 111
kitchen whiffs
    fishy 61
    tips for the fridge 87

L

lamb
    cuts xviii, 209
    leftover 85
    mince xviii, xxiii
    trimming ('frenching') shanks 120
    with rosemary 209
    Lamb and chickpea balls 41
    Lamb chops with anchovy sauce and
        bean purée 75
    Lamb, eggplant and potato pie 102
    Oven-braised lamb shanks 120
    Shepherd's pie 102
    Slow-roasted lamb shoulder with potatoes,
        anchovies and garlic 209
leeks
    Salmon, leek and potato chowder 55
leftovers
    defrosting 86
    freezer burn 87
    in fried rice 92
    inventing a new dish 84, 85
    meat 85, 99
    safe handling 86
    storing 84, 86
    suggested uses 85
    vegetables in soups 95
    vegetables in stir-fries 68
    what to keep 84
    what to toss 84

lemons
    buying and storing 150
    lemon juice to replace oil in hummus 29
    more ways with 151
    Chilled lemon sago 150
    Lemon and mushroom chicken pie 96
    Lemon and poppy seed muffins 12
    Lemon barley water 148
    Lemon curd 150
    Lemon delicious pudding 216
    Lemon herb butter 125
    Lemon syrup ricotta cake 187
    Penne with zucchini, lemon and mint 53
    Sardines with lemon and herbs 197
    Spiced lemon pickle 148
    Squid with capsicum and lemon 67
    Tuna and lemon dip 195
    Tuna, lemon and caper pasta salad 36
    see also preserved lemons
lentils
    Greek-inspired lentil salad 52
Light tuna salad with a spud 52
LSA (linseed, sunflower seeds and almonds) 4
Lucy's chocolate puddings 221
lunch
    containers 27
    drinks 48
    fridge and freezer supplies 27
    fruit juice 49
    keeping cool 48
    leftovers for 26
    quick fixes 49
    shopping for 27

M

Maltese tuna, pumpkin and rice pie 117
mayonnaise
    Basil mayonnaise 140
meat
    buying xx
    eating less 163
    getting your money's worth xviii
    portions xiv
    roasting 125
    storing xxiii
    thawing xxiii
meatballs
    freezing 118
    Italian meatballs with fresh tomato sauce 118

meatloaf
    Best-ever meatloaf 129
    Melt-in-the-mouth French toast 8
    Melt-in-your-mouth beef casserole 126
meringues
    fruit with 176, 177
    hints 174
    spooning or piping 175
    storage 174
    Chocolate cream and ginger meringues 176
    Demerara meringues 175
    Eton Mess 177
    Meringue fingers 174
    Passionfruit sauce 176
    Pavlova 177
    Plain meringues 175
Microwave porridge 6
Milky egg flip 4
mint
    uses 135
    Eggplant and feta salad with chilli and mint 201
    Mint pesto 141
    Penne with zucchini, lemon and mint 53
    Potato, mint and feta rösti 22
Miso chicken soup 52
Mixed greens, walnut and pear salad 200
mornay
    Crunchy tuna and egg mornay 57
Morning sunshine 4
Moroccan chicken couscous 53
Mozzarella and capsicum sandwiches 39
MSG (monosodium glutamate) 93
muesli
    storing 7
    Bircher muesli with berries 7
    Fruity muesli bars 46
    Soft and crunchy muesli 7
    Toasted muesli 7
muffins
    decorating 13
    freezing 12, 45
    reheating 12
    Apple and cinnamon breakfast muffins 12
    Bacon and corn muffins 30
    Cinnamon, sultana and buttermilk
        muffins 45
    Lemon and poppy-seed 12
    Orange and pear 12
    Raspberry and coconut 12
mushrooms
    Funghi pizza 214
    Lemon and mushroom chicken pie 96

mussels
  cleaning 198
  suggestions for 198
  unopened 199
  with pasta 198
  Mussel and parsley soup 198
  Mussel chowder 55
  Mussel, fennel and potato salad 201

N

No-knead bread 168
noodles
  Vietnamese chicken with vermicelli 68

O

oats
  Crispy oat, coconut and sultana biscuits 181
  Scottish oatcakes 173
  Sticky oat bars 46
  see also muesli; porridge
offal xviii
oils
  for salads 200
  pantry essentials xvi
Old-fashioned fish and potato pie 119
olives
  Chicken roasted with green olives 207
omelette
  Open-faced omelette with tomato, green onions
    and pesto 18
onions, crisp-frying in microwave 60
orange
  Morning sunshine 4
  Orange and pear muffins 12
  Orange flower water 172
oven
  cleaning xv
  preheating for baking 179
Oven-braised lamb shanks 120

P

pancakes
  freezing 10
  toppings 11
  Baked peach pancake 157
  Ricotta pancakes 11
pancetta
  Salsa di pomodoro with pancetta 161
  Spaghetti carbonara 70
pantry essentials xvi
parsley
  uses 135
  varieties 135
  Basil and parsley pesto 141
  Gremolata 78, 121
  Mussel and parsley soup 198
  Turkish bean salad 111
Passionfruit sauce 176
Passionfruit yoyos 178
pasta
  al dente 71
  cooking hints 71
  mussels with 198
  quantities 71
  with dried kidney beans 111
  Carbonara poached eggs 52
  Crunchy tuna and egg mornay 57
  Fettuccine with chicken and tomato cream 100
  Fish and risoni stew 78
  Ham and pasta salad 36
  Italian chickpea and pasta soup 54
  Pasta and beans with pork ragù 71
  Pastitsio 114
  Penne with zucchini, lemon and mint 53
  Ragù alla bolognese 124
  Sardine and chilli spaghettini 62
  Sausage and broccoli pasta 53
  Spaghetti carbonara 70
  Spaghetti puttanesca 65
Pastitsio 114
pastries
  Beef sausage rolls 32
  Chicken sausage rolls 32
  Spicy date pillows 172
  see also pies; tarts
pastry
  Shortcrust pastry 138

Pavlova 177
peaches
  preserving 153
  removing skin 153
  Baked peach pancake 15
  Fresh peach and plum compote 155
  Peach chutney 154
pears
  Mixed greens, walnut and pear salad 200
  Orange and pear muffins 12
  Pork chops with fennel and pear salad 52
peas
  Chickpea, pea and bean salad with aïoli 91
  Green-pea hummus 28
Penne with zucchini, lemon and mint 53
Perfect poached chicken 38
Persian baked chicken and rice 211
pesto
  classic version 141
  freezing 141
  Basil and parsley pesto 141
  Bruschetta with ricotta, tomato and pesto 14
  Mint 141
  Open-faced omelette with tomato, green onions
    and pesto 18
  Rocket 141
  Walnut 141
pickles
  Spiced lemon pickle 148
pies
  Lamb, eggplant and potato pie 102
  Lemon and mushroom chicken pie 96
  Maltese tuna, pumpkin and rice pie 117
  Old-fashioned fish and potato pie 119
  Shepherd's pie 102
Pikelets 11
pine nuts
  Apple and pine-nut cake 188
pineapple juice
  Pineapple sunrise 4
Pistou 108
pita bread
  for sandwiches 42
  Falafel pockets with eggplant 42
  Pita crisps 35
pizza
  barbecue-cooked 212, 213
  toppings 214
  Basic pizza dough 213

Basic tomato sauce 213
Funghi pizza 214
'Inferno' pizza 212
Shaved prosciutto, bocconcini and baby rocket
    pizza 214
plums
    preserving 153
    Chilli plum sauce 154
    Fresh peach and plum compote 155
    Plum tea cake 186
Poached eggs with rocket and prosciutto 16
pork
    apple sauce with 136
    buying xx
    crackling 205
    cuts xxi
    for roasting 205
    mince xxi
    storing xxiii
    substituting sausages for mince 71
    Italian meatballs with fresh tomato sauce 118
    Pasta and beans with pork ragù 71
    Pork chops with fennel and pear salad 52
    Roast belly of pork with apple and fennel
        stuffing 205
porridge
    salt in 6
    Microwave porridge 6
    Porridge with stewed rhubarb 6
potatoes
    cutting too small or overcooking 88
    instant 59
    mashed with garlic 123
    perfect creamy mash 88
    roasted 205, 209
    Lamb, eggplant and potato pie 102
    Light tuna salad with a spud 52
    Mussel, fennel and potato salad 201
    Old-fashioned fish and potato pie 119
    Potato, mint and feta rösti 22
    Salmon, leek and potato chowder 55
    Skordalia 88
    Slow-roasted lamb shoulder with potatoes,
        anchovies and garlic 209
preserved lemons
    flavour variations 149
    storing 149
    uses 149
    Preserved lemons 149

preserving 134
    in brandy 153
    sterilising jars 152
    stone fruit 152–3
    Preserved fruit 153
prosciutto
    Crispy chicken parcels 52
    Poached eggs with rocket and prosciutto 16
    Shaved prosciutto, bocconcini and baby rocket
        pizza 214
puddings
    Lemon delicious pudding 216
    Lucy's chocolate puddings 221
    Rhubarb bread and butter pudding 219
pumpkin
    microwaving 116
    Maltese tuna, pumpkin and rice pie 117
    Red beef and pumpkin stir-fry 72

Q

Quick minestrone 95
Quick tomato chutney 159

R

rabbit xxi
Ragù alla bolognese 124
Ranchers' eggs 21
Raspberry and coconut muffins 12
raw sugar 167
recycling
    baking paper 173
    foil 173
Red beef and pumpkin stir-fry 72
relish
    Tomato relish 158
rhubarb
    growing 219
    poisonous leaves 219
    Porridge with stewed rhubarb 6
    Rhubarb bread and butter pudding 219
rice
    for frying 94
    freezing cooked 92

GI rating 211
    leftover 92
    rinsing 94
    steaming 94
    storing cooked 92
    Maltese tuna, pumpkin and rice pie 117
    Persian baked chicken and rice 211
    Rice-stuffed capsicum 96
    see also fried rice
ricotta
    draining 203
    full-cream and low-fat 187
    Bruschetta with ricotta, tomato and
        pesto 14
    Crispy chicken parcels 52
    Ham and garlicky ricotta rolls 195
    Lemon syrup ricotta cake 187
    Ricotta and avocado toast topping 15
    Ricotta and grilled vegetable sandwiches 39
    Ricotta gnocchi with browned butter and sage
        sauce 202
    Ricotta pancakes 11
Roast belly of pork with apple and fennel
    stuffing 205
Roast chicken with tomato and fennel 76
Roasted capsicum 31
Roasted tomato and basil soup 159
rocket
    Poached eggs with rocket and prosciutto 16
    Rocket pesto 141
    Shaved prosciutto, bocconcini and baby rocket
        pizza 214
Roman stuffed tomatoes 163
rosemary
    uses 135, 209
    with lamb 209
rösti
    Potato, mint and feta rösti 22
Rumaki (Chicken liver and bacon bites) 195

S

sage
    uses 135, 196
    Browned butter and sage sauce 202
sago
    Chilled lemon sago 150

salads
  oils for 200
  Chickpea, pea and bean salad with aïoli 91
  Eggplant and feta salad with chilli and mint 201
  Greek-inspired lentil salad 52
  Ham and pasta salad 36
  Light tuna salad with a spud 52
  Mixed greens, walnut and pear salad 200
  Mussel, fennel and potato salad 201
  Pork chops with fennel and pear salad 52
  Simple green salad 207
  Steamed fish and green-bean salad 53
  The quickest Thai beef salad in the world 53
  Tuna and bean salad with pita crisps 35
  Tuna, lemon and caper pasta salad 36
  Turkish bean salad 111
salmon
  health benefits 58
  pink vs. red 58
  Asparagus and salmon chowder 55
  Salmon, leek and potato chowder 55
  Slightly spicy salmon fish cakes 58
Salsa di pomodoro 160
Salsa di pomodoro with herbs and garlic 161
Salsa di pomodoro with pancetta 161
sandwiches
  bread for 38, 42
  butter substitutes 38
  lunchbox ideas 38
  greens in 38
  poaching chicken for 38
  seasoning 38
  soggy 38
  toasted 15
  Chicken and mayo sandwiches 39
  Mozzarella and capsicum sandwiches 39
  Ricotta and grilled vegetable sandwiches 39
  Tuna and artichoke sandwiches 39
sardines
  canned 62
  fresh 197
  ideas for 62
  roasted whole 197
  Sardine and chilli spaghettini 62
  Sardines with lemon and herbs 197
sauces
  tips for smooth mornay 57
  Anchovy sauce 75
  Apple sauce 136

Basic tomato sauce 213
Browned butter and sage sauce 202
Cheese sauce 114
Chilli plum sauce 154
Fresh tomato sauce 118
Salsa di pomodoro 160
Salsa di pomodoro with herbs and garlic 161
Salsa di pomodoro with pancetta 161
sausages
  substituting for mince 71
  Sausage and broccoli pasta 53
Scottish oatcakes 173
seafood
  saving shells for stock 107
  Squid with capsicum and lemon 67
  see also mussels
Shaved prosciutto, bocconcini and baby rocket
  pizza 214
Shepherd's pie 102
shopping xiii–xxiii
  for lunch 27
  getting the best value at the supermarket xiv
  green shopping 131
  online xiv
  specials xiii–xiv, 130
  to avoid waste xiii, 85
Shortcrust pastry 138
Skordalia 88
Slightly spicy salmon fish cakes 58
Slow-roasted lamb shoulder with potatoes,
  anchovies and garlic 209
snacks
  'snack packs' 26
  Fruity muesli bars 46
  Sticky oat bars 46
Soft and crunchy muesli 7
soups
  Asparagus and salmon chowder 55
  Corn chowder 55
  Cream of tomato soup 159
  Easy vegetable soup 53
  French vegetable soup with pistou 108
  Italian chickpea and pasta soup 54
  Miso chicken soup 52
  Mussel and parsley soup 198
  Mussel chowder 55
  Quick minestrone 95
  Roasted tomato and basil soup 159
  Salmon, leek and potato chowder 55

Summery cold gazpacho 53
Spaghetti carbonara 70
Spaghetti puttanesca 65
Spanish-style toast 14
Speedy apple breakfast 4
Spiced lemon pickle 148
Spicy date pillows 172
squid
  preparing 67
  Squid with capsicum and lemon 67
Steamed fish and green-bean salad 53
stews
  Carbonnade of beef 206
  Fish and risoni stew 78
Sticky chicken 53
Sticky oat bars 46
stir-fries
  basil in 140, 143
  with leftover vegetables 68
  Red beef and pumpkin stir-fry 72
stock
  making 106
  storing 106
  Beef stock 107
  Chicken stock 107
  Fish stock 107
  Vegetable stock 107
Stocking the pantry xvi
stone fruit, preserving 152
sugar
  pantry essentials xvi
  types 167
sultanas
  Cinnamon, sultana and buttermilk
    muffins 45
  Crispy oat, coconut and sultana biscuits 181
  Fruity muesli bars 46
Summery cold gazpacho 53
Sunday roast chicken with stuffing 125
Sweetish colonial curry 99

T

takeaway food
  expense 25, 26
  MSG (monosodium glutamate) 93
  salt, sugar and oil content 25

tarts
    Apple tarte tatin 138
    Apple tarts 191
Thai-can-do chicken curry 52
Thai chicken with chilli and basil 142
Thai green chicken curry 64
Thai-style fried rice 94
The quickest Thai beef salad in the world 53
They love babycinos, now here come baby-
    burgers 53
Toasted muesli 7
toasts
    Bolognese topping 15
    Bruschetta with ricotta, tomato and pesto 14
    Comfort mince on toast 53
    Crostini con fegatini di pollo (Toasts with
        chicken livers) 196
    Melt-in-the-mouth French toast 8
    Ricotta and avocado topping 15
    Spanish-style toast 14
tomatoes
    more ways with 162
    peeling 65
    using up 158
    Basic tomato sauce 213
    Bruschetta with ricotta, tomato and pesto 14
    Cream of tomato soup 159
    Eggplant parmigiana 146
    Fettuccine with chicken and tomato
        cream 100
    Fresh tomato sauce 118
    Open-faced omelette with tomato,
        green onions and pesto 18
    Pastitsio 114
    Quick tomato chutney 159
    Ragù alla bolognese 124
    Ranchers' eggs 21
    Roast chicken with tomato and fennel 76
    Roasted tomato and basil soup 159
    Roman stuffed tomatoes 163
    Salsa di pomodoro 160
    Salsa di pomodoro with herbs and garlic 161
    Salsa di pomodoro with pancetta 161
    Spaghetti puttanesca 65
    Spanish-style toast 14
    Summery cold gazpacho 53
    Tomato and zucchini bake 112
    Tomato relish 158
    Turkish bean salad 111

tortillas
    Ranchers' eggs 21
trail mix, homemade 26
tuna
    tinned, for lunchboxes 27
    Crunchy tuna and egg mornay 57
    Light tuna salad with a spud 52
    Maltese tuna, pumpkin and rice pie 117
    Tuna and artichoke sandwiches 39
    Tuna and bean salad with pita crisps 35
    Tuna and lemon dip 195
    Tuna, lemon and caper pasta salad 36
Turkish bean salad 111

V

vanilla essence 167
vanilla extract 167
vegetables
    freezing 109
    in soups 95
    leftovers in fried rice 92
    leftovers in stir-fries 68
    Easy vegetable soup 53
    French vegetable soup with pistou 108
    Grated vegetable hash brown 95
    Quick minestrone 95
    Ricotta and grilled vegetable sandwiches 39
    Vegetable stock 107
Very retro curried eggs 60
Vietnamese chicken with vermicelli 68
Vinaigrette 201
vinegar
    pantry essentials xvi

W

walnut oil 200
walnuts
    Cheese and walnut biscuits 181
    Fruity muesli bars 46
    Mixed greens, walnut and pear
        salad 200
    Walnut pesto 141
wastage of food 85

wheatgerm
    for digestion 6
    storing 6

Y

yeast 167, 170
yoghurt
    making your own 4
    Coriander yoghurt 41
    Speedy apple breakfast 4

Z

zucchini
    Penne with zucchini, lemon and mint 53
    They love babycinos, now here come baby-
        burgers 53
    Tomato and zucchini bake 112

LANTERN

Published by the Penguin Group
Penguin Group (Australia)
250 Camberwell Road, Camberwell, Victoria 3124, Australia
(a division of Pearson Australia Group Pty Ltd)
Penguin Group (USA) Inc.
375 Hudson Street, New York, New York 10014, USA
Penguin Group (Canada)
90 Eglinton Avenue East, Suite 700, Toronto, Canada ON M4P 2Y3
(a division of Pearson Penguin Canada Inc.)
Penguin Books Ltd
80 Strand, London WC2R 0RL England
Penguin Ireland
25 St Stephen's Green, Dublin 2, Ireland
(a division of Penguin Books Ltd)
Penguin Books India Pvt Ltd
11 Community Centre, Panchsheel Park, New Delhi – 110 017, India
Penguin Group (NZ)
67 Apollo Drive, Rosedale, North Shore 0632, New Zealand
(a division of Pearson New Zealand Ltd)
Penguin Books (South Africa) (Pty) Ltd
24 Sturdee Avenue, Rosebank, Johannesburg 2196, South Africa

Penguin Books Ltd, Registered Offices: 80 Strand, London, WC2R 0RL, England

First published by Penguin Group (Australia), 2009

1 3 5 7 9 10 8 6 4 2

Design concept by Debra Billson © Penguin Group (Australia)
Additional design and layout by Kirby Armstrong © Penguin Group (Australia)
All photography by Chris Chen, except pictures on pages 48, 212 and 213 courtesy Kate Gibbs,
and picture on page 130 courtesy Andre Martin
Styling by Margot Braddon
Typeset in Granjon by Post Pre-press Group, Brisbane, Queensland
Colour reproduction by Splitting Image Colour Studio Pty Ltd, Clayton, Victoria
Printed and bound in China by 1010 Printing International Limited

National Library of Australia
Cataloguing-in-Publication data:

Gibbs, Suzanne.
The thrifty kitchen / Suzanne Gibbs, Kate Gibbs.
9781921382079 (hbk.)
Includes index.
Low budget cookery
Other Authors/Contributors:
Gibbs, Kate.

641.552

penguin.com.au/lantern